# NINETEENTH-CENTURY PIANO MUSIC

PERSPECTIVES IN MUSIC CRITICISM AND THEORY
VOLUME 3
GARLAND REFERENCE LIBRARY OF THE HUMANITIES
VOLUME 1799

# NINETEENTH-CENTURY PIANO MUSIC
## ESSAYS IN PERFORMANCE AND ANALYSIS

EDITED BY
DAVID WITTEN

GARLAND PUBLISHING, INC.
NEW YORK AND LONDON
1997

**Library of Congress Cataloging-in-Publication Data**

Nineteenth-century piano music : essays in performance and analysis / edited
by David Witten.
      p.    cm. — (Perspectives in music criticism and theory ; vol. 3)
(Garland reference library of the humanities ; vol. 1799)
   Includes index.
   ISBN 0-8153-1502-3 (alk. paper)
   1. Piano music—Interpretation (Phrasing, dynamics, etc.)  2. Piano
music—Analysis, interpretation.  3. Performance practice (Music)—19th
century.  I. Witten, David.  II. Series.  III. Series: Garland reference library of the humanities ; vol. 1799.
ML706.N58   1997
786.2'09'034—dc20
                                    96–34480
                                       CIP
                                       MN

Cover illustration of *Pictures at an Exhibition* by Modeste Musorgskii
(Saltykov-Shchedrin Public Library, St. Petersburg).

Printed on acid-free, 250-year-life paper
Manufactured in the United States of America

*Dedicated to pianists in practice rooms around the world*

# Contributors

*Charles Burkhart*
Queens College and Graduate Center, CUNY

*Camilla Cai*
Kenyon College

*John Daverio*
Boston University

*Cristina Capparelli Gerling*
Universidade Federal do Rio Grande do Sul, Brazil

*Antony Hopkins, C.B.E.*
Hertfordshire, England

*Nicholas Marston*
Oxford University

*Joel Sheveloff*
Boston University

*David Witten*
Cambridge, Massachusetts

# CONTENTS

# Acknowledgments

I wish to express my appreciation to all of the authors for their generous contributions to this book. I would also like to thank Michael Saffle, Leo Balk, and Phyllis Korper of Garland Publishing for their infinite patience during the preparation of the manuscript, and copyeditor Steven Lindberg for his prompt and precise answers to a multitude of questions.

Also, a very special and heartfelt thanks to Pavol Kozma, Karen Tomaszewski, Andrew List, June Komisar, and Ronni Komarow for the beautifully engraved music examples and illustrations, which are such an important part of this book.

D.W.

# INTRODUCTION

*Works of art are of an infinite solitude, and no means
of approach is so useless as criticism. Only love can
touch and hold them and be fair to them.*

Rainer Maria Rilke[1]

## I

NO READER needs to be reminded of the enormous contribution made to the piano repertoire by composers of the nineteenth century. Nor can one ignore the power that this repertoire holds over most pianists. Anyone who studied piano for even one year will remember the flush of envy when, at the end of a student recital, the Big Kids got to play Chopin's Waltz in C♯ Minor, or Schumann's *Aufschwung*. Yet, even as our emotions tell us that this repertoire is thrilling to hear and exciting to play, our intellect demands explanations. The essays in this book attempt to satisfy some of those demands.

Rainer Maria Rilke's point is certainly well taken — ultimately, there are no words to explain the beauty of music. In the end, we can only shake our heads in awe and wonder at the genius of artistic creation. Nevertheless, an analytical, critical look brings us closer to the music; at the very least, it provides a vocabulary with which to speak about our awe.

Analytical skills will decidedly improve the quality of life in the practice room. If the thoughtful pianist asks not simply *how* a phrase was written, but *why* it was written and *where* it is headed, that phrase will become imbued with an intelligence that will survive the difficult journey from the practice room to the concert stage, across the footlights, and to the ears of the receptive listener. The heart alone might produce an emotive but formless performance, but the heart and the mind working together will project the truth and beauty of a musical work of art.

In recent years, scientific journals and the news media have turned their attention to the advantages of music lessons. They report that students who study music will benefit because they will have an easier time mastering abstract constructs of science and higher mathematics. I believe the time has come for musicians to assert their own priorities, to give the pendulum a push in the other direction, and to unequivocally state that mathematics and the sciences are worthy of study because they prepare the mind to absorb great works of art and music. President John Adams understood these priorities (as did the Greek philosophers) and expressed related sentiments more than two hundred years ago:

> I must study politics and war, that my sons may have liberty to study
> mathematics and philosophy. My sons ought to study mathematics
> and philosophy, geography, natural history, naval architecture, navi-
> gation, commerce, and agriculture, in order to give *their* children a
> right to study painting, poetry, music, architecture, statuary, tapestry,
> and porcelain.[2]

# II

It is fair to say that this book *about* the nineteenth century could not have been written *during* the nineteenth century. The Greek historian Thucydides imagined Man standing in the river of time, facing the past and seeing events more and more clearly as they receded into the distance. In this manner, we are now in a position to perceive music of the nineteenth century more clearly than ever before. As the twentieth century completes its allotted hundred years, we have the luxury of contemplating the entire nineteenth century from a post-tonal, post-Freudian, post-Schenkerian vantage point.

The nineteenth-century world of music produced composers who were an unprecedented variety of idealistic dreamers, workaday craftsmen, socially misfit introverts, and highly individuated extroverts — in some cases, it seems that all of these traits coalesced within single individuals! Certain composers, unaffected by the work of their contemporaries, produced music in relative isolation (Schubert, Chopin, Musorgskii), while others thrived on interaction, influence, even on literary connections (Schumann, Liszt). It is not always sufficient, then, for today's analysts to merely look at the music. In addition to a consideration of theoretical or formal innovations, one must notice the social situation of the composer — pressures, opportunities, the degrees of acceptance by audiences and peers, and so forth — in order to gain proper perspective. The contributors to this volume have each taken a distinctive point of view, selected particular nineteenth-century piano works, and written essays that go beyond mere description in order to elucidate the composer's intent, enlighten the reader, and explain the affinity we feel with this repertoire.

# III

Several of the essays in this book reflect the influence of Heinrich Schenker (1868-1935), the pianist and theorist who, much like Freud in the realm of the human psyche, offered a theory that illuminated the underlying structure of music. In another setting, Nicholas Marston has written about the value of studying Schenker's original thoughts and speculations:

> If the time is now ripe to give Schenker the "authentic performance" treatment and (as the customary image has it) to peel off the layers of grime that have intervened between us and the real picture, we may hope to recover a stronger sense of the rich and enriching tension often to be felt between Schenker's theory and practice, a tension which is itself the product of his attempt to comprehend, in the fullest sense of that word, the tonal masterwork in all its unique, living particularity.[3]

In the opening chapter, I have written about the tremendous importance for performing musicians of analytical ways of thinking. Specifically, I discuss Heinrich Schenker, whose theories and graphs expose the bare bones, the structural skeleton of music, and Hans Keller (1919-85), whose wordless "functional analysis" clarifies the unifying elements of a given piece. I then add my own thoughts on the usefulness of *metaphor* in understanding and teaching music — particularly metaphors relating to motion. The concepts of my chapter are certainly not limited to readers interested in nineteenth-century piano music, but I believe that, within the pages of this book, they will reach an appropriate audience.

Nicholas Marston presents a chapter with his own translation and commentary of a previously unpublished essay by Heinrich Schenker himself: a discourse on Beethoven's "Eroica" Variations, Op. 35, which includes paragraphs aimed at performers.

Camilla Cai has contributed a thoughtful discussion about texture, an element of musical sound that has been given all-too-little consideration. She compares specific piano works of Felix Mendelssohn with those of his sister Fanny Hensel, a great talent who did not live in a sociologically correct era for women to gain recognition as composers.

Charles Burkhart, long an articulate spokesman for Schenkerian concepts, examines an element of organic unity seen in the music of Frédéric Chopin. Chopin had an extraordinary ear for perspective — when to shorten a section and when to lengthen it. Burkhart reveals a Chopinesque procedure found in various conclusions of works, a technique that paradoxically tightens as it expands, which he appropriately calls "concluding expansions."

In my later chapter about the Chopin Ballades, I have concentrated on a few structural ideas that illustrate Chopin's gift for long-range organization and control of his musical material. Though strongly influenced by Schenker's theories, I hope that I have wielded the technical terminology with a light hand — I realize that, for some readers, this may be their very first encounter with a stemless notehead.

John Daverio clarifies the generations-old controversy surrounding Robert Schumann's last compositions. Are they inferior works, products of his impending madness, or works of genius, prophesying the future of music? Focusing on Schumann's last published piano cycle, *Gesänge der Frühe*, Op. 133, Daverio unravels the arguments by invoking the poet Friedrich Hölderlin, an artist who also struggled with mental illness.

In the kingdom of transcriptions, Franz Liszt was royalty. Cristina Capparelli Gerling writes about Liszt's masterful talent for transforming a Schubert song into a solo piano transcription, a genre that reached the height of its popularity in the final decades before the advent of recorded sound. Liszt's own selection, ordering, and treatment of six songs from *Die schöne Müllerin* for his own "song cycle" reveals his boundless esteem and respect for Schubert.

Antony Hopkins has provided an illuminating survey of the shorter piano works of Johannes Brahms, from Op. 76 to Op. 119. While the subdivisions allow the reader to dip in and out of selected pieces, a straight reading through the chapter reveals the progressive, deepening maturity of Brahms' piano music.

Modeste Musorgskii has been the continual target of critics, detractors, and would-be apologists, from his well-meaning but patronizing colleagues, to recent analysts who somehow miss the mark. With precision, logic, and certainly with no apologies, Joel Sheveloff raises Musorgskii's *Pictures at an Exhibition* to its rightful status as one of the greatest epic masterpieces to emerge from the previous century.

Each contributor to this volume has a strong emotional and intellectual commitment to music, and each one writes through the prism of his or her own musical background. Their essays attempt to debunk a few myths, clarify some theoretical concepts, and, above all, stimulate the reader's intellectual curiosity about the piano repertoire of the nineteenth century.

David Witten
Cambridge, Mass.

# Notes

1. Rainer Maria Rilke, *Letters to A Young Poet,* trans. Stephen Mitchell (1903; reprinted, Boston: Shambhala Publications, Inc., 1984), 40.

2. John Adams, in a letter to his wife Abigail, 12 May 1780, quoted in *Bartlett's Familiar Quotations,* 15th ed., ed. E. M. Beck (Boston: Little, Brown and Company, 1980), 381.

3. Nicholas Marston, review of *Theory, Analysis and Meaning in Music,* ed. Anthony Pople, *Journal of the Royal Musical Association* 120 (1995): 297.

# NINETEENTH-CENTURY PIANO MUSIC

# CHAPTER ONE

# Stemless Noteheads, Flying Frisbees, and Other Analytical Tools

## David Witten

## I

A S ANY FREUDIAN will tell you, discovering the latent unity underlying the manifest dream content is a most satisfying, cathartic experience. As any mathematician will inform you, the highest goal in mathematics is to offer a simple, "elegant" solution. In the field of music, there exist equally insightful ways of thinking about great works, yet very few performing musicians ever learn about or benefit from those theories.

The last hundred years have produced enormously important musical theorists such as Hugo Riemann, Arnold Schoenberg, Heinrich Schenker, Rudolph Réti, and Hans Keller. Although their books and articles have never been widely read, these men became mentors to certain devoted circles of students, who in turn produced their own perceptive lectures, articles, and texts. In this manner the original ideas have trickled down; the process, however, has been painfully slow.

Too many music departments in the world are anachronistic holdouts. Theory textbooks often fail to include even one example of a Schenkerian graph or a Rétian interval. (Can one imagine an introductory psychology textbook without the name of Freud in the index?) It has been one hundred years since Schenker freed the first notes from their rhythmic moorings, allowing stemless noteheads to float freely to suggest their own contrapuntal contour. It has been more than a hundred years since Hugo Riemann articulated the concept of *Vierhebigkeit* (the tendency of phrases to group themselves in fours). And it has been more than twenty-five years since Edward T. Cone described "hypermeasures."[1] Yet an embarrassing number of theory professors continue to teach tedious chord-labeling with no mention of harmonic priority, levels of tension and resolution, or the presence of "up"-bars and "down"-bars. At best, an industrious student of such training may emerge equipped to harmonize chorales for a church choir in eighteenth-century Bavaria, but will never have pondered the Platonic balance of unity and variety, delighted in the inevitable rightness of wildly contrasting themes, or uncovered any "elegant" solutions lurking beneath the surface of the music.[2] Furthermore, that student will not be able to sit down and play "Happy Birthday" at the next party.

I do not believe it is necessary for performers to read earlier theoretical treatises in the original, or to use *Urlinie* or *Grundgestalt* in daily conversation. But in an enlightened music department, these concepts would be taught, debated, and refined; they would cross the halls from theory classroom to practice room and back again, and they would be absorbed through osmosis.

Let no performing musician fear that analysis will engage the mind at the expense of the heart. Intellectual curiosity is not a replacement for musical passion, but rather a supplement to it. As Alan Walker cogently explained in *An Anatomy of Musical Criticism,*

> An analysis merely explains rationally and logically what is already known and felt intuitively. It is an intellectual *enrichment,* and not a replacement or recompense for a *musical* understanding. . . . No musician needs to be told that the intuitive musical experience is a vehicle of truth far superior to that of rational thought.[3]

## II
## But does it "Schenk" out?

Heinrich Schenker's name is well known, but for a variety of reasons his influence on performers has been negligible. He has been overlooked, underexposed, and misunderstood. As William Rothstein writes in his trenchant essay, "The Americanization of Heinrich Schenker,"[4] Schenker's ideas are at odds with the American psyche; in short, Americans don't like to be taught dogma. Another problem, which may have delayed interest in Schenker until our current generation, involved discord among his own students. A spirit of friendly collegiality has at last replaced the behind-the-scenes disagreements, but Rothstein reminds us of the problems of the previous generation:

It has been seen as an exclusive and dogmatically minded cult, speaking an impenetrable jargon, whose members proselytize ceaselessly while constantly bickering among themselves over the proper tending of the sacred flame.[5]

Another dangerous problem: some students who do receive a smattering of knowledge about Schenker develop an attitude problem at the same time. "Oh, yeah, we did Schenker! Every piece is '3-2-1' — 'Thre-e-e Bl-i-i-nd M-i-i-ce,'" they will singsong for you. So much for valuing the latent unity beneath the manifest variety.

If only more Schenkerian-oriented teachers would be willing to compromise, to present "entry-level" Schenker. In a 1981 article, John Rothgeb advocated that undergraduates begin their studies with counterpoint and figured bass to prepare them for meaningful linear analysis later. He pleaded for a curriculum in which students learn to hear sonorities unfold, classes in which "the irrelevant and nonsensical indiscriminate application of Roman numerals to vertical structures is not allowed to rear its ugly head . . ."[6]

With regard to classroom presentation, Rothstein is quite level-headed and realistic:

> The right way, in my opinion, is never to force more of Schenker's approach onto anyone than can be truly absorbed and truly heard. If this means that most students and non-theorists generally are taught only how to interpret the foreground, well and good; that's more than most of them can do now, and besides, it's in line with Schenker's own ideas on musical education. *Backgrounds and even middle grounds are simply not for everybody.*[7]

In his article "Schenker's Theory of Levels and Musical Performance,"[8] Charles Burkhart offers several significant examples of how recognition of "hidden repetitions" (motives that appear both on the surface as well as on higher structural levels) can be helpful in actual performance. But should the performer explicitly "bring out" the structure? A pianist's knee-jerk (knuckle-jerk?) reaction to the identification of a structural note might be to give that note an accent; that reaction, however, is likely to be wrong. Choosing an illustration that everyone will recognize, Burkhart mentions the *appoggiatura*. Although the softer note that follows is in fact the structural note, the correct musical solution is to "lean" on the expressively dissonant *appoggiatura*. Of course, this is a surface detail, but performers would be well-advised to develop similar sensibilities at all structural levels. "It would clearly be tasteless to overemphasize the tones of the framework itself."[9] There are times when a hidden repetition *should* remain hidden.

Catherine Nolan and Janet Schmalfeldt have both addressed the issue of what to "bring out" in a performance and the larger issue of what performers and analysts can learn from each other.[10] This is a contentious topic. As Nolan remarks, "Many performers are suspicious of analysis because of a perceived conflict between analysis as an arid intellectual preoccupation and their more immediate concerns with artistic inspiration, creativity, or intuition."[11]

I would encourage analysts to address not only other analysts, but performers as well. Their insights ought to appear as commentary among the well-thumbed pages of music studied in practice rooms, not merely in journals read in silent reading rooms of libraries. We should not waste energy wondering whether the composers themselves were aware of their own *Urlinien* or *Ursätze*. Rather, we should strive for long-range, structural hearing as an attainable goal. If performers would learn to develop their harmonic nostalgia for the tonic, listeners would benefit as well. Pianist Murray Perahia, acknowledging his affinity for Schenkerian concepts, remarked in a 1994 interview, "I feel I become more free, not less, when I'm aware of these structures because I get away from the pedantry of measure-by-measure and into something much bigger."[12]

Even those pianists already enthusiastic about Schenker are often unaware of his writings specifically about performance. Schenker was himself an active performing pianist and never lost touch with performers' needs. At least thirteen of his analyses of specific pieces, with extensive commentary on performance, have been translated into English.[13] (His eighty-six-page manuscript, "On Performance," has yet to become readily available.) In his editions of Beethoven's Piano Sonatas, Schenker's fingering suggestions "point the performer — the performer, that is, who chooses to be so pointed — in the direction of the proper performance."[14]

We have much to gain not only from Heinrich Schenker's lofty and "spiritual bird's-eye view"[15] of music, but also from his very earthy involvement with piano-playing, teaching, and editing. I look forward to the day when his writings on performance are translated into various languages and made more widely available to all pianists, musicians, and teachers.

# III
## An analytical *enfant terrible*

Hans Keller (1919–85) was a vibrant, stimulating presence in England as music critic, analyst, and BBC radio personality. Influenced by

Schoenberg, Réti, and Schenker, as well as the psychoanalytic movement, Keller emphasized the value of uncovering the latent unity behind the manifest variety of a piece. He taught how contrasting themes are not merely related, but are in fact dependent on each other for the success of a work. The greatest compositions develop from a unified idea, whereas mediocre pieces simply bundle together diverse ideas. "Great music diversifies a unity; mere good music unites diverse elements."[16]

Keller repeatedly lambasted other writers who described but never explained music. He was renowned for his sharp-tongued, acerbic writing style. Particularly outraged by Cuthbert Girdlestone's flowery descriptive prose, he lashed out not only at Girdlestone, but also at his readers!

> And if you believe his metaphor that the chords "draw near you," "descending from realms above," you are so utterly stupid harmonically that, frankly, you aren't worth bothering about.[17]

Keller, however, did not neglect performers. The reason for a performer to probe and analyze, he argued, was to produce an organic, motif-conscious, and ultimately beautiful performance:

> A monotonous player has never understood the unity of a work, whence he is forced to substitute uniformity for it; an erratic player has never understood its diversity . . .[18]

Keller's articulate, pungent way with words led, ironically, to a growing impatience with them. He became frustrated by the limits of verbal discourse about music, and, in 1957, attempted to dispense with words altogether. Developing a method of using *music itself* to analyze music, he created "functional analysis," a musical presentation designed to enlighten the music-lover without the interference of a narrator or speaker. A typical "script," for example, would include Keller's own composed excerpts, laced into and around the actual composition. His musical fragments featured repetitions, motivic cells, "suppressed backgrounds," bits of rhythm — whatever it took to direct the alert listener's attention to underlying motivic connections within and among the movements. And at some point during the broadcast (try getting *this* approved on today's radio stations!), there would be a three-minute interval of silence, during which the listener might reflect, take notes, and absorb what he or she had already heard. Here is Keller's own comment about functional analysis:

There is nothing esoteric about functional analysis except music, which is esoteric to the unmusical. The purely musical method, that is to say, cuts straight across the sometimes unbearable divisions between musicologists and musicians, professionals and amateurs, music critics and music lovers. . . . Where the pure, musical application of functional analysis does not explain itself, it fails. Its success, on the other hand, may eventually mean *the twilight of twaddle.*[19]

Although two or three of Keller's functional analyses exist in print, reading them on the page is not the same as sitting back and listening to them. Functional analysis was meant to be heard, not seen. For that matter, any analytical essay in print is automatically at a disadvantage. To really get the most out of written music analysis, one must sit at a keyboard with both the analytical text and the score of the music carefully balanced on the music rack. Anything less, and the reader might fail to extract the full import of the analyst's message.

My own version of wordless analysis involves studying not only what the composer wrote, but also what the composer did *not* write. I try to abandon all previous knowledge of the piece and approach every phrase with childlike innocence. Imagining repetitive four-measure antecedent-consequent phrases and overly predictable $V^7$–I cadences, I create a hypothetical version that a simple-minded or mediocre composer might have written. Then, returning to the actual version, I can gain renewed appreciation for the artistic achievement. The best composers always rescue the phrase, evade stodgy squareness, and avoid a thumpy return of the tonic. As Keller wrote,

If you want to get the emotional impact of an interrupted cadence, you have to feel the emotional impact of its terms of reference — the perfect cadence which, in the creative event, never happens: the interrupted cadence happens instead. *All art is, in fact, "instead," even though not all "instead" is art:* the "instead" has to be meaningfully related to that which it replaces and contradicts.[20]

Keller's functional analysis has not produced any offspring — it is now only an historical curiosity. However, a stepchild may yet arise in the emerging computer age. CD-ROM, or some similar technology, could become a viable medium for the future of analytical instruction. CD-ROMs offer both aural and visual examples, and they are interactive. Although they are not yet widely used in classroom teaching, the few dozen that already exist in music have demonstrated an ability to promote active listening and to teach musical analysis.[21] I hope that this sophisticated computer wizardry will not degenerate into mere idle entertainment. The time is right for serious and savvy music educators to produce lively, interactive CD-ROMs. If placed in the right hands, this technology would indeed be capable of striking a fatal blow to ineffectual, passive listening. Hans Keller would have loved it.

## IV
## Any metaphor in a storm . . .

Metaphor has been defined as the hidden unity of the cosmos, revealing its points of convergence. Metaphor and her twin sister, Analogy, facilitate our understanding in art, music, and other modes of nonverbal communication. Though some metaphors may seem whimsical at first, the best ones have a way of growing profound at second glance. They invite us to make connections where none existed before. Even literature, an art form most decidedly *not* nonverbal, cloaks its greatest truths within the mantle of metaphor. The reader must be alert; if he or she doesn't "get" the metaphor, most of the message is lost. There are still some people who think *Moby Dick* is about a whale.

At the risk of invoking the posthumous wrath of Hans Keller, I maintain that metaphors are essential to the teaching of music. Music theorists have developed sophisticated constructs to get beneath the surface of the music, but their words too often sound cold and sterile. Valuable though they may be, those theories may become encrusted in abstruse academic jargon, impenetrable and uninviting to the performing musician. Music itself certainly communicates, so why shouldn't analysis? Music lacks its own syntactical vocabulary, and therein lies the problem. The solution is for teachers and analysts to shamelessly borrow words, analogies, and metaphors from other disciplines in order to elucidate their art. Metaphors are indeed the best gravel with which to pave the road to analytical, insightful music-making.

Marion Guck has written extensively on the subject of metaphor and its importance in lively, engaging analysis:

> Analytical methodology seems rarely to be meant to tap or to feed a passion for music. . . . I am inclined to highlight involvement, usually by integrating vivid, response-depicting language with more traditional, analytical language.[22]

Of course, metaphors and analogies, like those sprinkled throughout the paragraphs of this chapter, run the risk of lapsing into lavishly ornate prose. The danger of being too flowery or too philosophical, as Rothstein points out, is that the reader might "question the writer's intellectual solidity."[23] Flowery prose, by the way, is not the only threat to intellectual solidity — sexual metaphors, available and appropriate though they may be, may tempt the writer to stray beyond the "PG-13"-ness of scholarly discourse.[24]

It seems to me that, in particular, metaphors of movement are the most appropriate ones for music. Can one refer to reaching the "high" and "low" notes of a phrase without acknowledging the implied metaphor of motion necessary to get there? References to motion, to the effects of gravity, and to the energy of phrases attempting to *escape* gravity, go a long way toward elucidating musical meaning. Some of the very best music teachers, and certainly the practitioners of the Jaques-Dalcroze method of Eurhythmics, hold as their basic tenet the correspondence of physical movement to music. To quote pianist Reynaldo Reyes, "There is motion in all music, and music in every motion."[25]

The Roumanian pianist Dinu Lipatti, in a thoughtful and telling letter to a friend, wrote about the importance of keeping the musical line buoyant by respecting, even "accenting," the weak beats:

> To insist and stress the strong beat is to commit one of the greatest errors in music because this is nothing else but a diving board toward the weak ones; *these* bear the real weight.[26]

And addressing the 1996 graduating class of the New England Conservatory of Music, pianist Leon Fleisher spoke eloquently about our primal relationship with gravity:

> Whether we shuffle and slouch through life, or whether we carry ourselves erect and walk with a bounce in our step — that bounce is like a beat in the bar. Beats are not fence posts that chop up the landscape, or coffin nails hammered. Beats are like springs, impulses that carry the music on and on . . . The eagle searches out a draft of hot air and rises from the earth, catches it on the tip of its wing, and rises for miles and miles, soaring and dipping, without once flapping its wings. That is the manifestation of musical line.[27]

The phenomenon of music as motion has even been mentioned in the psychoanalytic literature. Richard Sterba wrote that we "recognize *pleasure in motion* as the essence of the musical experience."

The factor of movement in music, therefore, brings about not only a regression to early infantile kinesthetic pleasure, but also the intense pleasure of experiencing the dissolution of barriers between the self and the outside world.[28]

Sometimes a metaphor of motion can come to life, spark the imagination, and enlighten a performer even more than an analytical line of stemless Schenkerian noteheads. Concerning the second theme of Chopin's Sonata in B Minor, for example — one can learn more about this gravity-defying phrase by watching a well-thrown Frisbee than from reading all the analytical descriptions in the world.

The metaphor describing the tonic as the "home key" is well known and widely used, but we could go much further. Why not speak about the *pull of gravity* exerted by the tonic? The leading tone, a half step below the tonic, wants not merely to *lead* — it desperately wants to *cling* to its tonic. The dominant, a fifth above the tonic, offers a comfortable pathway, a chute down which to *slide home*. And speaking of sliding home . . . Leonard Bernstein occasionally used the baseball diamond as a metaphor for tonality during his distinguished *Omnibus* television series for children.[29]

Metaphors are the missing link between the analysis of music and the performance of music; they belong, therefore, in the teaching studio. Long after a lesson is over, the images will linger — the spring of the diving board, the elasticity of taffy, the weightlessness of the pole vaulter. The studio teacher can provoke a chain reaction of intuitive, metaphorical, analytical, and structural thinking in the student, leading to an awareness of the multileveled profundities of music. With these tools, each student will become his or her own best teacher, and move on towards musical maturity. Only then will the teacher have provided not merely the golden egg, but the goose that lays the golden egg.

## Notes

1. Edward T. Cone, *Musical Form and Musical Performance* (New York: W. W. Norton, 1968), 79.

2. "Students and musicians who want to learn something about harmony can find learned treatises and classical texts that, at their best, help prepare them for a gig in a provincial German town, circa 1760. Along with this useful knowledge comes a great deal of guilt, snobbery, and abuse." Eric Salzman and Michael Sahl, *Making Changes* (New York: McGraw-Hill Book Company, 1977), 9.

3. Alan Walker, *An Anatomy of Musical Criticism* (London: Barrie & Rockliff, 1966), 5.

I agree with the premise that analysis never presumes to prove the value of a work of art; its worth must be intuitively recognized. As a corollary to this premise, I believe every detail of a masterpiece holds significance and contributes to the successful outcome of the whole.

The premise of accepting a given text as definitive is certainly not new in the realm of analysis and exegesis; it is common procedure among students of the Greek classics and of Roman law, and, in the realm of Biblical exegesis, it was the fundamental assumption underlying the hermeneutical principles postulated by Midrashic scholars. Viewing the Torah as a unified, consistent text, capable of withstanding any amount of questioning and examination, Rabbinic scholars uncovered deeper meanings beyond a simple, literal interpretation. They proceeded from the premise that every syntactical peculiarity, every unusual word or superfluous prefix, held a greater significance than was apparent on the surface. By studying the seeming discrepancies, even postulating various alternatives differing from the original, they were able to come to terms with the Biblical text and succeed in offering valid explanations of the passage.

In musical analysis, it is useful to maintain a somewhat similar attitude of "respectful questioning." When the musical logic seems obscure, it is better to study the passage in greater depth, exploring the unifying structure, rather than to hastily attribute a lapse on the part of the composer. In other words, give the composer the benefit of the doubt.

4. William Rothstein, "The Americanization of Heinrich Schenker," in *Schenker Studies,* ed. Hedi Siegel (Cambridge: Cambridge University Press, 1990), 193–203.

5. Rothstein, "Americanization of Schenker," 195.

6. John Rothgeb, "Schenkerian Theory: Its Implications for the Undergraduate Curriculum," *Music Theory Spectrum* (1981): 149.

7. Rothstein, "Americanization of Schenker," 201. Italics mine.

8. Charles Burkhart, "Schenker's Theory of Levels and Musical Performance," in *Aspects of Schenkerian Theory,* ed. David Beach (New Haven: Yale University Press, 1983), 95–112.

9. Burkhart, "Schenker's Theory," 107.

10. Catherine Nolan, "Reflections on the Relationship of Analysis and Performance," *College Music Symposium* 33 (1994): 114–41, and Janet Schmalfeldt, "On the Relation of Analysis to Performance: Beethoven's Bagatelles Op. 126, Nos. 2 and 5," *Journal of Music Theory* 29 (1985): 12–18.

11. Nolan, "Reflections on the Relationship of Analysis," 116.

12. Michael Kimmelman, "With Plenty of Time to Think, a Pianist Redirects His Career," *New York Times,* 3 April 1994.

13. Sylvan Kalib, *Thirteen Essays from the Three Yearbooks "Das Meisterwerk in der Musik" by Heinrich Schenker: An Annotated Translation* (Ph.D. diss., Northwestern University, 1973).

14. Rothstein, "Heinrich Schenker as an Interpreter of Beethoven's Piano Sonatas," *19th-Century Music* 8, no. 1 (summer 1984): 24.

15. Heinrich Schenker, *Beethovens neunte Sinfonie* (Vienna, 1912) [man hat den Vortrag . . . aus einer Art geistiger Vogelperspektive . . . einzurichten], quoted and translated by Rothstein in "Heinrich Schenker as an Interpreter," 25.

16. Hans Keller, "The Chamber Music," in *The Mozart Companion,* ed. H. C. Robbins Landon and D. Mitchell (New York: W. W. Norton, 1956), 91.

17. Hans Keller, "K. 503: The Unity of Contrasting Themes and Movements," *The Music Review* 17 (1956): 41.

18. Keller, "Chamber Music," 93.

19. Hans Keller, "The Musical Analysis of Music," in Hans Keller, *Essays on Music,* ed. C. Wintle (Cambridge: Cambridge University Press, 1994), 127–28. Originally published in *The Listener* 58/1497 (5 December 1957). Italics mine.

20. Hans Keller, "Problems in Writing about Music," in *Essays on Music,* 4. Originally published in *Times Literary Supplement* (10 September 1969). Italics mine.

21. One company that has been producing many excellent music CD-ROMs is Voyager® [One Bridge Street, Irvington, NY 10533].

22. Marion A. Guck, "A Woman's (Theoretical) Work," *Perspectives in New Music* 32, no. 1 (winter 1994): 37. See also Marion Guck, "Metaphors in Musical Discourse: The Contribution of Imagery to Analysis" (Ph.D. diss., University of Michigan, 1981).

23. Rothstein, "Americanization of Schenker," 198.

24. See, however, Susan McClary, *Feminine Endings: Music, Gender, and Sexuality* (Minnesota: University of Minnesota Press, 1991).

25. Reynaldo Reyes, Professor of Piano, Towson State University, in conversation with author.

26. Lipatti correspondence, quoted in *Lipatti,* by Dragos Tanasescu and Grigore Bargaunu, ed. Carola Grindea, trans. Carola Grindea and Anne Goosens (London: Kahn & Averill, 1988), 142–43.

27. Leon Fleisher, in his commencement address at the New England Conservatory, 19 May 1996.

28. Richard Sterba, "Toward the Problem of the Musical Process," *Psychoanalytic Review* 33 (1946): 41, 42.

29. Leonard Bernstein, "Introduction to Modern Music" (*Omnibus* television broadcast, 13 January 1957). Reprinted in Leonard Bernstein, *The Joy of Music* (New York: Simon and Schuster, 1959), 183.

# CHAPTER TWO

# Notes to an Heroic Analysis: A Translation of Schenker's Unpublished Study of Beethoven's Piano Variations, Op. 35

## Nicholas Marston

## I

### *Introduzione col Basso del Tema*

IN 1930, SCHENKER published one of his most extensive and mature essays, namely his study of Beethoven's "Eroica" Symphony.[1] Although it might technically be defined as an article in a yearbook — it takes up almost the whole of the third and final volume of *Das Meisterwerk in der Musik* — it is commensurate in status with the individually published annotated, explanatory editions [*Erläuterungsausgaben*] of the late Beethoven piano sonatas. Like those publications, the "Eroica" study combines a close analytical reading of the work with comments on performance, editorial issues, and the (non-Schenkerian) secondary literature.[2] And while the "Eroica" study, unlike the *Erläuterungsausgaben*, is not complemented by an edition of the score, Schenker's text is complemented by a far greater and more detailed series of voice-leading graphs than had ever been possible in the *Erläuterungsausgabe* volumes.

Anyone writing about the "Eroica" can hardly fail to mention the fact that the main theme of the finale is not unique to the symphony but had been used by Beethoven on three previous occasions, and most notably in the important work for piano *Fünfzehn Variationen mit einer Fuge*, Op. 35, published in 1802.[3] Schenker is no exception — indeed, he makes the point that the symphony finale not only uses the same theme as the piano variations but adopts essentially the same formal model, too. His brief account of Op. 35 may be quoted in full:

In Op. 35 an *Introduzione col basso del tema* initially presents the bass of the theme that is to come and shows it in the large, small,

one-line and two-line octaves successively. Next the *tema* appears in
the two-line octave. Following this come fifteen variations, each in
the tonic key — except for Variation 6, which underlays the theme
with a purely artificial C-minor harmony, and Variation 14, which
employs mixture to introduce Eb minor instead of major. The chain
of variations is concluded by a *Finale alla fuga* which, in addition to
complete fugal subject-entries, employs all manner of abbreviations
of the first four half notes of the subject and even inversions. Finally
the fugue leads back to the *tema* which, now played *Andante con
moto,* first appears in the two-line octave and secondly in the left
hand in the small octave.[4]

Reading the symphony finale against the organization of Op. 35,
Schenker goes on to label measures 1–76 as the *Introduzione col basso
del tema,* with the *tema* itself following in measures 76–107. As for
the chain of fifteen mostly tonic-key variations in Op. 35, these are
not susceptible to orchestral, and least of all symphonic, transcription;
thus Beethoven writes instead a fugal section which, like the *finale
alla fuga* of Op. 35, has the function of contrasting various other
tonalities [*Klänge*] with the primary Eb.[5]

It is entirely to be expected that Schenker would have known
Op. 35 intimately both as a performer and as a theorist. What has not
emerged until recently, however, is that the summary account of
Op. 35 in the "Eroica" study represents as it were the public,
published face of a private, unpublished analysis of the piano variation
cycle itself. It is this unpublished analysis which is translated below
for the first time. Beyond its intrinsic interest as a detailed study of a
major Beethoven piano work about which there appears almost nothing
in Schenker's published output, the analysis is also significant in its
relationship to the analysis of the "Eroica."[6] This relationship will be
pursued at the appropriate point below; but we may begin with an
introduction to the Op. 35 study itself.

Like so much of Schenker's unpublished work, the Op. 35 study
is preserved today as part of the Ernst Oster Collection at the New
York Public Library. The main text is written out in the elegant hand
of Schenker's wife, Jeanette, on the recto side of thirty-six sheets of
paper; but Schenker himself revised the text thoroughly, sometimes
needing recourse to the unused verso sides in the process (see Figure
2.1). The numerous short musical examples which appear throughout
are also in Schenker's hand, although the staves for those examples
which were envisaged as part of the original text may have been
drawn by Jeanette prior to handing the manuscript to her husband for
his additions. In the section devoted to the fugue, four short staves
were drawn but left blank except for the addition of the numbers *2, 3,*

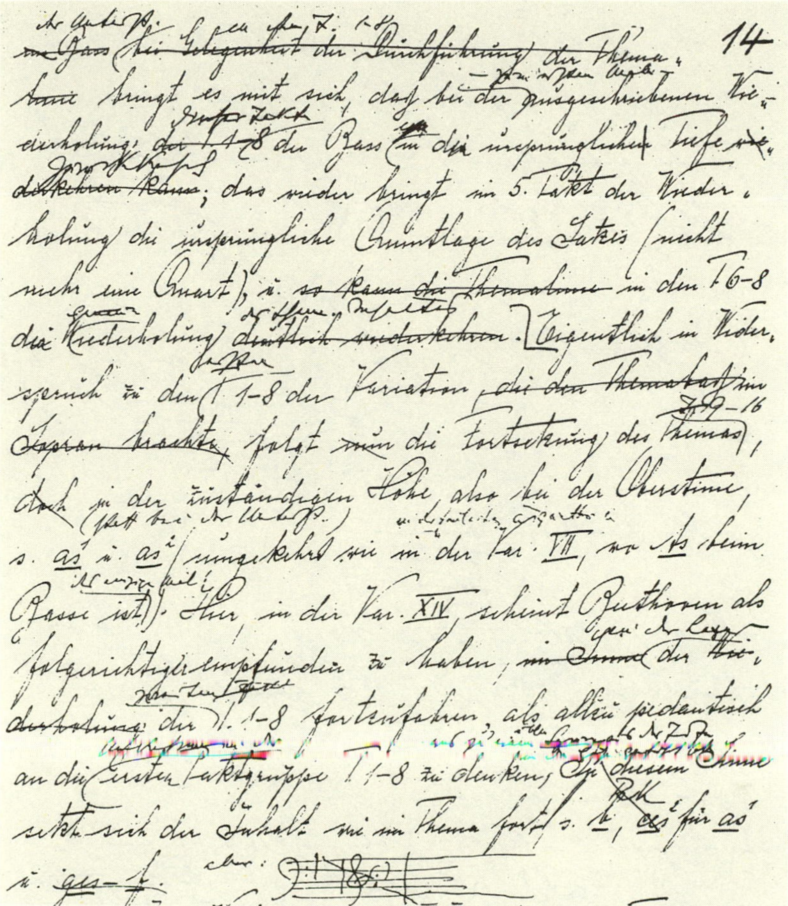

Figure 2.1a: Op. 35 text, p. 14r
New York Public Library, The Oster Collection, File 56, item 39 (recto). Reproduced by permission of The Music Division, The New York Public Library, Astor, Tilden, and Lenox Foundations.

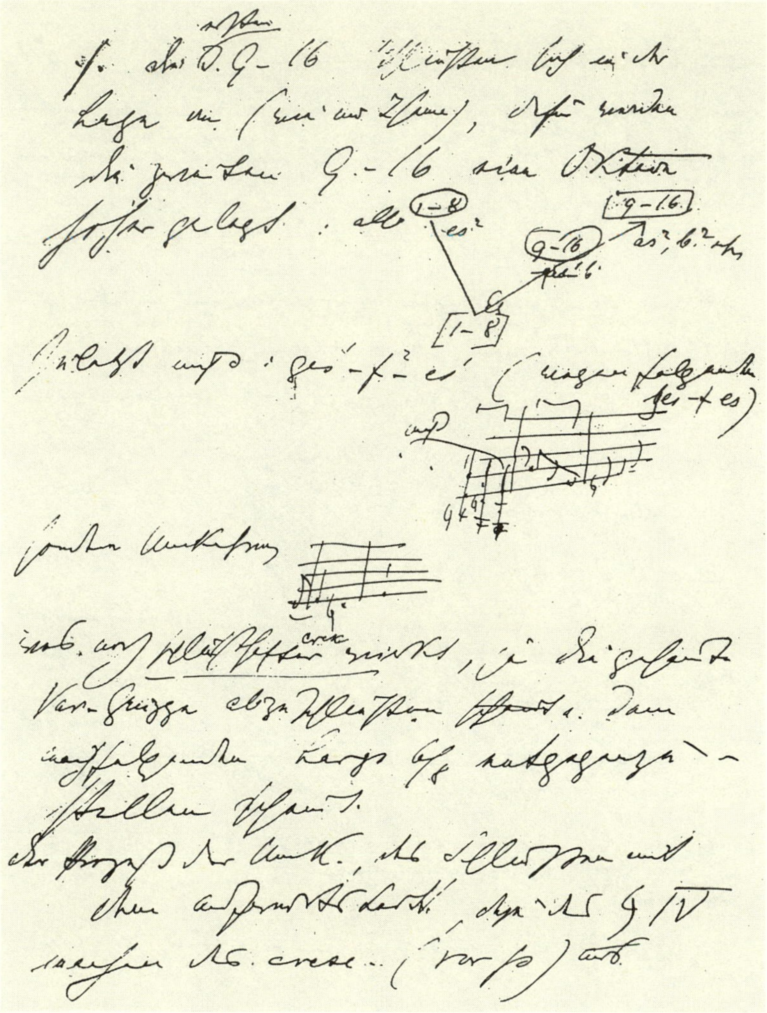

Figure 2.1b: Op. 35 text, p. 14v
New York Public Library, The Oster Collection, File 56, item 39 (verso). Reproduced by permission of The Music Division, The New York Public Library, Astor, Tilden, and Lenox Foundations.

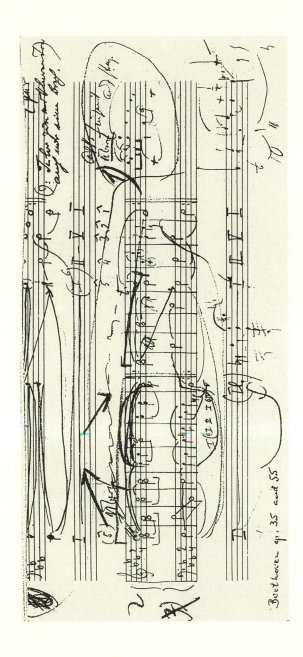

Figure 2.2: Schenker/Angi Elias: Analysis of the Op. 35 *tema*. New York Public Library, The Oster Collection, File 40, item 11 (verso). Reproduced by permission of The Music Division, The New York Public Library, Astor, Tilden, and Lenox Foundations.

and *4* to the latter three respectively. These numbers, together with the implied "1" omitted from the first of the four, prove to refer to four more extended musical "figures" found on three sheets of manuscript paper in the same file as the text.[7] Thus Schenker's study of Op. 35 appears to survive complete in the Oster Collection; or to be more precise, there seem to be no internal omissions of text or musical examples. The whole is rounded off with a touching inscription which supplies a date of 11 February 1927 for the completion of the copying: "Good night — more soon — kisses — Lie — Lie."[8]

Jeanette Schenker must have been copying from an original text in Schenker's own hand. Although that text apparently no longer survives, the Oster Collection does contain further autograph materials dealing with Op. 35. Although these cannot be discussed extensively here, they deserve mention since in some cases they bear directly on the Op. 35 study itself. Most important are two copies of the score of the work.[9] One is the edition by Louis Koehler and Richard Schmidt, published by Peters of Leipzig; the other is the edition published by Breitkopf & Härtel in the old Beethoven *Gesamtausgabe*. Although both scores carry extensive annotations by Schenker, including very careful fingering, the Koehler/Schmidt edition contains further markings of an analytical nature which complement directly many passages in the Op. 35 text; this edition was clearly Schenker's working score during the writing of the text. Next in importance comes a four-page series of notes on the Op. 35 variations. Written in Schenker's hand, in a mixture of ink and pencil, these notes again relate very closely to the text translated below and probably represent an early stage of Schenker's work on Op. 35.[10] Although it is natural to assume that these undated notes date from late 1926 or early 1927 — in other words, that they are essentially contemporary with the Op. 35 text — it is quite possible that they date from perhaps a decade earlier. Stored close to them in the Oster Collection are further fragmentary notes on Op. 35 and the "Eroica" Symphony which date from 1916.[11] Schenker's interest in this particular Beethoven variation cycle was evidently a long-term affair.

Despite its claim to internal completeness, the Op. 35 study is lacking in one important respect: it does not supply an analysis of the famous *tema* itself. Schenker refers the reader instead to the discussion of "diminution layers" [*Diminutionsschichten*] in *Free Composition* [*Der freie Satz*]. It was not until 1935, and after Schenker's death, that *Der freie Satz* was published;[12] and the published version contains no analysis of the Op. 35 *tema* nor any section entitled "Diminutionsschichten." Moreover, neither item appears to be present in the copious amount of draft material for *Der freie Satz* preserved in the Oster Collection.[13] But an analysis of the *tema* does survive elsewhere in the collection (see Fig. 2.2): originally written in the hand of Schenker's pupil Angi Elias but extensively modified by Schenker himself, this two-level graph interprets the upper voice as a $\hat{5}$-line *Urlinie*.[14] The $\hat{5}$ is reached only at measure 13 and is preceded by a slow *Anstieg* (Schenker uses the term *Aufstieg* here) from the triadic third, $g^1$ (m. 1) through $ab^1$ (m. 9) to $bb^1$ (m. 13).[15] Schenker notes that this ascent, which occurs one octave higher in the *tema* itself, is achieved through the technique of *Übergreifung,* whereby an ascending line is produced from a series of descending steps ($g^1$ descends to $f^1$ in measure 8 and $ab^1$ falls to $g^1$ in measure 13; the descending steps are marked by Schenker's pencilled brackets). This large-scale ascent to the structural $\hat{5}$ is foreshadowed in measures 1–5, where the same sequence of pitches ($g^1$–$f^1$–$ab^1$–$g^1$–$bb^1$) creates a stepwise progression from $\hat{3}$ to $\hat{5}$, followed by a stepwise descent to $\hat{2}$ over the dividing dominant in measure 8. The bass progressions accompanying the two $\hat{3}$–$\hat{4}$–$\hat{5}$ ascents differ in that $bb^1$ in measure 5 is set over root-position tonic harmony while in measure 13 the bass has itself moved up to g as part of the large-scale arpeggiation from I (m. 1) to the structural V (m. 15), with the result that the structural $\hat{5}$ occurs above a I♮ harmony. The foreground graph shows that Schenker originally planned to indicate the structural $\hat{5}$ as implicit from the outset of the theme: he included a bracketed $bb^1$ (an unstemmed black note) in measure 1 and linked it via a broken slur to the appearance of $bb^1$ in measure 13. Both the notehead and the slur, although not the bracketed $\hat{5}$ above measure 1, were subsequently deleted; and Schenker's pencilled middleground sketch, squeezed in following the foreground graph, makes no reference to an upper-voice B♭ prior to measure 13.[16]

The survival of this analysis of the Op. 35 *tema* is undoubtedly fortunate in view of Schenker's omission of such an analysis from the Op. 35 study itself. Yet it is important to remember that the graphs shown in Figure 2.2 are not necessarily those to which Schenker refers the reader of the study; they are undated, and it is entirely possible that they were prepared in connection with the "Eroica" study rather than that of Op. 35. For this reason it is prudent to comb Schenker's comments on the Op. 35 variations for evidence of his interpretation of the *tema* at the time when the study itself was written. As will become clear from the following discussion, that interpretation turns out to be more or less identical with the one graphed by Elias.[17]

Schenker's remarks on Variations 1 and 2 suggest that he heard the upper voice of measures 1–4 less in terms of *Übergreifung* than as the composing-out of a double neighbor-note motion around the triadic third, $g^2$. The reference to the "decisive" $bb^2$ in Variation 3, measure 5 suggests, however, that this is already the *Kopfton* of the *tema*, approached by an initial arpeggiation from $g^2$.[18] The descending stepwise progression $bb^2$–$ab^2$–$g^2$–$f^2$ in measures 5–8 is already recognized in the discussion of Variation 2; yet the example in which Schenker illustrates this point casts some doubt on the precise relationship of $g^2$ to that "decisive" $bb^2$. Schenker's example (Ex. 2.5 below) brackets $bb^2$ and slurs the neighbor-note motion $g^2$–$ab^2$–$g^2$, thereby suggesting that the basic upper-voice motion in measures 1–8 of the theme is not a $\hat5$–$\hat4$–$\hat3$–$\hat2$ descent preceded by an arpeggiation from $\hat3$ to $\hat5$ but rather a straightforward $\hat3$–$\hat2$ progression in which the motion between $g^2$ and $bb^2$ is regarded as a triadic embellishment of the *Kopfton* $g^2$. Further reconsideration of the structure of measures 1–4 is encouraged by the initial comments on Variations 4 and 5, where Schenker refers to the progression $g^2$–$ab^2$–$bb^2$ as being conformant to the theme.[19] On this reading, $ab^2$ in measure 3 is not an upper neighbor to $g^2$, but rather a passing note connecting $g^2$ to the "decisive" $bb^2$ in measure 5; and this reading corresponds to that illustrated in Figure 2.2, although in the Op. 35 text Schenker does not refer to the use of *Übergreifung* in the ascent from $g^2$ to $bb^2$.

If Schenker's remarks on the first half of the *tema* suggest some indecision as to the choice of *Kopfton* — $g^2$ or $bb^2$, $\hat3$ or $\hat5$ — his comments on measures 9–16 of Variation 11 seem to argue strongly for the higher pitch. He makes explicit reference to the "$\hat5$ and $\hat4$" of the thematic line in measures 13–14 of Variation 11, observing that they "must be supplied from the course of the bass and upper voice";[20] the completion of the line with $g^1$–$f^1$–$eb^1$ in the left hand of measures 15–16 is also made plain. And a further identification of $bb^2$ as the *Kopfton* of the thematic *Urlinie* comes in the discussion of Variation 13, where Schenker observes that the "forthcoming $\hat5$" is prepared by the ostinato $bb^2$ present from the very outset of the variation. As suggested above, his comments on earlier variations might lead one to assume that the "forthcoming $\hat5$" is located in measure 5, where $bb^2$ first appears in the *tema*. But this is not so: his subsequent remarks on Variation 13 once again support the analysis of the *tema* shown in Figure 2.2. Schenker observes that conformity to the *tema* properly requires measures 9–12 of Variation 13 to be governed by $ab^2$ in the upper voice. But if Beethoven had followed the demands of the theme at this point in Variation 13, $ab^2$ in measures 9–12 would have created the effect of a descending motion from the ostinato $bb^2$ of measures 1–8. Such a descent would, in Schenker's view, be contrary to the "upward direction of the theme"; thus Beethoven substituted $bb^2$ for the $ab^2$ expected in measures 9 and 11.

The reference to the "upward direction of the theme" clearly implies the slow *Anstieg* of measures 1–13 illustrated in Figure 2.2, and this finally helps to put Schenker's previous comments into their full perspective. In short, it appears quite safe to assume that the analysis shown in Figure 2.2 conforms wholly to the interpretation of the *tema* implied by Schenker's analysis of the Op. 35 variations.

As noted above, Figure 2.2 may have been prepared not in connection with the Op. 35 study of 1927 but with the "Eroica" study published in *Das Meisterwerk* in 1930; indeed, the middleground graph of the *tema* published in that study is essentially identical to the one in Figure 2.2.[21] But all of the foregoing discussion of the *tema* has been predicated on the assumption that it is a free-standing, closed, autonomous tonal stucture rather than part of a larger composition. It is to that larger context that attention must now turn. We shall begin by examining Schenker's analysis of the "Eroica" finale; for while the Op. 35 study may have served him as a preliminary to the analysis of the symphony, the latter can help to suggest further ways of understanding the Op. 35 study itself. Beyond this, the "Eroica" finale analysis can help to frame a Schenkerian understanding of the overall structure of Op. 35, an issue which Schenker signally failed to address.[22]

Unlike Op. 35, the "Eroica" finale is not a conventional variation set but a unique formal design with no strong precedent. And Schenker's analysis of it is likewise unconventional within the confines of his mature theory; as another commentator has remarked, it "is one of several examples from Schenker's large output of analytical work that radically contradicts popular myths about his techniques."[23] Schenker understood the background structure (in his own terminology, "die erste Schicht") of the finale as a $\hat{3}$-line *Ursatz*, with the *Urlinie* unfolding as $g^2$–$f^2$–$eb^2$. In two further graphs he demonstrated the introduction of $g^2$ via an upper neighbor, $ab^2$, and the appearance of two descending third-progressions from $\hat{3}$. The first of these third-progressions unfolds over measures 76–107: that is, over the course of the *tema* at its first appearance. A chromatic ascent from $eb^2$ then leads back to $g^2$ at measure 254, whereupon the second third-progression begins and is completed at measure 277. Schenker argues that because $g^2$ at measure 254 is supported by chord III$^{\natural}$ (functioning here as V of C), only the second third-progression has "*Urlinie*-status" (*Urlinie-Bedeutung*). Schenker reads the remainder of the movement essentially as a repetition, in the three-line rather than the two-line octave, of all the material presented in measures 1–277: two descending third-progressions, introduced by an upper neighbor, with "*Urlinie*-status" accorded the second progression only. The first third-progression is again associated with the reappearance of the *tema* in measures 349–80.[24]

Not the least unconventional aspect of Schenker's analysis of the "Eroica" finale is his proposed $\hat{3}$–$\hat{2}$–$\hat{1}$ || $\hat{3}$–$\hat{2}$–$\hat{1}$ *Urlinie*, with its suggestion (note the double vertical bar) of a divided, or interrupted, form. The reduplicative structure — in effect, Schenker hears four $\hat{3}$–$\hat{2}$–$\hat{1}$ descents, the second and fourth of which are structurally superior to the first and third — could be held to underline the relationship of this movement to classical variation form, in which the structure of the theme is replicated in each of the succeeding variations.[25] Yet whereas in that formal context the structure of the theme is decisive for the structure of each variation, a further peculiarity of Schenker's "Eroica" analysis resides in the fact that he is at pains to play down the structural role of the theme in relation to the larger movement: the descending third-progression unfolded by the theme (mm. 76–107) is not accorded *"Urlinie*-status." As noted above, Schenker first grounds this reading in the setting over chord $III^{\natural}$ of the $g^2$ which begins the second $\hat{3}$–$\hat{2}$–$\hat{1}$ descent (m. 254). The logic of this argument is hard to perceive; and at a later stage Schenker appeals instead to the thematic character of the "basso del tema," which functions almost as a secondary theme in contrast to the *tema* itself. He notes further the extent to which the *tema,* taken simply by itself, suggests a $\hat{5}$-line *Urlinie* unfolding from $bb^2$: as we now know, this interpretation of the theme had sufficed him in the Op. 35 study. The neighbor note $ab^2$ at the outset of the movement points strongly towards the initial $g^2$ of the theme, however; it is the importance of this factor, and the weight of subsequent events in the movement, which leads Schenker to read the movement as a whole in terms of a $\hat{3}$-line *Urlinie* rather than the ostensible $\hat{5}$-line one exhibited by the *tema*. And in concluding his remarks on the two middleground graphs of the movement, he observes that it is precisely the fact that the outer voices of measures 107–277 are at last freed from any strict thematic function which allows the contrapuntal structure to assimilate all the foreground content, even when that content is itself thematically based.[26]

In summary, it may be said that Schenker's analysis of the "Eroica" finale recognizes a potential contradiction between the ostensible *Urlinie* of the *tema* and that of the movement as a whole. Schenker resolves the contradiction in favour of the larger movement, and does this by playing down the structural significance of the *tema* itself; indeed, the closing remarks just discussed seem to imply that he regarded as mutually incompatible the functions of closed thematic statement and large-scale (middleground) contrapuntal structure.

How, if at all, does the analysis of the "Eroica" finale cast a retrospective light on the Op. 35 study? Although Schenker at no stage openly articulates a potential conflict between $\hat{3}$ and $\hat{5}$ as *Kopfton* of an *Urlinie* in Op. 35, his analysis of the fugue posits what he would later have interpreted as an interrupted $\hat{3}$–$\hat{2}$ || $\hat{3}$–$\hat{2}$–$\hat{1}$ structure: this despite the fact that the fugue, as Schenker is at pains to demonstrate, relates very closely to the structure of the *tema* (he refers to "eine Fugen-Variation") which, as we have seen, is clearly interpreted as possessing a $\hat{5}$-line *Urlinie*. The Op. 35 fugue, moreover, was understood by Schenker to be the correlate in the piano variations to the "free" section spanning measures 107–277 in the "Eroica" finale:[27] the correlate, that is, to the section in the finale to which he attributed structural significance ("*Urlinie*-status"). This raises the possibility of reading the fifteen variations and fugue of Op. 35 against the middle-ground model provided by measures 1–277 of the "Eroica" finale analysis: the ostensible $\hat{5}$-line *Urlinie* of the *tema* and the following variations would be regarded as subordinate to a larger (and, in the case of Op. 35, interrupted) $\hat{3}$-line *Urlinie* closing at the end of the fugue, as illustrated in the graphs accompanying Schenker's analysis (Examples 2.20, 2.21, and 2.23 below). And the analogy to the "Eroica" finale analysis may be pursued further. Op. 35 does not, of course, end with the fugue: its cadential tonic is elided with the beginning of a thematic reprise-variation (mm. 133–64) in a slower tempo, *Andante con moto*. This is followed by a further variation (mm. 165–96) and a coda in which Schenker located the "concluding descent" [*Ablauf*] $g^2$–$f^2$–$eb^2$. Thus the *Andante con moto* section equates to the second part of the "Eroica" finale in Schenker's analysis: it is "essentially a repetition, . . . which discloses nothing new about the *Ursatz*."[28]

To segment Op. 35 in the manner just outlined — to distinguish the fugue from the preceding fifteen variations on one side and from the *Andante con moto* on the other — would seem entirely unexceptionable, not least because Beethoven's own headings support such an approach. But Schenker's study argues for a slightly different segmentation, with the final *largo* variation being heard as separate from the preceding fourteen. Although he does not elaborate on the reasons for this interpretation, there is much to support it. In particular, Variation 15 has a recapitulatory function in at least three senses. Firstly, and most obviously, it re-establishes the tonic major following the turn to the minor mode in Variation 14; secondly, the melodic register and line of the theme are recapitulated very accurately, despite the highly florid decoration that prevails throughout. Thirdly — though this point is closely related to the last — the opening of

Variation 15 restores the melodic primacy of $g^2$ following the increasing emphasis on B♭ in various registers in Variations 9–13.[29] Indeed, the sense of this restoration of the triadic third in Variation 15 is heightened by the fact that the coda which links it to the ensuing fugue ends poised on chord III$^{\sharp}$, functioning locally as the dominant of C minor: the triadic third is treated now as a chord root as well as a melodic pitch.[30]

The argument for the importance of G, and specifically the opening $g^2$, in Variation 15 plays into the larger claim being made here: that the unorthodox $\hat{3}$–$\hat{2}$–$\hat{1}$ || $\hat{3}$–$\hat{2}$–$\hat{1}$ *Urlinie* that Schenker discerned in the "Eroica" finale is discernible in Op. 35 also. Whereas a crucial factor in Schenker's argument favoring $\hat{3}$ over $\hat{5}$ in the "Eroica" finale was the upper-neighbor-note status of a♭$^2$ in the introductory bars, pointing clearly as it does towards a forthcoming significant $g^2$, such is not the case in Op. 35. Instead, the work opens with an arresting tonic chord, and $g^2$ ($\hat{3}$) is announced immediately as the very first upper-voice pitch. That opening chord and pitch are then "remembered" at several crucial junctures later on: at the beginning of the *tema*, and correspondingly at the return of that material in the *Andante con moto;* and of course at the beginning of Variation 15. Finally, it is from $g^2$ that Schenker reads the "concluding descent" [*Ablauf*] in the Coda (mm. 196ff.) to the whole work. The periodic remembrances — reutterances — of the opening chord are vital to the sense of the triadic third $g^2$ as *Kopfton* of the work.

Assisted by Schenker's "Eroica" analysis, this commentary has now accomplished a shift of focus from Schenker's Op. 35 study to the study of Op. 35 itself. And implicit in the immediately preceding paragraphs is the suggestion that, from a Schenkerian perspective, what might be called the real structural "action" in Op. 35 is deferred until the beginning of the fugue; the main business of all the music up to that point is merely to prolong the initial structural $\hat{3}$. That such a reading entails a severe downgrading of the importance of the individual variations will be obvious; and while many will be understandably antagonistic towards it, there is no denying that the distribution of Schenker's text relative to the sections of the work reinforces that reading in some measure. Schenker's analytical remarks on the individual variations are hardly extensive; there is a distinct increase in engagement with the music of the fugue, supported by the much more elaborate accompanying voice-leading diagrams. In his earlier analysis of the Variations and Fugue on a Theme of Handel, Op. 24, by Brahms, Schenker had characterized variation form as intrinsically "loose" (*locker*), and sought to demonstrate the means by which Brahms was able to make it more organic. In Schenker's view, the organicism of Brahms's variations lies not in their composing-out of a single *Ursatz* overarching the entire work but rather in the "generative" nature of their sequence whereby the first variation begets the second, the second the third, and so on.[31] Such concerns are barely evident in the text relating to the Op. 35 variations; there are occasional references to relationships between variations (for example, the origin of the sixteenth-note upbeat to Variation 2 is traced to the last measure of Variation 1, and the octave-arpeggiations in Variation 10 are traced to the pervasive B♭ of Variation 9), but Schenker's main concern appears to be the relationship of each variation back to the theme itself. The issue of large-scale organicism is not addressed.

It may have been the difficulty in applying his concept of the *Ursatz* as guarantor of the organic unity of tonal masterworks to the "loose," additive organization of works in variation form that held Schenker back from publishing more studies of such works in the 1920s and after.[32] Whether he intended to publish the Op. 35 study at any stage is in fact uncertain at present.[33] It does not follow the general format of the essays in *Das Meisterwerk*, in which analytical commentary, remarks on performance, observations on manuscript sources, and critique of secondary literature are treated separately; indeed, neither of the last two categories is treated at all. The Op. 35 study may have been undertaken simply as a preliminary to the study of the "Eroica" that was to appear three years later; but it deserves to be read again, and not merely in this "preludial" sense but in its own right as an informed and informative study of one of the great variation works of the nineteenth-century piano repertoire.

# II
# Translation

The following translation of Schenker's study of Beethoven's Op. 35 follows the text copied by Jeanette Schenker and incorporates all of Schenker's revisions and emendations, except in the few cases (identified in the notes below) where these are illegible. Deleted passages and original versions of revised passages have not been translated. In the musical examples, clefs, key signatures, accidentals, and similar material sometimes omitted by Schenker have been supplied silently. All of the footnotes and all material in square brackets are editorial.

For permission to transcribe and translate the study, and to reproduce Figures 2.1 and 2.2 above, I am indebted to the Music Division, The New York Public Library, Astor, Tilden, and Lenox Foundations. I am grateful to Robert Kosovsky for assistance with materials in the Oster Collection, and to Max Paddison for his detailed critical reading of an earlier draft of the translation.

## *Fifteen Variations (with fugue) for the pianoforte, Op. 35, by L. van Beethoven[.]*
### *Dedicated to Count Moritz von Lichnowski[.]*
### *Composed in 1802*

*[Mm. 0–16]* Preceding the theme (where else could it go?) there is an introduction which brings in the thematic bass. The use of the deepest piano bass register suggests that one should think of this bass as being played on the double bass; but it was obviously inappropriate to render something conceived for double bass as a mere undoubled line on the piano. Performance of this bass depends upon a non legato for the half notes; thus the hand must be lifted on the second beat, provided of course that pressure sufficient to establish the effect of a half note has been applied. In measure 6 one should avoid a legato slur between Eb and E;[34] the *ff* and *p* in measures 10 and 12 form a unit, such that the *p* represents as it were the dying sound, an echo, of the *ff*. The performer is best advised to imagine a decrescendo during the rest in measure 11:

| [Measure] | 9 | 10 | 11 | 12 |
|-----------|---|-----|------|---|
|           | -- | *ff* | (>) | *p* |

*[Mm. 17–80]* Now the thematic bass rises from the depths into higher octaves: one octave higher in the *a due*, two in the *a tre*, and three in the *a quattro*. Meanwhile the first counterpoint, which — naturally — embodies the outline [*Aufriß*] of the theme, takes shape already in the *a due*.[35] This feature recurs in the *a tre*, in the first part of which a three-voice texture is effected initially by means of registral differentiation. In the *a quattro* this counterpoint appears in the inner voice, since the top voice carries the former bass. Now at last the theme appears. (For an analysis see "Freier Satz," "Diminutionsschichten."[36])

## Variation 1

In measure 2 $ab^2$ appears in addition to $f^2$ through reaching-over; likewise $bb^2$ as well as $g^2$ in measure 4 [Ex. 2.1].[37]

EXAMPLE 2.1

## Variation 2

The two upbeat sixteenth notes basically derive still from the last measure of Variation 1. In measures 1–4, $g^2$–$f^2$ and $ab^2$–$g^2$ stand out clearly; in measures 5–8 there is a voice-inversion: not only are the notes of the bass transferred to the upper voice (see $e^3$–$f^3$–$d^3$–$eb^3$–$a^2$–$bb^2$ [mm. 6–8; Ex. 2.2]), but this inversion is prepared already within measure 5 by an inversion of the *inner voices* also: that is, [thirds are replaced by sixths; Ex. 2.3]; thus it is the $eb^3$ at the summit of measure 5 which first makes possible the takeover of the bass notes by the soprano [Ex. 2.4].

EXAMPLE 2.2

EXAMPLE 2.3

EXAMPLE 2.4

The $bb^2$ does not appear until the fourth eighth note of measure 6, and in the inner voice; $ab^{[2]}$–$g^{[2/1]}$–f follows from this $bb^{[2]}$ in the next two measures [Ex. 2.5].

EXAMPLE 2.5

The passagework at the fermata must be subdivided.[38] In the penultimate measure the true thematic line is in the inner voice (l.h.).

*Variation 3*
Here, in a departure from the thematic line, we find $eb^2$–$d^2$ and $f^2$–$eb^2$
[mm. 1–5], but the decisive $bb^2$ is clear nonetheless in measure 5. Still
within measure 5 the thematic line enters the bass: see the continuation
with Ab–G in measures 6–7. Meanwhile the top voice takes over the
former bass ([thus, an] inversion [Ex. 2.6a]).

EXAMPLE 2.6a

One should not overlook the fact that the progression to II over the
chromatic note e, which in the theme takes place across measures 6/7,
occurs already across measures 5/6 here in Variation 3. This hastening
of events then makes possible a retardation which is expressed by the
repetition of ab–g from the thematic line in measure 7 (see the inner
voices [Ex. 2.6b][39]).

EXAMPLE 2.6b

*Variation 4*
Measures 1–5 in the top voice correspond to the theme (see $g^2$–$ab^2$–$bb^2$); on the second beat of measure 5 the top voice takes over the thematic bass and the bass takes over the top voice. $Eb^1$ and $f^1$ are avoided on the second beats of measures 1 and 3 [respectively] since they would have created $\substack{6\\4}$ harmonies.[40] The [left-hand] figuration turns downward on the second beat of measure 15 so as to enable a smooth progression of sixteenth notes down from $bb$ [Ex. 2.7].

EXAMPLE 2.7

*Variation 5*
The top voice in measures 1–4 conforms to the theme, with $g^2$–$ab^2$–$bb^2$; in measures 5–7 the thematic line is continued in the bass, and returned to the top voice at last in measure 8 with $g^1$–$f^1$. The right-hand eighth notes should be read as syncopated from the last eighth note of measure 4 onward. Thus the third-arpeggiation $bb^2$–$g^2$ is followed by descending octave-arpeggiations: $bb^2$–$bb^1$, $g^2$–$g^1$, $eb^2$–$eb^1$. This reading is confirmed by the octave $bb^1$/$bb$ on the fourth eighth note of measure 6. In measures 9–12 the imitation between the outer voices is to be brought out above all. The increased number of voices [*Mehrstimmigkeit*] in measures 13–14 results from the retention of the lower note of the octave-arpeggiation, which is a motivic element [Ex. 2.8].[41]

EXAMPLE 2.8

*Variation 6*
With the exception of one pitch ($e^2$ instead of $eb^2$ in m. 7) the theme is transposed note-for-note to C minor. However, this is fundamentally an Eb-major theme, not a C-minor one; the decisive factor is $bb^2$ in measure 5, which can be understood only as the fifth of the Eb triad and not as a seventh. (As a seventh, the $bb^2$ could function only as a passing note and would need to be understood here as coming from the octave $c^3$ [Ex. 2.9].

EXAMPLE 2.9

But it is the fifth-boundary [*Quintgrenze*] alone, and not passing notes, that determines the composing-out of a triad [*Klang*]!) The first part [of the variation] must clearly turn toward F minor, hence e² on the fourth eighth note of measure 7 (see above).

Concerning the performance of the broken octaves in the left hand, note that on each downbeat the first sixteenth note should be made the propulsive force [*Antrieb*] [Ex. 2.10]; an elastic thrust [*ein elastischer Stoß*] will of itself carry the remaining sixteenth notes along.

EXAMPLE 2.10

In crossing from the lower to the higher notes [in the broken octaves: *Beim Übergang von den Untertasten auf die oberen*] this thrust must be renewed on the fourth eighth note of measures 6, 13, and 14, despite the fact that the fourth rather than the first eighth note is involved here.[42]

*Variation 7*
Literal correspondence to the theme, and accordingly the introduction of the g² as the melodic pinnacle in measure 1, would have required that the arpeggiation be in ⁶₄ position [Ex. 2.11].

EXAMPLE 2.11

Beethoven uses the $^6_3$ inversion so as to circumvent the $^6_4$, and this results in $eb^3-f^3$ at the pinnacle instead of $g^2-ab^2$. The arpeggiation in measures 5–6 may be considered as two half-arpeggiations, $bb^2-g^2-eb^2$ and $bb^1-g^1-eb^1$; fingering and performance should be arranged accordingly.

## Variation 8
The thematic line proceeds through $g^2-f^2$ in measures 1–2, $ab^1-g^1$ across measure 3/4, and $bb^1-bb^2$ in measures 4–7/8. The *sf* in measure 11 must be understood within a prevailing *p* rather than a *ff*, the [notated] *ff* notwithstanding. This can mean only the *p* in measure 9; see also the *p* continuation across measure 12/13. The upper voices are inverted, sixths replacing thirds, from the fourth eighth note of measure 14 onwards.

## Variation 9
The thematic bass is given out clearly in the short left-hand grace notes. In order to make it clear on the piano the half note Bb must, despite the *sf*, be reduced to the value of a quarter while at the same time giving the effect of a half; thus the left hand must be withdrawn from the key on the second beat. In measure 7 in particular, the eighth-note Bbs should be played faintly so that the neighboring, or rather preceding, short grace notes may stand out clearly. The same holds for measures 9 and 11. The thematic line (g–ab–bb [mm. 1–6]) is clearly perceptible in the upper voice.[43] The performance of the double stoppings requires that they be grouped clearly by register: see my [performance] manual.[44]

## Variation 10
The ascending and descending octave-arpeggiations (Bb–bb–bb^1–bb^2 and the reverse) in Variation 10 are clearly related to the pervasive Bb of Variation 9. The thematic line $g^2-ab^2-bb^2$ in measures 1–4 is easy to find, as is its continuation. While contrasting with the left-hand octave-arpeggiations [of Bb], the unbroken octaves Cb/cb/cb^2/cb^3 in measure 10 offer at the same time a parallelism.. Some technical preliminaries: in the left hand [the fingering is] 5 4 3 2 progressing up through the arpeggiation, and 3 3 1 5 back down. A diminuendo is necessary in both hands on the first beat of measures 1 and 3; measure 5 should also begin *p*, with the crescendo commencing only thereafter. The clashes [*Reibungen*] on the first quarter note of measures 6 and 7, 14 and 15 must be brought out clearly.

*Variation 11*
The upper voice [in mm. 1–4] deviates from the thematic line, substituting eb²–d² and f²–eb² for g²–f² and ab²–g²; in measure 5 bb² is of course sounded clearly, in accordance with the theme (bb² in measure 3 already hints at this). In measures 13–14 the 5̂ and 4̂ [of the thematic line] must be supplied from the course of the bass and upper voice;[45] g¹–f¹–eb¹ (3̂–2̂–1̂) appears in the left hand in measures 15–16. In measures 13–16 particularly the performer must project the bass line as a unity: the interlocking of the right hand as it crosses over [the left] on Ab — and there is a *sf* on this note[46] — must give the same effect as would the progression G–Ab if confined to the left hand.

*Variation 12*
Here too [in mm. 1–5] we have eb²–d², then ab²–g², and finally bb², as in Variation 11. In measures 7–8 the bass is taken over into the top voice [and] the middle voice states the thematic line strictly.[47]

*Variation 13*
In terms of keyboard texture this is the most sonically powerful [*schallkräftig*] variation: [there are] eighth-note triplets, thick chords in the middle registers, right- and left-hand leaps of at least an octave allied to an ostinato bb² (*sf*) in measures 1–8, and thereafter arpeggios which simultaneously maintain the large leaps. Since bb² is a fixed element from the outset, there arises a natural allusion to the forthcoming 5̂. The actual thematic line is in the inner voices: see g¹ in measures 1–4, ab¹ in measure 5, and bb¹ in measure 7. Because of the ostinato bb² the bass in measures 6–8 employs a fourth-progression Eb–D–C–Bb which precludes the thematic fourth-progression bb¹–ab¹–g¹–f¹ in the inner voice: hence the alteration [to bb¹–a¹–bb¹–ab¹: Ex. 2.12].

EXAMPLE 2.12

If, as properly required by the theme, ab² were set as the pinnacle in the measure-group 9–12, this would signify a descent in relation to the bb² of measures 1–8 and would thereby conflict with the upward direction of the theme. For this reason bb² is retained as the pinnacle in measures 9 and 11 where one would actually expect ab². Related to this veiling of the true summit [*Höhe*] is the fact that Beethoven overshoots it also in measure 13 and substitutes eb³ for bb²! The cause of the one is the cause of the other. It goes without saying that the real thematic line follows the voice leading, irrespective of the artificial summit [*vorgeschobene Höhe*]. The initial upbeat eighth note connects back to the preceding variation (compare Variation 2).

Regarding performance, this variation belongs in the ranks of almost insoluble technical problems; the right- and left-hand leaps in particular can be overcome only in a frankly violent manner which originates, however, in the realm of pure Spirit.[48] No amount of technical study [*Etüdenwerk*] or digital dexterity can lead one through the difficulties; only Spirit can force a way through (compare Beethoven's exercises in Nottebohm[49]). Players often unconsciously make things easy for themselves either by reducing speed or by playing the first eighth note of the left-hand [triplets] in octaves (by which means the wide leaps are obviated or reduced), or even by omitting the last eighth note [of the triplet] altogether for fear of being unable to reach the next bottom note [*Grundton*]. In measure 11 the bass f on the last eighth note belongs to the arpeggiation, and therefore should be fingered 5 rather than 3.

*Variation 14*: Minore
There is an inversion of voices in measures 1a–8a:[50] the thematic bass appears in the top voice (compare the Introduction, *a quattro*) and the theme in the bass, with gb[1]–f[1], ab–gb and Cb–Bb.[51] The origin of the neighbor note Cb in measure 5a may be explained as follows: the upper-voice eb[2] precludes the Bb required in the bass by virtue of the theme because of the resultant $^6_4$ setting; thus a neighboring Cb substitutes for Bb. The initial effect is that of VI; but the inner-voice 8–bb7 motion has a tonicizing effect which also finally brings in ab[1]–gb[1]–f[1], in accordance with the theme. In measure 7a fb[2] as bII replaces f[2] (compare the thematic bass). On the third eighth note of measure 7a, however, it finally emerges that not VI but rather ♮IV was basically intended [Ex. 2.13].

(1)                                                              (2)

I ————————— ♮IV — V

EXAMPLE 2.13

A consequence of the registral descent of the lower voice during measures 1a–8a is that in the written-out repetition of these bars — the first occurrence of this feature — the bass returns to its original register; in return, this brings the original $^5_3$ (as opposed to $^6_4$) setting in measure 5b and the exact repetition of the thematic content in measures 6b–8b.

Measures 9a–16a stand in complete contradiction to measures 1a–8a in that the theme continues here in the proper register, that is, in the upper (instead of the lower) voice: see a♭$^1$ and a♭$^2$ [mm. 9a–10a, 11a–12a] (contrary to the Introduction, *a quattro*, and Variation 7, where A♭ appears in the bass for the only time!). Here in Variation 14, it seems that Beethoven felt it more logical to maintain the register of measures 1b–8b, and overly pedantic to think back to the inversion of voices in measures 1a–8a, which would have led to an ugly *leap* from the lower to the upper register.[52] It is in this sense that the content continues as in the theme: see b♭, c♭$^2$ for a♭$^1$, and g♭–f [mm. 12a–15a]. But [see Ex. 2.14]:

EXAMPLE 2.14

Measures 9a–16a are confined to one register (as in the theme), and therefore measures 9b–16b are set an octave higher, thus:

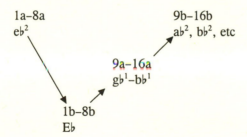

[In mm. 15a–16a] g♭$^1$–f$^2$–e♭$^1$ has ultimately to be replaced by the inversion [e♭$^1$–d$^1$–e♭$^1$] because of the ensuing g♭$^{[1]}$–f$^{[1]}$–e♭$^{[1]}$ progression [Ex. 2.15].

EXAMPLE 2.15

[This inversion] functions with even greater *closural force* to conclude the entire group of variations and seemingly to set them in opposition to the ensuing Largo, 6/8.

The procedures of the inversion and the ascending leading note close with its associated ♮IV constitute the *crescendo* (preceding *p*).

In relation to performance one need only recall that the two left-hand b♭s [Ex. 2.16] in measures 10[a] and 12[a] (not counting the repetition of mm. 1–8) are part of the thematic bass and must therefore be set off from the eighth notes in the middle voice and in the preceding measures.

EXAMPLE 2.16

*Variation 15*: Maggiore 6/8, Largo
*[Mm. 1a–8a, 1b–8b]* Here for the first time, the clearly traced $g^2$-$f^2$, $ab^2$-$g^2$ progression is accompanied by a different bass [Ex. 2.17] which in the last analysis actually amounts to the same thing. In measure 6a $eb^1$ replaces the chromatic note (E) in the thematic bass; consequently A♭ also replaces A on the last eighth note of measure 7a. The written-out repetition is filled with more widely flowing ideas. (The procedure of writing out the repeat had already been prepared in Variation 14.)

EXAMPLE 2.17

Notwithstanding the clear arpeggiations g–e♭ and d–f in measures 1a and 2a, third-progressions are displayed in the diminutions: $g^2$-$f^2$-$eb^2$ in measure 1a and $f^2$-$eb^2$-$d^2$ in measure 2a, likewise $ab^2$-$g^2$-$f^2$ and $g^2$-$f^2$-$eb^2$ in measures 3a and 4a [Ex. 2.18]. The first-mentioned arpeggiations take priority, since the imitating accelerated third-progressions are merely embellishing the resolutions of suspensions.[53]

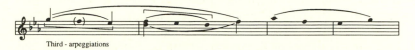

Third - arpeggiations

EXAMPLE 2.18

In measure 5a the bass reaches G, and thus stands a third higher here than the bass in measure 5 of the theme. But since conformity to the thematic bass made an eventual return to the E♭ root unavoidable, E♭ had stronger claim in measure 6a than the chromatic E, which sounds better as proceeding from E♭ (as in the theme).

The measures corresponding to the repetition (mm. 1b–8b) bring even richer embellishment: already on the sixth eighth note of measure 8a the upward run leads on to faster figurations. Firstly, in measure 1b the third-progression $g^2$–$f^2$–$eb^2$ is clearly expressed even by the sixty-fourth notes (see $f^2$–$eb^2$ within the last eighth note). In this measure the $g^2$ extends from the first quarter note to the two $g^2$s on the fourth and fifth eighth notes. In measure 2b even the minor-third progression $f^2$–$eb^2$–$d^2$ is still incorporated at the end of the figuration, which has taken on the character of a mordent. Measures 3b and 4b may be described similarly [to mm. 1b–2b]. In measure 5b there is a continually intensified note-repetition which leads on to trills in measure 6b. The voice leading remains unaltered even in measures 6b, 7b, and 8b; the only difference is that the diminutions are expressed in sixty-fourth notes.

*Performance.* The broad *Largo* requires a more diverse shading. Note the *crescendo–sf–diminuendo* in measures 1a and 2a; the bass should be drawn into the expression of the crescendo. Contrary to measure 2a, the crescendo in measures 3a–4a no longer leads to a *sf* but to a *p*; this is related to the fact that a crescendo must begin in measure 5a, but it goes without saying nonetheless that the expression of the [4–3] suspension in measure 4a requires a diminuendo. The dynamics in measures 5a and 6a conform to the corresponding bars of the theme*: crescendo–sf–decrescendo–p,* except that the last two indications occur already in measure 6a here rather than in measures 7 and 8, as in the theme. The alteration is connected with the suppression of the chromatic note (E) in the bass.

In bar 1b the *p* marking for the arpeggiation on the third eighth note is the means whereby Beethoven indicates that the downbeat $g^2$ continues to sound on. The $g^2$ on the first quarter note must resonate across this arpeggiation to link up with $g^2$ on the fourth and fifth eighth notes; this will create the impression of a sustained $g^2$ through which the sixty-fourth-note figuration runs delicately until the third-progression takes shape on the last eighth note. Here in measure 1b both the interpolated *p* and the sixty-fourth notes preclude a crescendo as in measure 1a. Only in measure 2b does a crescendo occur, one that in no way seeks to contradict the 4–3 suspension (for such a suspension invariably demands a diminuendo) but rather aims towards the *sf* in the bass. This arrangement [of dynamics] more or less repeats that in measures 1a–2a, except that the crescendo is deferred by one measure in measures 1b–2b because there are diminutions in the bass as well [as in the upper voice]. A *sf* on the downbeat b♭ in the bass [of m. 2b] would be unbearable, unthinkable. The bass figuration in measure 2b alludes back to that of the right hand in measure 1b.[54]

The acceleration [*Steigerung*] of note values in measure 5b must be brought off convincingly, and caution is therefore required particularly on the first and second eighth notes. The transition from the thirty-second-note triplets on the fourth eighth note through the sixty-fourth notes on the fifth to the sixty-fourth-note triplets on the last eighth note must be felt and played as an acceleration, since on the last eighth note each sixteenth is expressed by six sixty-fourth notes [Ex. 2.19a] as opposed to only four on the fifth eighth note [Example 19b]: the acceleration lies in the progression from the duple to the triple division.

(a)

(b)

EXAMPLE 2.19a and b

*[Mm. 9a–16a, 9b–16b]* In measure 9a, as in the theme, the diminution is controlled by the upward progression b♭–a♭, but articulated in thirty-second notes here in accordance with the variation, which makes it possible to repeat the figuration within the same measure. The left hand, moving in the opposite direction and falling from a♭ to b♭, likewise brings in the counterpoint twice. In measure 11a the figures from measures 9a–10a are imitated at the third above, so that b♭$^1$ in measure 13a is reached by means of the arpeggiation b♭ (m. 8b)––d$^1$ (m. 9a)––f$^1$ (m. 11a)––b♭$^1$ (m. 13a). Here in the variation the passing note A♭₁ is required in the bass between B♭₁ and G₁ (see mm. 9a–13a). The repetition of these measures introduces faster note

values throughout: sixty-fourth notes instead of thirty-seconds, and a particularly abundant [*reich*] arpeggiation (in one-hundred-and-twenty-eighths) in measure 15b.

*Performance*. Despite the *p* dynamic, a♭$^1$ on the fourth eighth note of measure 9a must obviously be stressed, and there should be a crescendo to a♭$^2$ in measure 10a; conversely, the initial a♭ of the left-hand figure requires accentuation. The same holds for measures 11a and 12a. There should be a crescendo and diminuendo during the trill on the last eighth note of measure 12a. The sixty-fourth-note arpeggio in measure 13a is easy to bring off if one thinks less in terms of four octave-leaps than of two double-octave-leaps (G$_1$–g–g$^2$). The bass note [A♭$_1$] in measure 14a should indeed be played staccato but sustained by the pedal up to the third eighth note; thereafter the right-hand quarter note must sound on alone. In measure 15b, notwithstanding the placing of the thumb on the g (where the figure is transferred to the right hand), it is advisable to use the thumb again on b♭ and likewise again on b♭$^1$, and at the end of the figure to proceed smoothly from the fifth finger on g$^1$ to the fourth on e♭$^1$.[55]

## Coda

The Coda brings a parallel to Variation 6, that is, to that variation in which the fundamentally inappropriate key of C minor was used for a singular harmonization [of the theme]. This parallelism represents justice in the highest sense of the term: reparation is offered, fervently if also belatedly, for something long past. Just as C minor had eventually to be supplanted by E♭ major in Variation 6 if the next variation were to proceed again in the tonic key without extensive modulation, so in the Coda a full close in the C-minor tonic is avoided: the harmony leads [*der Satz führt*] to the dominant of C minor which, however, is better understood as III in E♭ here. During the arpeggiations in the final measures of the Coda the inner-voice quarter notes should be drawn upon in order to enhance the *crescendo*.

## Fugue [Ex. 2.20]

One needs only to have probed the true content of the [fugue] subject and to have glanced at the repeated A♭ in measure 125[ff.] and the continuation in measures 129–32 to sense from these features that Beethoven wanted to express the theme even through the fugue. Whoever considers Beethoven incapable of thus transforming a [variation] theme into a fugue-variation understands absolutely nothing of the force [*Tragkraft*] of a musical ear of genius; he will neither comprehend nor believe it.

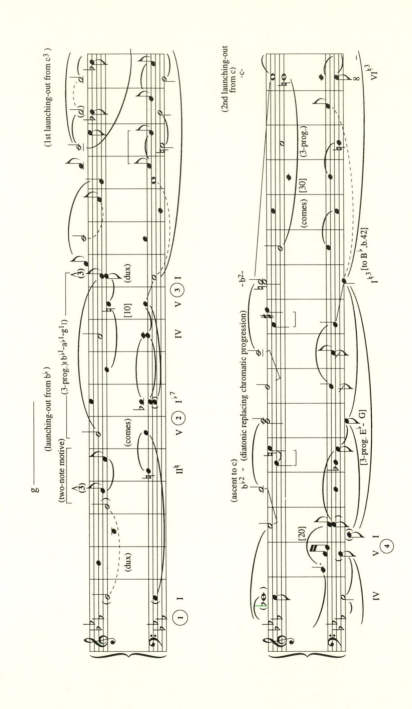

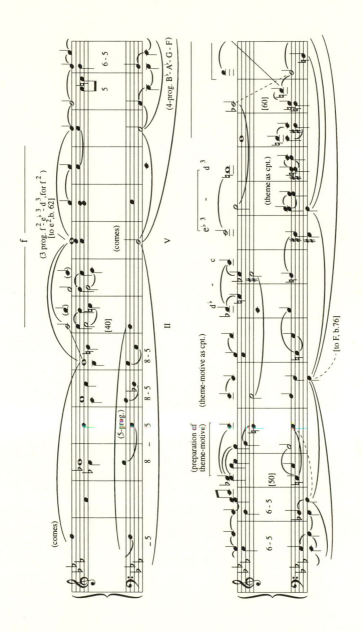

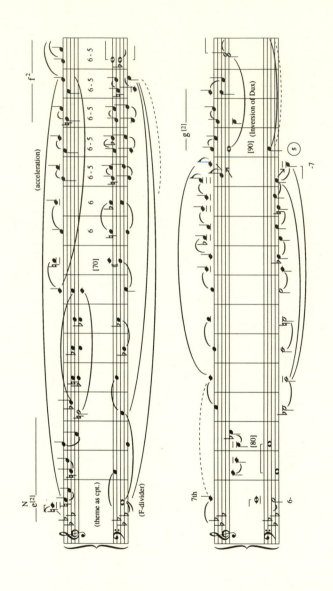

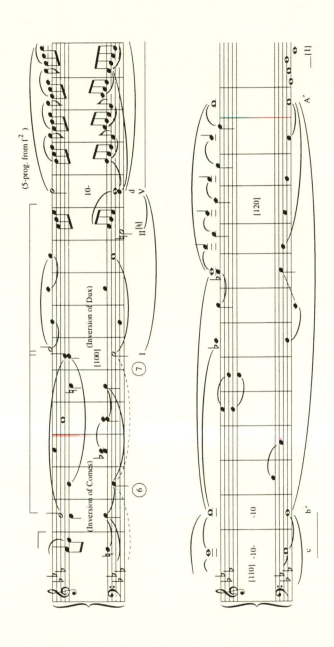

EXAMPLE 2.20.  Schenker's graph of the Fugue of Op. 35

The first four measures of the subject set forth the content of measures 1–4 of the thematic bass; the substance of measures 1–2 of the actual variation theme first emerges with $g^1$ and $f^1$ on the last eighth note of measures 4 and 5. The answer is stated in measures 6–11; its distinguishing feature is the third-progression $bb^1$–$ab^1$–$g^1$, which contrasts with the two-note motive [$g^1$–$f^1$] of the subject. This is related to the bass arpeggiation, which of course holds fast to Eb major;[56] there is certainly no question of Bb major in measures 5–6. (The theory that makes such claims is utterly erroneous.[57]) The distinction between subject and answer is maintained throughout the course of the fugue. The counterpoint to the answer follows on initially from the sixteenth-note figure in the subject, but from measure 7 it takes the route prescribed by the bass arpeggiation. The subject enters again in measure 11, bringing the two-note motive g–f (see the last eighth note of mm. 14 and 15). Counterpoint 1 at first shapes the third-progression $bb^{[2]}$–$ab^{[2/1]}$–$g^{[1]}$ in measures 11–14, as if repeating the third-progression in the answer;[58] but right above the two-note motive of the subject in the bass the upper voice launches out [*holt . . . aus*] with the progression from $c^3$, so that the advance towards g as $\hat{3}$ now presents a more extended route than does the third-progression in the answer.[59] This creates a special emphasis on $c^3$ as well as on the endnote g. Admittedly, the $bb^2$ is left out in measure 16; this would seem to have come about since $bb^2$ appears in measure 17. In measure 18 the $ab^2$ likewise is dropped; again, this was possible because in measures 19–20 the bass, as if summarizing, takes up the linear succession [*Folge*] $c^{[1]}$–bb–ab–g and completes the progression. The third bass arpeggiation lasts until measure 20; like every arpeggiation it is a unity, which permits no talk (as demanded by Theory) of an "episode" beginning in measure 16. One would have a formal section begin in the middle of a passing motion [*Durchgang*]!![60] Theory claims such a logical absurdity! Strictly speaking, the counterpoint in measure 14 follows the traces of that in measure 9, except that the augmented-fourth leap is filled in by a triplet and the momentum of the triplet drives the figure on up to $c^3$ — what psychological justification![61]

In measures 20–42 [the upper voice] launches out a second time from c in search of the route to $f^2$, and this results in a linear succession that is even more emphatic than the preceding one since it presses further forward (bb–ab–g/c–bb–ab–g/c–bb–ab–g–f). In measures 20–32 there is a neighbor-note motion in the upper voice: $bb^2$–$ab^2$–$c^3$–$b^2$ (mm. 21, 23, 25, 27). The meaning [of this motion] is grasped through the voice leading in the bass, which leads ultimately to the triadic root G in measure 27 (see the third, Eb–F–G); the root G represents III. The answer is built into this III: see the third-progression $g^1$–$f^1$–$e^1$ in measures 28, 31, and 33. Another, modified answer begins in measure 33; it brings in the third-progression $c^2$–$bb^1$–$ab^1$ initially in measures 33–38, but also continues further in the following bars, to $g^1$ in measure 39 and thereafter — following a transfer to the two-line register — directly to $f^2$ via $ab^2$–$g^2$–$f^2$. The new answer is set in VI ($C^{\natural 3}$), which is followed in measure 40 by II, so that $f^2$ in measure 42 coincides with V. Thus the extended route [to $f^2$] is supported by a richer scale-degree progression: I–III–VI–II–V. Concerning the transformation of the chromatic step $bb^2$–$b^2$ (mm. 21–27) into a diatonic neighbor-note sequence, see "Erl[äuterungen]" and the examples in *Der Tonwille* and the yearbook, vol. 1.[62] However, it is decisively important to grasp the fact that both entries of the answer in measures 28–33 and 33–38 are built into the one arpeggiation.[63] Bach [*recte*: Beethoven] does not treat the entries as separate formal units functioning as bearers of tonality, but has them occur in passing, as it were, while at the same time having a cadential progression unfold. It would seem that the occurrence at this point of [fugal] entries exclusively was not inevitable since some alternative to them would have been conceivable, and the [musical] content could also have been otherwise. And what key, moreover, might be surmised for the two entries? Would Theory wish to speak of C minor in the first case and of F minor in the second? One sees the contradiction by comparing this outcome with that provided by the scale degrees.

*Mm. 42ff.* In measure 42 $f^2$ is at last reached above the dominant.[64] A further elaboration of V extends to measure 89. In measure 42 $f^2$ is the fifth of the dominant, but the goal of the motion, intended to make the voice leading more compelling, is the seventh; it is reached in measure 89. This fact urges a retrospective view: it turns out that [in the upper voice] measures 1–42 are controlled by $g^1$ (and $g^2$); four bass arpeggiations are needed for the expression [*Ausdeutung*] of this g, and $f^2$ falls in the middle of the fourth [see Ex. 2.21].

The reduction [*Aufriß*: Ex. 2.21] shows a twofold neighbor-note motion in the upper voice and a concluding stepwise ascent to the seventh. The first neighbor-note motion in measures 42–52 is accompanied by a fourth-progression in the bass (Bb–Ab–G–F, mm. 42, 45, 49, and 52); in the second, the fifth-divider C in the bass is set against the lower neighbor note $e^2$ (m. 62). But since the triadic root F in measures 52 and 76 is itself only the fifth-divider of the dominant Bb, the bass motion presses back again to the root Bb in measure 89.

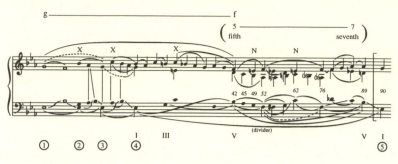

EXAMPLE 2.21

As for the detail, the answer appears in the bass in measures 42–45. An ascending motion begins in the upper voice in measure 46, ostensibly with the aim of transferring the neighbor note to a higher register [Ex. 2.22]. Note $db^3$–$c^3$ (mm. 50–51) and $eb^3$–$d^3$ (mm. 56–58), which lead one to expect $f^3$–$e^3$ in measures 60–62; $f^1$–$e^2$ enter in place of these notes owing to a sudden downward transfer, so that $f^2$ from measure 42 finds the neighbor note $e^2$ in the correct register in measure 62. Following the neighbor note $f^2$ now appears, likewise in the correct register, in measure 76.

EXAMPLE 2.22

The arpeggio $db^3$–$bb^2$–$g^2$ in measures 50–51 prepares the arpeggiation which is a motive in the [variation] theme and which serves as a counterpoint to the subsequent entries in measures 52–55 and 57–62. Thus the fugal entry is counterpointed by the arpeggio-motive of the theme for the first time. The progressions $f^1$–$f\sharp^1$ in measures 52–55 and $g^2$–$ab^2$ in measures 57–60 accord with the bass, which seeks a path from the triadic root F to the divider C ([see] mm. 52 and 62). In measures 62–65 the subject enters in the bass and is likewise counterpointed by the arpeggio-motive. A fifth-progression begins in the bass in measure 65 and extends to F in measure 76. A change of technique takes place with [the arrival on] Ab in measure 69, inasmuch as the fifth-leaps pass to the upper voice. A further change occurs in measures 73–76, where the leaps accelerate. In measure 69 the bass $c^1$ picks up $c^1$ from the middle voice (see $c^1$, m. 79), so that the outer voices proceed in sixths in measures 69–72. From measure 73 onward the contrapuntal setting [*Satz*] is 6–5, 6–5, 6–5 (ostensibly 6–8, 6–8, 6–8). Sixteenth-note motion resumes in measure 77, and is prepared by the sixteenths at the end of measure 76. The underlying sense of the sixteenth notes in measures 77–78 is $f^2$–$g^2$–$ab^2$. The third-progression $Db$–C–$Bb$ provides the content of the bass in measures 77–89 (see Ex. 2.21). This pitch-sequence accompanies the third-progression $f^1$–$eb^1$–$d^1$. The bass head note $Db$ in measure 77 serves in the first instance to connect up with the F-minor triad which has been the controlling harmony since measure 52. $Db$ first yields to D, the third of the [dominant] root $Bb$, in measure 89. In the realization [of mm. 77–89] $Db$–C is repeated in the bass in measures 81–82, where also the $ab^2$-register rings out again (see $ab^2$, m. 78). Beginning in measure 81 the outer voices rise up through a sixth: see $ab^2$–$f^3$ in the upper voice (mm. 82 and 89) and correspondingly C–$Ab$ in the bass; and, first in the bass, the turn back down to the root $Bb$ which links up with $Bb$ in measure 42, at the same time as the upper voice, moving in the opposite direction, sounds $bb^1$–$ab^2$ in order to confirm the $ab^2$ of measures 78–82 as the seventh of the dominant triad.

The fourth bass arpeggiation concludes in measure 90; $g^1$ reappears with the entry of the inverted subject so that a repetition of g–f, the outcome of the upper-voice motion up to this point, may take place.

*M. 90.* The Line has again reached $g^{265}$. The subject appears in inversion. In measures 90–91: the arpeggio of the [variation-] theme-motive still used as a counterpoint. In measures 95–100: the answer in inversion. In measure 100: upward transfer of the Line, $g^2$ replacing $g^1$; the subject in inversion here. In measure 105 $f^2$ falls on the dominant. This $f^2$ marks the end of the second $g^2$–$f^2$ progression,[66] so that the content of measures 1–8 of the [variation] theme is treated to a repetition which corresponds to the repetition in the theme [itself]. In its pursuit of the design of the theme the fugue also now strives to establish $bb^2$, and this takes place in measures 105–23. For a voice-leading diagram see [Ex. 2.23].

[In Ex. 2.23] we see a fifth-progression which, owing to the registral transfer of the second note ($eb^3$ for $eb^2$, m. 110), gives rise to the illusion of a fourth-progression since $bb^2$ and not $bb^1$ eventually appears at the end of the fifth-progression. The diagram further shows the [downward] unfolding $d^3$–$ab^2$ in measures 111–16 and the upward unfolding $g^2$–$c^3$ in measures 117–18; the upper voice proceeds only through $d^3$–$c^3$, of course. The dominant in measure 105 is in $^6_3$ position, and so the bass must continue onward to the root.

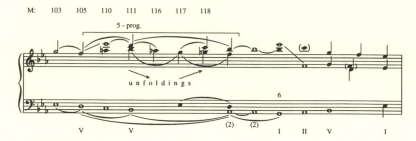

EXAMPLE 2.23

An opportunity for this is provided by the steps in the fifth-progression, which are accompanied step-by-step in the bass. The [dominant] root arrives in measure 111. Contrary to the theme, but as in many of the variations, the passing note Ab is interpolated here between the [dominant] root and the I⁶₃ in measure 130. Above Ab comes bb² itself, creating a ⁴₂. The alterations made to the upper voice in measures 130–32 are easy to understand: strict accordance with the theme would require c³ over the bass Ab in measure 131 and g²–f² in measure 132.

The fugue debouches into a slowed-down statement of the [variation] theme, *Andante con moto;* here, to the detriment of work as a whole, the character of the keyboard writing becomes downright orchestral; compare the conclusion to the finale of the "Eroica" Symphony.[67] The a² and bb² [*recte*: a¹ and bb¹] which introduce the trill in measure 141ff. should be fingered 1 1; the trill should be fingered 1 2.

The Coda (m. 196 [ff.]) brings the concluding descent [*Ablauf*][68] g²–f²–eb².

11. II. 27

# Notes

1. Heinrich Schenker, "Beethovens Dritte Sinfonie zum erstenmal in ihrem wahren Inhalt dargestellt," in *Das Meisterwerk in der Musik: Ein Jahrbuch von Heinrich Schenker* 3 (1930; reprint, New York: Georg Olms, 1974): 25–101.

2. The *Erläuterungsausgaben* of Opp. 109, 110, 111, and 101 were published in Vienna by Universal Edition in 1913, 1914, 1916, and 1921, respectively. However, the reader who enjoys Schenker's characteristically dismissive assessments of contemporary and earlier writings on the piano sonatas in the *Erläuterungsausgaben* turns in vain to Part IV (*Literatur*) of the "Eroica" study in search of further such material. "Most of what has been written about the Third Symphony in theoretical, biographical and analytical studies," writes Schenker, "does not yet actually count as music literature: it has no connection whatsoever with music, let alone with Beethoven's Third Symphony. I can safely leave it to the reader to verify this for himself" ("Beethovens Dritte Sinfonie," 100). Only Nottebohm's partial transcription of the main sketchbook for the "Eroica" and an essay by August Halm are deemed worthy of any mention.

3. The other two works in which the theme appears are the Contretanz, WoO 14, No. 7, and the Finale of the ballet music *Die Geschöpfe des Prometheus*, Op. 43, No. 16. On the relationship of the "Eroica" finale to Op. 35, see Lewis Lockwood, "The Earliest Sketches for the *Eroica* Symphony" and "The Compositional Genesis of the *Eroica* Finale," in Lockwood, *Beethoven: Studies in the Creative Process* (Cambridge, Mass.: Harvard University Press, 1992), 134–50 and 151–66 respectively. On the sketches for Op. 35, see Christopher Reynolds, "Beethoven's Sketches for the Variations in E♭ Op. 35," in *Beethoven Studies* 3, ed. Alan Tyson (Cambridge: Cambridge University Press, 1982): 47–84.

4. Schenker, "Beethovens Dritte Sinfonie," 75.

5. Schenker, "Beethovens Dritte Sinfonie," 75. See also Fig. 45, where the formal descriptions borrowed from Op. 35 are applied directly to a high-level voice-leading graph of the "Eroica" finale.

6. There is no entry for Op. 35 in Larry Laskowski, *Heinrich Schenker: An Annotated Index to His Analyses of Musical Works* (New York: Pendragon Press, 1978), which of course deals only with Schenker's published work.

7. The text and separate musical examples are all part of File 56 in the Oster Collection: see *The Oster Collection: Papers of Heinrich Schenker: A Finding List*, compiled by Robert Kosovsky (New York Public Library, Music Division, 1990), 225, 227. However, the final page (p. 36) of the text is not identified as such and is listed separately from the remainder: see File 56, items 6 and 26–60. The musical figures illustrating the analysis of the fugue are File 56, items 7–9. Items 7 and 8 preserve two versions of a foreground graph; item 7 appears to represent a fair copy, with some revisions, of item 8 and is the source for the transcription that appears as

Ex. 2.20 below. The material for Op. 35 in File 40, item 11 is misidentified in *The Oster Collection*: see the main text and n. 13 below.

8. "Lie — Lie" was a pet name for Schenker's wife, Jeanette.

9. See items 31 and 32 in the catalogue of scores: *The Oster Collection*, 341.

10. See File 83, items 155–58.

11. See File 83, item 146, dated 8 October 1916; item 147 (undated); and item 151, dated 1 November 1916. All the material in File 83, including the four-page document referred to above, was apparently destined for a theory of form. This "Entwurf einer neuen Formenlehre" was already in Schenker's mind as early as 1913; in the Op. 109 *Erläuterungsausgabe,* he undertook to deal more extensively with the issue of the large-scale unification of the variation set in the *Entwurf*: see *Beethoven: Die letzten Sonaten: Sonate E-dur Op. 109. Kritische Einführung und Erläuterung von Heinrich Schenker* (1913; rev. Oswald Jonas, Vienna: Universal, 1971), 38. See also the reference to the *Entwurf* in *Free Composition*, trans. and ed. Ernst Oster (New York: Longman, 1979), 1:130.

12. For an English translation of *Der freie Satz* see *Free Composition*, ed. Oster.

13. See Files 20–23, 35–38, 51, 74, 76, 79, and File A; see further *The Oster Collection*, Appendix 1 (370–81).

14. The graphs are located on the verso of File 40, item 11; in the reference to the *a due* from Op. 35 in *The Oster Collection*, 157, is incorrect. The pencil sketches on the bottom staff appear to relate not to Op. 35 but to the first movement of the Sixth Symphony, other graphs for which appear on the recto of item 11 and elsewhere in File 40. The annotation "Beethoven Op. 35 and 55" in the bottom left-hand corner is in the hand of Ernst Oster.

15. Compare Schenker's analysis of the sixteen-measure variation theme in the second movement of Beethoven's "Appassionata" Sonata, Op. 57: Schenker, "Beethoven: Sonate opus 57," *Der Tonwille* 4/1 (1924): 14. Schenker reads the upper voice as a slow arpeggiation from a♭ (m. 1) to a♭$^1$ (m. 14), which functions as the *Kopfton*. This analysis was subsequently incorporated into *Free Composition*, 2: fig. 40, 8.

16. File 40, item 11 is clearly a fragment from a larger sheet of manuscript paper; the fact that the foreground graph of the Op. 35 theme was originally numbered "3" and then renumbered "2" suggests that a background graph has been lost. Schenker's pencilled middleground sketch, numbered "1," is clearly a modified copy of Elias's partially obscured fair copy of this level on the top staff of the paper.

17. It should be noted that while terms such as *Ursatz* and *Urlinie* used in the following paragraphs do not appear in Schenker's Op. 35 text, they do occur in writings published prior to this: see, for example, *Das Meisterwerk in der Musik* 1 (1925; reprint, New York: Georg Olms, 1974); also "Brahms: Variationen und Fuge über ein Thema von Händel, Op. 24," *Der Tonwille*, 4/2–3 (1924): 3–46. Schenker's avoidance of such terms throughout the

Op. 35 study is thus striking, and may reflect his growing awareness of the difficulty of applying his now more mature understanding of *Ursatz* and *Urlinie* to works in variation form.

18. See also the remarks on Variations 8 and 11.

19. See also the remarks on Variations 10 and 13.

20. The only B♭ (5̂) literally present in measure 13 is b♭ in the left hand. It is unclear whether Schenker heard the progression of this inner-voice pitch to a♭ in measure 14 as providing the 5̂–4̂ motion, or whether the bass A♭ played by the right hand in measure 14 is to be understood simultaneously as the 4 of the "thematic line" and as part of the *basso del tema*.

21. Schenker, "Beethovens Dritte Sinfonie," Fig. 47.

22. On the question of Schenkerian analysis and variation form, see my "Analysing Variations: The Finale of Beethoven's String Quartet Op. 74," *Music Analysis* 8 (1989): 303–24, and the secondary literature cited therein.

23. Esther Cavett-Dunsby, "Schenker's Analysis of the 'Eroica' Finale," *Theory and Practice* 11 (1986): 43. See also her *Mozart's Variations Reconsidered: Four Case Studies (K. 613, K. 501 and the Finales of K. 421 (417b) and K. 491)* (New York: Garland Publishing, 1989), 66–72.

24. See Schenker, "Beethovens Dritte Sinfonie," Figs. 43–45 and the associated text on pages 74–75.

25. Cavett-Dunsby observes that "the reduplicative structure of Schenker's level-two graph ("Beethoven's Dritte Sinfonie," Fig. 44) of the movement . . . has a family resemblance to the sectional structure of conventional variation form" ("Schenker's Analysis," 43).

26. Schenker, "Beethovens Dritte Sinfonie," 75–76.

27. Cf. "Beethovens Dritte Sinfonie," 77: "Hier [m. 107] setzt der Anstieg . . . ein. . . .; er beginnt mit einem angewandt fugierten Satz, der ungefähr dem *finale alla fuga* in Op. 35 entspricht."

28. "Beethovens Dritte Sinfonie," 74: "Was nun folgt ist im Grunde eine Wiederholung, . . . die über den Ursatz nichts Neues mehr aussagt." While it is tempting to regard the *Ablauf* here as denoting a structural 3̂–2̂–1̂ *Urlinie*-descent, this is probably to read too much into a term which Schenker typically uses in a less specific sense: see, for example, the essay on Chopin's Etude in G♭, Op. 10, No. 5, *Das Meisterwerk* 1 (1925): 164, where Schenker refers to the "Ablauf der Urlinie" in the sense of its overall course rather than the concluding 3̂–2̂–1̂ descent. In any case, the analogy to the "Eroica" finale being drawn here requires us to regard the 3̂–2̂–1̂ descent at the end of the fugue as being structurally decisive. With this in mind, it is interesting to observe the much stronger language used by Schenker in describing the corresponding point (mm. 258–77) in the "Eroica" finale itself: "Nun fällt g² als die 3̂ urliniemäßig zu es². . . . die Urlinie fällt zu es² in T. 277" ("Beethovens Dritte Sinfonie," 82). Of the repetition of 3̂–2̂–1̂ in the three-line octave at the end of the finale he has nothing to say.

29. The audible shift of emphasis from G to B♭ at the beginning of the variations might be interpreted with reference to the theme, in which a similar shift is effected: see the analysis of the theme discussed above.

30. The importance to the large-scale structure of Beethoven's variation cycles of the recapitulatory or "restorative" procedures touched upon here is further explored in William Kinderman, *Beethoven's Diabelli Variations* (Oxford: Clarendon Press, 1987), and my own *Beethoven's Piano Sonata in E, Op. 109* (Oxford: Clarendon Press, 1995).

31. Schenker, "Brahms: Variationen und Fuge über ein Thema von Händel, Op. 24," 6, 35.

32. Apart from the study of Brahms Op. 24 and the slow movement of the "Appassionata" Sonata (n. 15 and 17 above), see the condemnatory study "Ein Gegenbeispiel: Max Reger Op. 81: Variationen und Fuge über ein Thema von Joh. Seb. Bach für Klavier," *Das Meisterwerk in der Musik* 2 (1926; reprint, New York: Georg Olms, 1974): 171–92.

33. The correspondence relating to *Das Meisterwerk* in the Oster Collection (see File 54) throws no light on the question of publication; Schenker's diary, preserved in the Oswald Jonas Memorial Collection at the University of California, Riverside, might be more informative but was unavailable for the purposes of this study.

34. Schenker writes "von *es* zu *e*," as if referring specifically to the octave below middle C. His use of register notation is occasionally inconsistent, and the observation made here clearly applies across all three octaves.

35. By "*Aufriß*," Schenker presumably means the middleground progression $g^1$-$ab^1$-$bb^1$ and its continuation: see Figure 2.2 and the accompanying discussion in the introductory essay above. It is the retention of this *Aufriß* in the counterpoints of the *a tre* and *a quattro* to which Schenker refers in the following sentences.

36. See Figure 2.2 in the introductory essay above.

37. The short musical examples relating to the variations and numbered here from 2.1–2.19 are unnumbered in the manuscript; the four examples relating to the fugue are numbered 1–4 by Schenker but have been incorporated into the larger numerical sequence here as Examples 2.20–2.23.

38. "Der Lauf in der Fermate ist einzuteilen." Schenker's working score of Op. 35, ed. Louis Koehler and Richard Schmidt (Leipzig: C. F. Peters; Oster Collection, printed scores, No. 31) indicates a basic three-part subdivision comprising the arpeggiated descent from and return to $d^3$, the triplets (or sextuplets) descending from $f^3$ to d, and the chromatic scale rising from B♭. The markings in the score indicate further that Schenker thought of the descent from and return to $d^3$ as spanning two 4/4 measures: the fermata lasts for two beats, and the following sixteenths are articulated as six quarter notes: 4 + 4 + 4 + 5 (quintuplet) + 4 + 4.

39. See the two-note descending motive bracketed by Schenker in Ex. 2.6b; the opposing stem directions distinguish the inner-voice repetition of a♭–g in measure 7 from the immediately preceding statement in the bass.

40. In Schenker's working score (see n. 38 for details) the right-hand $e\flat^1$ on the second beat of measure 1 is erroneously omitted, leaving only the pair $b\flat/g$.

41. Schenker presumably understood the octave-arpeggiation to be established as a motivic element by the syncopations in measures 5–6.

42. This is probably the most obscure passage in the essay. Schenker's working score (see n. 38) shows a pencilled slur from the lower to the higher note of the broken octave on the fourth eighth note of measures 6, 13, and 14 respectively, but it is uncertain why he felt that these three junctures required special treatment by the performer.

43. In Schenker's working score (see n. 38), $g^1$ (m. 1), $a\flat^1$ (m. 3) and $b\flat^2$ (m. 6) are highlighted in pencil by upward stems and partial beams.

44. "Der Vortrag der Doppelgriffe verlangt eine deutliche Gliederung in Lagen": another somewhat obscure passage relating to performance issues (compare n. 42). *Lagen* might also refer to hand positions on the keyboard, analogous to those on stringed instruments (note the corresponding use of the string term *Doppelgriff* here). Materials relating to Schenker's projected textbook on performance ("Eine Lehre vom Vortrag") are contained in File 13 of the Oster Collection (see *The Oster Collection*, 45–46).

45. While the bass supplies A♭ (4) in measure 14, there is no upper-voice B♭ (5) in measure 13; only the left-hand inner voice supplies this note.

46. Schenker's working score (see n. 38) indeed carries a *sf* on the right-hand A♭ in measure 14; however, the autograph manuscript and first edition (Leipzig: Breitkopf & Härtel, 1803) give *f*, in accordance with the previous measure.

47. In fact the lower right-hand voice in measures 5–8 presents the *basso del tema*.

48. Schenker's use of the terms *geistig* and *der Geist* in this and the next sentence poses obvious problems in translation; for a roughly contemporary use see "Vermichtes: Gedanken über die Kunst und ihre Zusammenhänge im Allgemeinen," *Das Meisterwerk* 1 (1925): 209–10. The English translation by Ian Bent translates *Geist* as "spirit": see *The Masterwork in Music: A Yearbook, Volume 1 (1925),* ed. William Drabkin (Cambridge: Cambridge University Press, 1994), 115–16.

49. Gustav Nottebohm, "Clavierspiel," *Zweite Beethoveniana: nachgelassene Aufsätze,* ed. Eusebius Mandyczewski (Leipzig: C. F. Peters, 1887), 356–63.

50. In dealing with the written-out repeats in Variations 14 and 15, Schenker distinguishes parallel bars by various means, often referring to "die erste T. 1–8," "die zweite T. 9–16," and so on. For the purposes of the translation the suffix a or b has been appended silently to all relevant bar numbers.

51. Each pair of notes is slurred in the manuscript.

52. The continuity of the manuscript becomes problematic at this point. The sentence translated "It is in this sense . . . g♭–f" is partially deleted, and

the following two paragraphs, written on folio 14v, are cued in following "as in the theme," which makes little sense. The placement of the text found on folio 14v is therefore somewhat tentative here, as is the retention of the preceding sentence and accompanying Ex. 2.14.

53. This point applies only to the "accelerated" third-progressions in measures 2a and 4a, where 4–3 suspensions occur above the bass.

54. Schenker is referring presumably to the third eighth note in measure 1b (r.h.) and the first eighth note in measure 2b (l.h.).

55. This fingering is entirely corroborated by Schenker's working score (see n. 38).

56. The encircled numbers 1–7 in Ex. 2.20 and 1–5 in Ex. 2.21 identify the sequence of bass arpeggiations in the fugue; the numbering is Schenker's own.

57. Compare this and subsequent withering references to traditional fugal theory with Schenker's remarks in "Das Organische der Fuge," *Das Meisterwerk in der Musik* 2 (1926): 93–4.

58. This observation is not entirely supported by Ex. 2.20, which shows a neighbor-note progression $g^2$–$ab^{2/1}$–$g^1$ in measures 11–14.

59. There is an apparent question mark above "Comes" at the end of this sentence in the manuscript.

60. *Durchgang*, usually translated as "passing note," presumably refers here to the "more extended route" from B♭ to G discussed in connection with measures 11–20.

61. " — welche psychologische Begründung!" Above this phrase in the manuscript there are some illegible additions in Schenker's hand.

62. The essay "Erläuterungen" was first published in *Der Tonwille*, 4/2–3 (1924): 49–51, and reappeared in 4/4 (1924): 40–42. It was subsequently included in *Das Meisterwerk* 1 (1925): 201–205 and 2 (1926): 193–97; for an English translation by Ian Bent, see *The Masterwork in Music*, ed. Drabkin, 112–14.

63. That is, E♭–G–B♭ (mm. 20, 27, 42): see Ex. 2.20.

64. In the manuscript there is an illegible pencilled insertion following "$f^2$."

65. Schenker uses the term *Linie* here; in this context it has connotations of *Urlinie* as he understood it at this period, and also of the *Thema-Linie* — itself essentially an *Urlinie* — frequently referred to in the analysis of the variations.

66. The manuscript has "die 2. Reihe (?) $g^2$–$f^2$": the question mark is not an insertion by Schenker but appears within the main text. Was Jeanette Schenker questioning the propriety of the term *Reihe* here?

67. Schenker refers to the takeover of measures 133–96 of Op. 35 in measures 349–96 of the "Eroica" finale.

68. On the meaning of *Ablauf*, see n. 28 above.

# CHAPTER THREE

# Texture and Gender: New Prisms for Understanding Hensel's and Mendelssohn's Piano Pieces

## Camilla Cai

## I
## Texture reconsidered

ALTHOUGH the term *texture* is used easily and frequently in musical discussion, there are few comprehensive definitions of it.[1] One recent standard source, *The New Grove Dictionary of Music and Musicians*, gives texture only a three-paragraph description.[2] Texture is "any of the vertical aspects of a musical structure." The description does not explicitly mention the horizontal nature of texture, but the elements of texture listed are homophonic or polyphonic (contrapuntal) treatment, the number of parts, the spacing of chords, the "thickness" of sonority, the "lightness" or "heaviness" of performing forces, and "the arrangement of instrumental lines in an orchestral work." Other usages of the term are "melodic texture" which indicates "changes of pace or density in a melody" and "harmonic texture" which indicates "the rate of harmonic change." There is no mention of range or instrumental color as part of texture, nor of the changing nature of texture in time, the rhythmic nature of texture, or of the possibility that texture can influence or be part of form. No mention is made of the implications of texture for the performer, for whom working with it as a daily matter involves choosing tone color, balancing lines with other masses of sound, and projecting differing levels of importance to the listener.[3] The process of recreating texture from the written score, though vital to effective performance, is neglected.

Certain important aspects of musical texture must be added in order to round out the concept: texture at its most fundamental level can be conveyed by a single sound, and this quality is a function of timbre.[4] These individual timbral sounds combine to make both vertical (high-low) *and* horizontal (time-related) patterns; both are basic to texture. The vertical components are described by the range of sounds; their spacing and number within that range are called density. The horizontal components of texture are described by the frequency of the sounds in time and the patterns of their changes in quality or density. These would include melodic pacing, harmonic rhythm, rhythmic drive, and formal structural properties. Fundamentally, however, the two-directional axis — high-low elements in tension with time-related elements — define texture.

The concept of texture belongs to many fields: art, literature, religion, linguistics, physics, geology, psychology, and others. As used in the fine arts the definition can further illuminate its meaning in music: "[t]he representation of the structure of a surface as distinct from color or form."[5] Thus, texture in art is a tangible surface that can be described in and for itself. The structure of that surface includes two important aspects: something that can be seen, and something that can be touched or felt by the hand. Since texture in the fine arts is both visual and tactile, it can be described from both angles.

If the visual is difficult to describe in words, so the tactile aspects of texture, usually called "touch," are even more difficult to articulate and analyze. "This feels smooth," "this feels rough," are typical relative and flexible descriptions. Adding to this difficulty of tactile description are the subjective and emotional reactions that influence the understanding of touch as part of texture. In many cases it is these reactions to a work of art that first draws in both artist and viewer. Though other aspects of an art work also bring forward personal responses, texture does so in an unusually strong way through this basic reaction to the element of touch. If we are to understand texture more fully, we cannot ignore these personal, subjective, and emotional elements that touch imposes on texture.

Standard, nonmusical dictionary definitions of texture include further images useful to music: "[t]he appearance of a fabric resulting from the woven arrangement of its yarns or fibers" and "[t]he composition or structure of a substance; grain: *the smooth texture of ivory.*"[6] These two definitions are close to the fine-arts definition in that they suggest a physical object, a woven thing or something with grain, something to be touched. The three definitions together also bring us close to the musical one in that they refer to texture with words like *fabric* or *grain*.

These definitions suggest the possibility that musical texture also contains this additional quality of touch. And indeed, touch, in music as in art, is present as a highly subjective element, primarily evident to the composer or performer. The feel of the keyboard, the tactile knowledge of how the hands feel moving over it, will be part of how the player and composer understand the piece. The player is the most privileged and complete listener because he/she experiences all these aspects of texture directly. The ability to touch the piece is not an incidental or purely technical matter. The listener, even at a distance, can imagine this sense of touch, and can appreciate it indirectly through watching and listening.[7] Texture, including this aspect of touch, will be the first thing apparent to the listener, and the first thing that can be described. This primacy of grasp, alone, suggests texture's importance.[8]

Most authors have placed texture in conjunction with another element.[9] In art, authors connect texture with color or form.[10] In literary criticism, texture and structure or text are paired.[11] In language studies, texture has been linked to structure.[12] In musical writings, there is also juxtaposition with other elements: texture with timbre, tonality, or sonata form.[13] Texture has been highly useful to these authors in such a tandem role, and, as we will see below, texture connects equally well with rhythm, melody, and form.

I propose, however, that this paired or secondary role for texture — where it has sometimes been labelled as the "surface" element or the one of lesser importance — may come from gender stereotyping of the concept of texture itself. Since both the wording of its definition and the intimate nature of texture and touch discussed above have deeply embedded feminine imagery, texture is vulnerable to stereotyping. Let us first examine the wording of the definition of texture: described primarily as a woven thing, texture directly suggests fabric. Traditionally, creating a fabric's texture, that is, the act of weaving, is an area of almost exclusively feminine knowledge; women have always worked with fabric in their daily lives, creating its contours and textures through sewing, embroidering, crocheting, and knitting. These processes have produced crafts, not art, which historically have been of lesser value in the public sphere.

Much more powerful than these historical facts are the mythic underpinnings surrounding weaving. Buried deep in the cultural consciousness, images of weaving demonstrate strong connections not only to the feminine, but to the negative, the mysterious, and the dangerous. Arachne, changed into a spider for challenging Athena in a weaving contest, was condemned to spin for eternity. Penelope, wife of Odysseus, had her endless weaving described as a *deception* toward her suitors, and for Helen, wife of Menelaus, her weaving was seen as the sinister mapping of the history of Troy.[14] In Norse mythology when Brynhild wove the deeds of Sigurd into her tapestry, she embodied the fears of the Catholic Church who at times forbad this "magical art" of weaving. Such witchcraft that could entwine curses and charms into tapestries and seal the fates of those depicted was clearly dangerous.[15] Weaving, as a little-understood, but feared activity of women, is central to these mythic depictions. It is not surprising that the result of weaving, the fabric and its texture, could evoke negative responses and distancing mechanisms.

Furthermore, texture — through its element of touch — includes sensual aspects, and the sensual aspects, in turn, are closely linked with ideas of the feminine. These sensual aspects may additionally require discussion of emotional components, and emotional content — often the center of musical appeal — is also invariably feminized. Texture, as a thing to be touched, suggests that there is a physical object present to touch or feel. There are two parts here: touching the fabric, a feminized object, and the act of touching, touching by or of a woman. In either case, these connotations suggest images that are domestic and/or private, two ideas further associated with the feminine.

Texture is described as the exterior of the music, the immediately apparent, the "trappings" of the piece. Within this description is embedded yet another feminine image: texture with exterior sensuousness or "surface voluptuousness."[16] The texture, in this formulation, may be boldly appealing, possibly even suggestive, and thus it resembles the cultural stereotype of, for example, a well-dressed or perhaps even a partially dressed woman. Texture, as a sensuous exterior, hints at the possibility of more intimate touching and, thus, in yet another way, includes the feminized sensuality.

Perhaps because of the difficulty in describing texture, it has also been labeled "inexact," "ambiguous," "amorphous," or "auxiliary."[17] With some regularity these adjectives are also considered feminine attributes. Texture is *not* described as abstract, mathematical, formal, or as something developed through mental activity. It stands apart from a planned *Ursatz* or an overarching structural principle, that is, from rational or unemotional principles, often also called important or masculine principles. Texture, then, as the amorphous facade of the piece, belongs to the realm of women. These feminine images and connotations — connected to texture more often than to melody, harmony, and rhythm — particularly assign to texture the added property that it is an element of lesser importance.[18]

An awareness of the feminized definition permits a new perspective from which to view texture in the piano compositions by siblings Mendelssohn and Hensel. To compare only their forms and structures in traditional ways brings with it standard and inherent judgments about value and quality, judgments that traditionally give the highest value to pieces with tightly structured, closely balanced forms and pieces with motivic development. The judgment is often unfavorable for pieces differently constructed. Hensel, by choosing longer and freer forms than Mendelssohn, would thus have her accomplishments devalued.

## II
## The comparison

The siblings make an excellent pair for musical comparison. Their close personal relationship, their common training as pianists and as composers, their lifelong involvement in music, their interest in piano music, and, specifically, their interest in each other's music suggest that study of their compositions will provide new information about their musical personalities.[19] Differences in their handling of texture will reveal individual approaches to composition, and analysis of these patterns will suggest gender as one influence on their choices.

There are events, both cultural and personal, which suggest the powerful influence of gender roles on Hensel and Mendelssohn. For example, in spite of their seemingly equal educations (mentioned with a kind of bravado in every life account of Hensel) there was, from the beginning, a fundamental difference of experience for the aspiring performer-composer children. From the feminine patterns of her daily life, Hensel knew from earliest childhood that her future, and especially her future in music, would be different from Mendelssohn's.[20] This understanding would have colored the relevance of every music lesson and every composition assignment, even though the musical information presented to the children may have been the same. Hensel's future was to be a woman within a society that assigned men and women different tasks. Her father Abraham's warning to her at age fourteen, near the time of her confirmation, that music was an ornament for a woman and a profession for a man, was simply one more fatherly reminder of lessons already well absorbed.[21] Hensel's envious pleas to Mendelssohn to relate the details of his musical travels display her longing for the privileges awarded him, but those pleas contain no rebellion against her own female lack of privilege.[22]

As young adults, the differences of their life experience became externally obvious. Hensel received little stimulus within the family to train herself in all areas of composition (for example, *Singspiele* or opera) or to prepare her music for wider audiences.[23] She was not encouraged to perform publicly, as Mendelssohn was, and she participated solely in the family's musical salon. However brilliant that salon was, she was not challenged and evaluated as Mendelssohn was on his gentleman's tour of Europe.[24] Prominent musicians helped him polish his musical skills, and through these associations he built a network of colleagues and influential friends who furthered his career.

Hensel's and Mendelssohn's basic personalities were, of course, different, and the degree to which these basic differences were determined by gender is impossible to assess. But *how* they expressed themselves was cultural and determined by their gender roles. Since disciplined learning was central to their lives from earliest childhood, they developed into individuals and musicians who were highly critical of their own work. Hensel's self-criticism was turned inward with her self-deprecating attitude and her constant doubting the value of her work: "It won't be much but it will be something. . . . I'm happy if I succeed in writing down some notes, without having much of an idea at the start as to how it will turn out afterwards. Later, of course, I fret if it's bad."[25] If she used composition as an outlet to express strong feelings, perhaps the unnumbered piece in F minor (discussed below) could be considered an example of it. In Mendelssohn the same self-critical attitude was reflected in holding himself (and others) to high standards, but it was also directed outward. He exhibited annoyance toward the busy public side of music; he only partly contained hostility toward colleagues; and he showed contempt for the feminine, even when it concerned his own work.[26] Public expression of this kind was a culturally accepted masculine model not available to Hensel.

Mendelssohn felt keenly the outside pressure on him to be successful as a musician. Publishing *Songs without Words* seems to have been an obligation rather than a pleasure.[27] This attitude alone could have inhibited his work. When, later, his new *Songs without Words* had to be written to resemble earlier ones and had to be done quickly, this too may have placed limits on his creativity.[28] Even Robert Schumann hinted that in the fourth collection "certain turns of phrase, repetitions [from earlier collections], seem almost to be mannerisms."[29] That such a critic saw lack of inspiration lends credence to the interpretation of compositional constriction for Mendelssohn.

There were advantages accorded to Hensel, both by her native talent and through her situation in the home. She was the better pianist of the two, according to Mendelssohn himself, and these skills at the piano meant that piano music was her most natural and comfortable medium. Since most other media were not available to her, she could concentrate in large part on her strongest area, and thus expand and develop to a high degree a personal idiom for the piano. Mendelssohn's public duties brought pressures from every direction to write in all mediums, denying him the same concentrated focus. In spite of Hensel's unhappiness over the lack of public recognition,[30] she was, as an adult, freer than Mendelssohn in several other ways. She did not need to please the paying public or the commercial publishers, she had no professional commitments to distract her attention, and she was answerable only to a small number of people. By performing in her own salon environment where criticizing a hostess would have been rare, she could develop her music as she wished. The lack of constant criticism and judging allowed her, though she may not have been aware of it, freedom from public pressure to conform. It let her develop a style that was at once more idiosyncratic and less disciplined than Mendelssohn's.

Hensel had constraints on her time, however, in ways different from Mendelssohn. She had a large household to manage and supervise, for which much of the work was not related to music. Composing, for her, was a sideline, done for her own enjoyment and for her salon, but only when there was time available.[31] Even her beloved salon mixed pleasure with responsibility for she was both hostess and manager of this large and complex event. Mendelssohn, on the other hand, devoted himself entirely to music, dividing his time only between conducting and composing. Their attention to composing was, by the circumstance of these gender roles, vastly different.

Hensel and Mendelssohn had not only differing amounts of time to spend on composing but also a different purpose in doing so. For Mendelssohn composing was a primary occupation, and through his compositions he established his reputation and the public press judged his worth. Hensel was primarily a salon hostess, and her success in this role was judged by the guests who visited. This role included composing and performing music, but equally important were planning interesting programs, presenting high-quality performers, inviting entertaining guests, easing contact among these strangers, providing clever and witty conversation, managing the serving staff, seeing to the food, arranging for its presentation with expensive, polished silver, providing an elegant and inviting gathering space, in all, smoothly presenting an afternoon of entertainment and pleasure for others.[32] The standards for success in this role in cosmopolitan Berlin were high. That Hensel herself was particularly talented in composition and performance added special luster to her reputation as a hostess, but music alone did not define her as it did Mendelssohn. Their two occupations — his, composer and conductor, hers, hostess and musician — had standards of excellence and spheres of influence that only barely overlapped.

That Hensel's pieces resemble Mendelssohn's shows the force of the values of the dominant masculine musical culture. Hensel studied music with men and by men. While she was being taught to compose "like a man" (resembling a man, yet not a man), she was also being imbued with the feminine values of the same culture. By being a composer at all she chose a position that put her in conflict with cultural values of her time, and although she did use the musical-technical language of men, she accepted a woman's place by choosing genres and an instrument appropriate to a woman.[33]

But did her position of tension, a woman using a man's language, affect her handling of that musical-technical language? Does a feminine voice speak at all in Hensel's compositions, beyond their position as nineteenth-century character pieces for piano, that is, as a genre acceptable for women composers? I suggest that through the particular network of compositional choices she makes, that she has a distinctly feminine voice. This is not an essentialist stance, however; no particular compositional device can be singled out as "feminine" or "feminine-sounding." While Hensel's special interest in texture, for example, shows in her criticisms of Mendelssohn's pieces,[34] one cannot listen to her pieces and to Mendelssohn's and determine the composer's gender. The problem is more complex, the differences more subtle. It is only collectively that Hensel's musical choices suggest a leaning to aspects of music that are traditionally labelled feminine, and even then these leanings are best observed by direct comparison to similar pieces by Mendelssohn.

Hensel's strong interest in the surface or texture of the music suggests a feminine leaning through two of the stereotyped images for this concept mentioned earlier. The one image is that musical surface is analogous to exterior feminine dress; the second compares music to woven cloth. Both nineteenth-century feminine dress and woven fabric (*das Gewebe*), though not part of the musical-technical language of Hensel's time, would have had strong importance for a nineteenth-century woman like Hensel in preparing herself for presentation at her elegant salon. Since her attire and her music were both important parts of this same event, it is intriguing to connect similar aspects of the two.[35] That her music would be imbued with the same sense of attention to surface and texture as her attire seems entirely possible. By according texture this important position in her music, she can move ahead to use it in interesting ways. As we will see below, in her piece titled "No. 7," texture becomes the unifying force that replaces form in importance.

# III
# Piano pieces

The pieces for piano, in particular, invite our attention. Examining only these pieces eliminates the need to compare different instrumental colorations that affect texture in larger pieces. This limitation is not an artificial one. Hensel wrote only a few oratorios and one orchestral piece because she did not regularly have such performing forces available to her.[36] Her few works in these groups do not form a body of music comparable to Mendelssohn's large output. The same is true for Hensel's chamber pieces. As for the songs of both brother and sister, they possibly could be compared, but the nature of both the texts and the human voice add further complexities to such a comparison.

Hensel and Mendelssohn were actively involved with the piano throughout their lives and were excellent pianists who wrote for themselves and others. However, their piano repertoires are not completely parallel because they have a difference of purpose. Hensel's pieces were written for herself, her own enjoyment, and for performance in her private salon. She and a few close friends performed them, but they were not dedicated to others, or available to a wider public (until the last two years of her life).[37] When she wrote her pieces she had little hope or expectation that they would be published, gain a public, or be reviewed in the press. Mendelssohn's piano pieces were also for his own performance, but used at both private gatherings and salons as well as in public concert halls throughout Europe. This provided his pieces with a wider, more varied audience than that found in Hensel's Berlin salon. In addition, Mendelssohn dedicated pieces to specific women, both amateur and professional pianists; more importantly, he catered to a large anonymous buying public that sought out his published editions for home use.

Mendelssohn's and Hensel's common use of this personal and mostly private idiom comes not only from their own connection to the piano as performers, but also from performance settings which intensified the personal: an intimate room with people sitting near the piano and sharing the music closely with the performer. Even for the buying public, Mendelssohn would have expected a similar setting, though the performances would have been amateur and the homes less sumptuous.[38] The feel of the keyboard, the textural aspect mentioned above, would have been an important part of this intimate setting to a young, female amateur pianist. For the young man sitting or leaning nearby to admire her, there would also have been the textural feel of his armchair, the piano itself, or even the texture of his own imaginings. Such intimate places and occasions appropriate for Hensel's and Mendelssohn's piano pieces suggest that a similarly intimate quality may be embodied within the pieces themselves. These pieces do share a large common ground through their texture, the feel of the keyboard, and their emotional appeal.

To choose comparable pieces of Hensel and Mendelssohn for study we will put aside for the moment their slight differences of function and place. (These differences will be relevant to certain aspects of composition in the comparison of individual pieces below.) Pieces chosen have obvious and widely applied textural similarities; they also share other clusters of common traits. Because of these other similar traits, the variables in the study are more limited, and this permits a clearer focus on textural issues. The title of a piece, though it often suggests the genre to which a piece belongs, has not been relevant to the selection process. Two pieces titled, for example, "Sonata," "Capriccio," "Scherzo," "Prelude/Fugue," or "Etude," can be successfully compared using traditional formal analysis since both composers are fairly consistent in their understandings of these genres. These categories do not help clarify textural issues because two sonatas that are formally of a kind may not have significant textural elements in common. On the other hand, a Mendelssohn prelude might very fruitfully be compared with an untitled work of Hensel's because of their similar textural type. A few of Mendelssohn's piano pieces can be excluded from this study entirely. His variations and his fantasy on "The Last Rose of Summer" are unique, and nothing in Hensel's work overlaps with them. The form in the former and the foreign tune in the latter dictate so strongly to these pieces that elements of texture exist in service of the corresponding characteristic.

Three conclusions will emerge. Hensel and Mendelssohn use apparently similar textures in similar pieces for different compositional purpose, i.e., what seems initially a straightforward commonality contains important underlying differences of approach. Secondly, Hensel and Mendelssohn's different purpose in using a common texture leads to a different handling of other elements. Finally, these individual ways of handling elements of music may derive from their gender roles.

# IV
# Three-part texture

Mendelssohn's main group of *Songs without Words* are defined by their three-part texture. This texture provides an excellent place from which to view the points of convergence and difference in Hensel and Mendelssohn. This three-part texture has both vertical and horizontal components. To use the metaphor of fabric again, the warp (lengthwise strands) and the woof (crosswise strands) vary in thickness and these variations give each fabric its unique quality. For example, arpeggios call attention to the warp, or the horizontal, while block chords call attention to the woof, or the vertical. Such figurations are not new with Hensel and Mendelssohn, but they exploit the textural differences with particular effectiveness.

Mendelssohn's Op. 53, No. 1, is a typical example that illustrates three-part texture.[39] The melodic voice is uppermost, independent of inner voices, singable in the soprano range, and fairly regular and balanced in its phrasing with short, discrete two-measure units added together to build larger, mostly eight-measure phrases. The middle or inner voice is a filler of arpeggios divided between the two hands and constructed of chord-filling notes with occasional, mildly chromatic coloring. The bass voice is independent of the middle voice and forms a contrapuntal support for the melody. It is, of course, also the harmonic support. Each of the three voices maintains a consistent rhythmic and textural pattern. There are a few minor deviations: an example is the inner voice that splits into two parts in measures 28–29, 40–42, and 47–48.

A piece of Hensel's that, by its similarity, eliminates as much as possible the effect of variant factors is her Op. 6, No. 1.[40] Not only is the texture similar but also the key, meter, tempo, and length. These many common characteristics suggest some kind of further connection between the pieces — that their musical alliance might be supported with a close historical concordance. If there is any connection at all — that is, if one composer knew the other's piece and used it as a model or inspiration — it would be that Mendelssohn's 53/1 influenced Hensel's 6/1. Mendelssohn's piece existed already by 4 June 1841, when Mendelssohn refers to the whole Op. 53 *Stichvorlage* in a letter, and the piece itself was subsequently published 15 August 1841.[41] Hensel's piece exists in an autograph of 11 November 1846,[42] and was published in 1847. She would certainly have seen Mendelssohn's published set by 1846, but there is no evidence specifically linking her piece to his earlier 53/1.

Even without direct historical evidence linking the two, it is worth noting that both pieces stand first in their respective opus numbers. Hensel may have composed this 1846 piece, not for her own performance as she did for most of her compositions, but for its place as the first piece of a published set. All Mendelssohn's *Songs without Words* sets published before her piece of 1846 begin with a piece in the same flowing three-part texture,[43] but 53/1 is the most striking in its possibility as a model for 6/1. One might suggest that Hensel, not yet confident of her ability to capture public approval, rejected extant pieces, wrote a new piece to open Op. 6, and modeled it closely on Mendelssohn's known and successful opening piece.

To consider the similarities more closely: the pieces are in the same key (A♭ major), and of approximately the same length, Mendelssohn's is 64 measures; Hensel's, 61. The tempo markings are almost the same: Mendelssohn's 53/1 is *Andante con moto*, and Hensel's 6/1 is *Andante espressivo* (originally *Andante cantabile*). Their time signatures produce the same metric effect through their subdivision: Mendelssohn's 12/8 meter and Hensel's C meter both use triplet eighths as the predominant accompaniment pattern. The pieces are closely parallel in their rondolike form; twice they bring back A material in the tonic (Mendelssohn at mm. 24 and 43; Hensel at mm. 33 and 49). They are similar in a detail of elaboration, both have solo melismas (Mendelssohn at mm. 23–24, 42–43, 59–60; Hensel at mm. 22–23, 30–32), and they use the same overall tonic-dominant harmonic motion, stating it early in the piece. Mendelssohn moves to the dominant area already in measure 11; Hensel modulates to the dominant by measure 11.

Their similar three-part texture is the overriding likeness between the two pieces, but their individual handling of this texture shows subtle differences of usage. One comparison demonstrates how they handle stability at the opening of the piece: Mendelssohn grounds his beginning with two-and-one-half measures of simple, descending arpeggios. See Ex. 3.1.

EXAMPLE 3.1a. Mendelssohn, Op. 53, No. 1, mm. 1–4

EXAMPLE 3.1b. Hensel, Op. 6, No. 1, mm. 1–6

To this textural constancy he adds harmonic stability: the introduction is tonic and the melody begins fully on the tonic. Hensel begins her piece more precipitously with only one half-measure of rising arpeggio texture which barely anchors the tonic; her melody begins over an already falling bass line (note G in m. 1) that begins the move away from the home key (Ab major) to a Cb-major coloring in measure 4. The common principle in both composers, it seems, is that the degree of opening stability is a function of the combined effects of texture and harmony. The pieces differ in that they apply this shared principle to produce an opposite effect; Mendelssohn seeks stability, Hensel, instability.

We can also look to Hensel's unnumbered piece in F minor[44] and Mendelssohn's Op. 38, No. 5, for a similarly veiled relationship of texture. This pairing of pieces has suggested itself for two reasons. They have an especially compelling historical connection because Hensel sent her unnumbered piece to Mendelssohn in late October of 1836 and Mendelssohn wrote Op. 38, No. 5, only six months later, 6 April 1837, as he was seeking to fill out the set that would be published as Op. 38 in May/June 1837.[45] As I have argued elsewhere, the musical similarities of texture, melodic shape, harmonic progression, and accompaniment type are so convincing that, in spite of significant differences in the amount of material used and in their differing scopes, Mendelssohn seems to have modeled his piece directly on Hensel's.[46]

The veiled textural aspect that conveys commonality, yet comes from a different vantage point, is their use of octaves to intensify a line. For Mendelssohn the use of octaves is an exception; he rarely chooses this technique within his *Songs without Words*.[47] For Hensel, octaves are a normal part of her piano style, possibly developed because she imagined her own piano sound not quite powerful enough without them. In any case, many of her pieces display long passages of this virtuosic doubling of line. Hensel's unnumbered piece, in measures 70–73, has a typical usage; Mendelssohn's exceptional use within 38/5 (mm. 10–11, 14–18 and elsewhere) suggests that Mendelssohn is paying homage to Hensel with a technique otherwise foreign to him in this genre of piano music. See Ex. 3.2.

EXAMPLE 3.2a.  Hensel, Unnumbered Piece, mm. 70–73

EXAMPLE 3.2b.  Mendelssohn, Op. 38, No. 5, mm. 10–11

Individual lines of the three-part texture have different meaning to Hensel and Mendelssohn. The top voices, or the melodic lines, have, in Mendelssohn's 53/1 and Hensel's 6/1, different ranges, and this feature affects their textural quality. Though both top voices are uppermost and independent of inner voices, Mendelssohn's melody is singable in the soprano range. Hensel extends her melody beyond a comfortable soprano range, reaching a fifth above and an augmented fourth below Mendelssohn's, and she includes large leaps that, while easy on the piano, would be difficult vocally. Hensel's range and melodic handling suggest a free and spacious texture; Mendelssohn's suggest a controlled environment and restricted texture.

In comparing Hensel's unnumbered piece and Mendelssohn's 38/5 we find similar patterns. Hensel uses the wider range and creates the more open sound. Her unnumbered piece rises to $ab^3$ within the second theme (m. 27) and much of her developmental material lies in this high range, while Mendelssohn reaches his highest note ($e^3$ in m. 28) at only one of the two *ff* places in the piece. Even Hensel's opening melody which started in the middle range ($c^1$) soars up to $c^2$ already in measure 2 (See Ex. 3.3). Mendelssohn, who also begins his melody in the middle range ($e^1$), rises only to $c^2$ in his opening four measures.

EXAMPLE 3.3a. Hensel, Unnumbered Piece, mm. 1–4

EXAMPLE 3.3b. Mendelssohn, Op. 38, No. 5, mm. 1–4

The melodic phrasing of these upper voices show their differing approaches to the forward motion of the melodic texture. The structure of Mendelssohn's 53/1 melody is mostly regular and balanced — short, discrete two-measure units build larger, mostly eight-measure phrases. Rests are often used as phrase delineators. Mendelssohn's forward melodic motion is sectional and regular, giving a start-and-stop effect to the texture. This motion becomes predictable, or at least reliable, because of the repetitions of phrase patterns. In contrast, Hensel's melody in 6/1 is a long, spun-out line, almost without cadential moments. The first time her melody pauses is in measure 33 (with a half-rest), and at that moment, for the first time, there is the support of a real cadence in the tonic. In between, Hensel's wavelike phrasing ebbs and flows, avoiding regular or expected patterns that might allow the listener to anticipate the phrase conclusion. The opening four swells (mm. 1–8) are of uniform size (two measures each, beginning in the middle of the measure). The continuation swells are more irregular: four measures (mm. 9–12), two measures (mm. 13–14), one measure (m. 15), one measure (m. 16), six-and-one-half measures (mm. 17–23), and, finally, nine measures (mm. 24–32).[48] Ex. 1 demonstrates one way that these swells connect. In measures 3 and 5 the *appoggiatura* resolutions (respectively, $c^2$ to $bb^1$ and $db^2$ to $cb^2$) suggest melodic pause, but Hensel immediately confounds that expectation by continuing the melody with a quarter note on beat three. Measure 11 (not shown in the example) has a similar elision: four eighths lead directly into a return of the opening melody on the dominant. This return of melodic material is apparent only in retrospect because, in the moment, those pitches suggest just another crest in a forward-moving wave. Hensel's phrasing shows an attitude different from Mendelssohn's toward the span of anticipation in music and toward the importance of directional focus: Hensel takes a long view; Mendelssohn, a closer one.

Interaction of the three components of texture is also handled differently. Mendelssohn's descending arpeggios in 53/1 form a middle voice that is distinct from the bass voice and the upper voice. See Ex. 1. This separation of voices gives Mendelssohn's piece a clear three-part texture, at the same time that it limits the possible range of the middle voice. His three-part texture has three distinct contrapuntal areas, though not strictly contrapuntal lines in the Bachian sense. In Hensel's 6/1 the widely spaced arpeggios span from the bass note up into the treble range. The bass note, included as part of that arpeggio, has a double function as a member of both bass and middle voices. Hensel's sound texture, with this wide range, is free-wheeling, open, and expansive. The arpeggios make the piece technically difficult, but the middle part is free of linear restraint.

Mendelssohn's bass voice in 53/1 exhibits its linear character more clearly than does Hensel's in 6/1. Mendelssohn's contrapuntal bass voice moves forward mostly by dotted halves, and it supports a steady harmonic rhythm that changes quite regularly with the half-measure (the dotted half). Hensel's bass voice also supports a steady harmonic rhythm moving by the half-measure, but the linear character of the bass line is obscured, not only by its inclusion in the middle voice as just mentioned, but also through Hensel's notational method. The quarters of beats one and three (a stem is missing in measure 6) lack clarifying rests for beats two and four. In addition, beats two and four often have an unstruck quarter note tied over from the last inner-part eighth of the former beat. Those tied quarter notes, either an octave higher than the original bass note or another note within the same triad, suggest a new note for the bass voice. The bass line, therefore, can be described in two ways: a supporting part of leaping quarter notes, as well as the linear voice moving in tandem with the harmonic motion.

The handling of the middle voice in relation to the other voices is another crucial element in clarifying Hensel and Mendelssohn's differing approach to contrapuntal effect. In the unnumbered piece Hensel has the bass notes (chord anchors) spaced in time between the pulsing inner-chords for the left hand. See Ex. 3. The inner voice has little direction of its own. The bass line is essentially supporting and only occasionally linear, while the right-hand melody is positioned relatively far from the inner voice and is completely independent. Mendelssohn's 38/5 has similar inner, pulsing (but also syncopated) chords that are so close as to almost interfere with the low-placed, limited-range melody. Yet, in spite of the closeness of melody and inner voice, his three parts of the texture always remain distinct, and his contrapuntal bass line is fully independent.

In both of Hensel's pieces just discussed, 6/1 and the unnumbered piece, her three-part texture has been shown to be less distinct than Mendelssohn's in his pieces 53/1 and 38/5. Hensel's textures are more flexible and irregular, and the pieces more pianistic and virtuosic. Her melodies, with their wider range and more expansive phrase structure, are more spun out, and give significant pianistic effect. In contrast, Mendelssohn's pieces are less exploratory of pianistic elements and of the pianist's capabilities, and their textures are more anchored and consistent throughout.

Two causes suggest themselves. First, differences in range and arpeggiation type can be the result of their differing purposes and their differing performance settings. Mendelssohn's *Songs without Words,* which he wrote mainly for his public, needed to be more limited in order to be technically accessible to the amateur. Hensel's pieces, which she wrote both for her own pleasure in private and for her own performance at her elite salon, could have a freer, less constrained approach to both technical difficulty and composition in general.

The other difference, the handling of the linear aspect of texture, may result from differing attitudes toward counterpoint. I suggest that Hensel's avoidance of clearly defined contrapuntal lines in these pieces could have its source in a specifically feminine reaction to her musical education in counterpoint with Carl Friedrich Zelter, their composition teacher. Zelter emphasized the study of Johann Sebastian Bach and encouraged their education in the contrapuntal style. On the surface it seems that the two children had the same instruction. It is well known that Hensel played all the Preludes of the *Well-Tempered Clavier* from memory at the age of thirteen, and that Mendelssohn directed the revival of Bach's "St. Matthew" Passion at the age of twenty. Mendelssohn's youthful studies in counterpoint show that the style was vitally important to him, and that he learned it amazingly quickly.[49] We lack direct information about Hensel's rate of learning and her talent for counterpoint because her early exercises do not survive, but on 10 December 1824, Zelter wrote to Goethe that she had completed her thirty-second fugue.[50]

Zelter, however, is likely to have given out mixed messages as a teacher. Not only was he a person with little tact,[51] he was a product of his time. He knew as well as Hensel that subjects such as mathematics, physics, and music theory belonged to the male intellectual world of the day, and that women were not considered capable of learning in these areas.[52] Since contrapuntal study, the pinnacle of music theory, was central to Zelter's teaching, if there is any area of her education from which Hensel, as a female child, might have felt excluded, it would have been counterpoint. It is entirely possible that in time counterpoint became less important or interesting to her, and even that she ultimately found it more difficult than Mendelssohn. Many women have displayed such patterns of gradually diminishing accomplishment during their education.[53] If we consider Hensel's ambivalence about her compositional skills (mentioned above), it is likely that she came to doubt her ability to write counterpoint and therefore chose to use it less than Mendelssohn.[54] It is also possible that she sufficiently accepted society's norms concerning female pursuits to reject counterpoint for herself, believing it not appropriate for her and her salon, coming from a woman. Such a stance contains a face-saving component; it could mask even strong dislike for counterpoint without ever being interpreted as criticism of Mendelssohn's use of the technique.

# V
# The complex of texture
# and rhythm as it affects form

For both Hensel and Mendelssohn, texture's relation to rhythm is particularly close. Since rhythmic elements determine how tightly or loosely woven the texture (or fabric) is, rhythm will define texture's consistency (the warp or motion in time). For the siblings a change in rhythm will usually be accompanied by a textural change, after which both features remain stable for a period of time.

Two similar pieces, most likely written within a year of one another, give a strong sense of the importance of this conjunction of texture and rhythm. Hensel's piece, without title but the designation No. 7, is part of a ten-piece set; if one were to suggest a title it would most likely be *Song for Pianoforte*.[55] Mendelssohn's comparable piece, Op. 117, is titled both *Album Leaf* and *Song without Words*.[56] Mendelssohn knew Hensel's No. 7, which was completed 8 July 1836, because she sent it to him in late October of that year. Since Mendelssohn's Op. 117 is dated as *probably* written in 1837, there is the good possibility that he considered Hensel's piece in writing Op. 117.

Many musical similarities suggest that these two pieces are relevant to one another. They are both in minor mode and C meter. They have similar tempo markings — *Allegro agitato* for Hensel and *Allegro* for Mendelssohn. They show a similar melody type and shape — a rising line with expressive leaps of sevenths and sixths that reverse the direction of the line. See Ex. 3.4, the second full measure of melody. They include a triplet accompaniment against duplets and triplets in the melody. They have a similar number of measures — Hensel's 114 measures (with repeats, 128) to Mendelssohn's 96 measures (with repeats, 154 measures). Finally, they have clearly defined, soaring melodies that lie at a distance from the rest of the texture, Hensel in her opening section (mm. 1–14 and elsewhere) and Mendelssohn in his A section (mm. 1–60). Their differences, however, are also striking. Mendelssohn does not borrow Hensel's form, her extensive modulations, or her developmental techniques.

EXAMPLE 3.4a. Hensel, No. 7, mm. 1–4

EXAMPLE 3.4b. Mendelssohn, Op. 117, mm. 1–6

Their strongest common element is that the accompaniment texture is tied to a single rhythmic pattern almost throughout. Chords are repeated (Hensel) or arpeggiated (Mendelssohn) in half-measure units that are built of two triplets supporting a single harmony. This pattern is relentless in Mendelssohn's Op. 117; Hensel eases it a bit by using the triplets melodically (mm. 28 and 29 and elsewhere) and developmentally (mm. 34 and 35 and elsewhere). The dominating presence of the texture and rhythm complex in both pieces comes from the fact that (1) it is established early — Hensel at the beginning of the piece, Mendelssohn in his two-measure introduction, and (2) it continues in a position of prominence to the end.

Their texture and rhythm complex, alike in principle, produces a different sense of forward motion. In Hensel's piece the accompanying texture has an open sound because the bass notes are widely spaced in relation to the midrange chords. The bass notes gain prominence because of this separation of range, and the bass line stands out as an important forward-moving force. Hensel's midrange part, using insistent, pulsing repetition of block chords, also provides impetus for motion, and this forward motion later supports developmental ideas. Mendelssohn's arpeggios have no special focus on their lowest notes (which often function as pedals), and because of this the accompaniment lacks Hensel's force. Also, because Mendelssohn's arpeggios only gradually unfold into chords, their forward drive is weak. This texture has a smooth, lulling sound, and the piece remains rhythmically static. The physical sensation of playing these two different textural/rhythmic patterns further reinforces this differing sense of urgency in the two pieces. For Hensel's piece the hand motion would be a quick muscular repetition from the wrist, while for Mendelssohn's piece it would be a loose flow that balances the hand from finger to finger. As skilled pianists both Hensel and Mendelssohn would have been aware of this important difference of textural sensation, forceful for Hensel and caressing for Mendelssohn.

In addition, although both pieces are *Allegro* and might be performed at the same tempo, the perception of passing time will also be differently interpreted through the different sense of touch for each piece. The metaphor of fabric can assist in explaining this perceptual difference: the passing of time (the lengthwise strands or warp) is a relentless constant for both pieces. The two differ, however, in their woof, the strands across the fabric: thick, bumpy strands for Hensel, thin, smooth strands for Mendelssohn. Hensel's "bumps" (chords) are visually more taxing to scan and more difficult for the hand to produce; thus, these "bumps" in Hensel's piece call attention to themselves, making the process of passing by them (in music, passing by them in time) seem more agitated and intense.

Rhythmic conflict of three against two is frequent in both pieces, and through its repetition this conflict takes on the characteristic of a textural component. Hensel and Mendelssohn, again, take different paths of exploration. Hensel uses melodic duplets against accompaniment triplets to create a continuous conflict, and melodic triplets appear only at the close of her phrase (m. 4), as a coming-together to relax tension. See Ex. 3.4. Mendelssohn uses an opposite plan; he opens with melodic and accompaniment triplets which, through their congruence, create a relaxed atmosphere. He employs the conflict of melodic duplets against triplets mostly in the decay of melodic phrases as they descend toward their close (m. 5). There the duplets move comfortably because their descending motion softens inherent conflict between duplets and triplets. In spite of Hensel's rough, driving texture with mostly conflicting rhythmic patterns and Mendelssohn's smooth, lulling texture with mostly congruent rhythmic patterns, their compositional goals are similar in that both pieces use the combined rhythmic and textural pattern to provide an important element of unity.

Hensel's and Mendelssohn's choices, which created complex textures and rhythms in No. 7 and Op. 117, also influence their approach to form. Within her development section and his B section they have in common a desire to reconsider and develop the A material. Hensel, however, begins this process with a textural development already in the first section. In measure 9, beat 3, to measure 14 the bass line moves up into the accompaniment-triplet range where it acts as a contrapuntal line opposing the melody. Over that partially altered texture — one that retains repeating triplet chords — Hensel completes the cadential gesture of the opening material. More importantly, in her development section Hensel has variety of subtextures. New versions of the opening texture of the piece emerge: measure 34 brings octave triplets, retaining the triplet motion but using it for chromatic motion to a new key. Measure 39 returns the pulsing triplet texture of the opening, measure 46 uses octave triplets for a transition, and measure 50 brings single chords supported by the familiar accompaniment triplets, now in single notes or with octave doublings. Measure 54 brings the ever-present triplets in a distinctive sprightly *staccato*, retaining the chordal triplet accompaniment texture from the opening section but now in one-beat groups. Compare Ex. 3.4 with Ex. 3.5.

EXAMPLE 3.5.  Hensel, No. 7, mm. 54–57

This *staccato* passage also has a melodic resemblance to measure 1 of the opening theme, but the *staccato* texture is more distinctive than the static melodic material. Common to all these textural changes is that each new subtexture brings with it an element of the former one, as if it were developed or evolved from it. "Developing texture" can be a useful term for this process, as "developing variation" is for a similar process in Brahms's music.[57]

Developing texture can be used as a way of interpreting Hensel's formal structure. No. 7's formal structure grows gradually and organically; it does not fit neatly into a preplanned structure. See Diagram 3.1. The measure 54 *staccato* passage (X in the diagram; the music is Ex. 3.5) that evolved gradually from the opening section is so distinctive that it gains a life of its own with new responsibilities. First it prepares the A$^1$ return in measure 62; then, elevated to an item in itself in measure 74, it closes A$^1$, and finally, in measure 97 it stabilizes tonic harmony in the coda. The opening texture of the piece, as evolved into this sprightly, distinctive, contrasting material becomes a structural force. Understanding this evolution of texture gives meaning to the *staccato* passage and explains Hensel's formal design.

| A | Development | | | | | A$^1$ | | Coda | | | |
|---|---|---|---|---|---|---|---|---|---|---|---|
| | | (A) | (A)  X | tr | | X | | (A) | X | Codetta | |
| i | III | ♭ii | iv  (V–i) | | V | i | (V/iv–iv)(V/v–v)V | i⁶ | i  (V–i) | i | I |
| 1 | 15 | 39 | 43  54 | | 60 | 62 | 74 | 89 | 97 | 103 | 111 |

DIAGRAM 3.1. Hensel, No. 7

Hensel's approach to form in No. 7 — built by developing the texture and rhythm — is more unusual than Mendelssohn's straight-forward appropriation of A–B–A form for Op. 117. Mendelssohn's B section texture (m. 60) does grows out of the A section in that he moves the existing arpeggio pattern to the inner voice and alters the spacing between melody and inner voice. However, the B-section melody, built exclusively of the top notes of the arpeggios, almost loses itself within the arpeggio texture. Supporting half-note chords give a full sound on beats 1 and 3 and emphasize regularly spaced melody notes, and the texture remains steady and consistent through-out. The B-section range is yet more confined and the sound more subdued and repetitive than that of the A section, but, overall, his two textures are similar. After the B section Mendelssohn returns to the A section verbatim. By so exactly completing the requirements of a balanced A–B–A design, he demonstrates that form, not texture, controlled the progress of his piece.

Hensel's piece, based on textural development, is dynamic and expansive; Mendelssohn's piece, based on formal principles, is balanced and smooth. Differently said, in considering texture (and its related rhythmic properties) Hensel uses it actively to build form, Mendelssohn uses it passively to reflect form. This is not to be understood as compositional "role reversal": that Hensel is masculine because of forceful texture and driving rhythms, that Mendelssohn is feminine because of caressing texture and gentle rhythmic patterns. Though these devices typically have such gender stereotyping, they are used here to serve larger compositional goals. Hensel uses her forceful devices to emphasize textural development, unfolding expansiveness and freedom, while Mendelssohn, by making texture and rhythm less central, brings formal balance to the fore.

# VI
## The texture and rhythm complex
## supporting form and melody

Finally, four pieces with strongly similar textures and rhythmic patterns make a good group for viewing form and melody against the backdrop of the textural and rhythmic alliance considered above. In Hensel's three pieces, *melody* is the most important element, while in Mendelssohn's piece, *form* is primary. Melody seems to create and drive Hensel's form; while form seems to suggest Mendelssohn's melody and phrase type.

Historical and internal evidence together suggest the following compositional order for these four pieces: Hensel's 5/5, Mendelssohn's 38/5, Hensel's 2/2, then Hensel's 8/1. Hensel's Op. 5, No. 5, without autograph or composition date, but published in 1847, may be the earliest of the four, possibly before 1835.[58] The piece was not necessarily composed close to its publication date since Hensel drew from her entire repertoire to make up her published sets. The texture type of 5/5 is a common one for Hensel, used in pieces both early and late; it is, however, an unusual type for Mendelssohn. I suggest, therefore, that Hensel's 5/5 may precede Mendelssohn's 38/3. Then 38/3's unusual texture could be explained as deriving from 5/5. Mendelssohn's Op. 38, No. 3, is the earliest firmly dated piece of the four considered here. The autograph, dedicated to "Clara Wieck" in Düsseldorf, is dated 2 January 1835.[59] It was published in May/June of 1837. Next in the sequence comes Hensel's Op. 2, No. 2. Dated in the autograph 15 November 1841, as part of an unpublished collection called *Das Jahr*, it is titled "September, Am Fluße."[60] She published it five years later, in 1846, as No. 2 of the collection called *Vier Lieder für das Pianoforte,* Op. 2.[61] When she worked with it again to prepare it for publication possibly she was encouraged to write yet another piece with similar texture. Such a piece, Op. 8, No. 1, exists in an untitled autograph of 14 May 1846.[62] The family published this last piece posthumously as Op. 8, No. 1, in 1850.[63]

The type of three-part texture that links these four pieces is made up of a supporting bass line and a distinct melodic line. The triplet subdivisions that make up the third part are arpeggio break-ups of the harmony; they provide the filling voice. Their similar triplet figurations give a sense of urgency to these four pieces that also have in common a fast tempo. 5/5 is *Allegro molto vivace*, 38/3 is *Presto e molto vivace*, and 8/1 is *Allegro moderato*. Even 2/2 marked *Andante con moto* has strong forward drive that Hensel encouraged in her autograph with the marking *Andante con moto quasi Allegro.*[64]

The last three pieces — Mendelssohn's 38/3, Hensel's 2/2, and her 8/1 — have a particularly strong resemblance in the shaping of the arpeggio voice. Mendelssohn's 38/3 has six sixteenths, usually a rise, then a fall. For Hensel's 2/2 and 8/1 the arpeggio is also grouped by six, a rise and then a fall, with an additional three-note group that usually rises. Hensel's 5/5 is only slightly different; the six-note arpeggio is usually internally bidirectional and overall falling.

For all four pieces, the textural aspect is more important than the metrical. The time signatures that define the meter vary: 5/5 is in 2/4 meter, 38/3 is in 3/4 meter, 2/2 is in 6/8 meter, and 8/1 is in 3/8 meter, but in each case the meter is weakly defined because downbeat accents are separated by the many arpeggiated sixteenths (twelve in 5/5, eighteen in 38/3 and 2/2, and nine in 8/1). This long span between downbeat accents promotes fluid motion of the sound and produces a textural effect rather than a metrically accentuated one. A subtle difference in their handling of this weakly defined meter will be relevant to formal considerations discussed below: in 38/3 Mendelssohn uses the weak meter to hint at an ambiguity in the designated 3/4 meter — the possibility that it might contain elements of 6/8 meter (see Ex. 3.6b, mm. 18 and 19) — while his introduction and two interludes display pure 3/4 meter throughout. This difference contributes to a sense of separateness for the introduction and interludes.

EXAMPLE 3.6a. Hensel, Op. 5, No. 5, mm. 41–46

EXAMPLE 3.6b. Mendelssohn, Op. 38, No. 3, mm. 18-19

Hensel, on the other hand, does not disturb her metrical pattern. In
2/2 she never leaves the 6/8 meter; in 8/1 she keeps the 3/8 meter
without ever suggesting hemiola (i.e., 3/4 meter); and in 5/5 — 2/4
meter with triplet subdivisions of sixteenths — the piece never leans to
cross meters, though it does use gentle melodic syncopation (mm. 5-7
and elsewhere).

Hensel's 5/5, Mendelssohn's 38/3, and Hensel's 8/1 also have in
common occasional interruptions of the steady sixteenth-note motion,
leaving only eighths to move forward. This sudden alteration of both
texture and rhythm directs a strong focus to those measures and to the
bare metrical underpinnings of the piece. Hensel in 5/5 (m. 44) uses
the device to open up and expand the time-space, as a built-in lull
during which the phrase gathers momentum before surging forward.
See Ex. 3.6a. Single eighth notes make the effect additionally striking.
For Mendelssohn in 38/3 (mm. 18-19) block chords, a sudden *f*, and
an *sfz* call additional attention to his combined texture and rhythm
change. In 8/1 (mm. 119, 121, 131, 133), Hensel again uses the
device for suspended moments, as pauses between phrase surges. In
all, these unexpected reductions to basic meter provide suspension and
breathing space for Hensel, dramatic emphasis for Mendelssohn.

Though these pieces share textural and rhythmic patterns, form
and melody are handled differently. Hensel's 5/5 (possibly the earliest
of the four) has the freest form. There are competing analyses, none
entirely satisfactory: A-B-A$^1$ or A-A$^1$-A$^2$ (mm. 1, 49, 91), A-B-
Development-A$^1$ (mm. 1, 17, 49, 91), or A-B-A$^1$-C-A$^2$ (mm. 1, 17,
49, C at 56 or 63, 91). See Diagram 3.2 for a more detailed description. In that diagram the sections labeled B, C, D, and Development
are flowing continuations of A's melodic material, not borrowings of
A motives that are developed. The sections are not clearly delineated
with strong cadences, although there is an almost exact return of the
two opening measures of A in measures 49-50. Hensel's formal
ambiguity is different from that of a sonata-rondo where exploring the
tension between the two formal designs may be a compositional goal.

Rather, her structural organization seems an incidental result of the forward motion of the melodic line. In this piece of 143 measures, Hensel's melody is without breathing spaces (rests) except for one short passage of ten measures (mm. 65–74). The melody, within the first phrase mark of twenty-four measures, has continuous phrase surges or waves that are balanced and regular two- and four-measure groupings. See Diagram 3.3. They could be considered standard phrase groupings except for their linking mechanisms. Each wave concludes with a "tail" that overlaps into an "upbeat" of the next wave, making labels such as "tail" and "upbeat" arbitrary (See Ex. 3.7, mm. 16 to 17, 18 to 19).

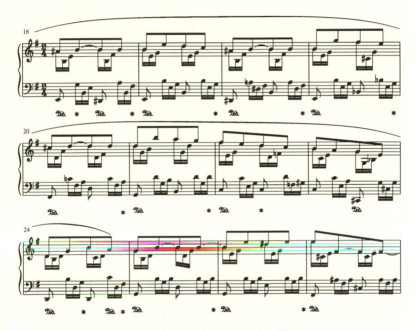

EXAMPLE 3.7. Hensel, Op. 5, No. 5, mm. 16–27

A particularly telling such link is illustrated in measure 25. Although the piece cadences for the first time in measure 25 and that cadence is tonic (G major), even here Hensel's resolution is blurred by the forward motion of the melody that flows past measure 25 without a break until measure 65. Constant "tails and upbeats" focus the listener's attention on the forward, wavelike motion of the melodic line. Another composer might have chosen rests to separate melodic elements in order to emphasize their structural formation. Hensel's melody, as a result of her linking devices, becomes a single entity that accommodates constant and continuous expansion.

In contrast, Mendelssohn's 38/3 (from 1835) does not link his phrase sections. His piece also has a clear and standard overall form, Introduction–A–B–A–Coda (mm. 1, 7, 22, 54, 63); there is a slight ambiguity in that B is derived from A material, but this is a familiar *Songs without Words* device. More unusual are the two interruptions of the B section, measures 30–33 and 44–45. See Diagram 3.4. In applying a principle of interruption Mendelssohn seems at first to parallel Hensel's return to her opening measures 1–2 at measures 49–50.

| A  | A¹ | B | C | D | Development | | | | | | A² | A³ | |
|----|----|---|---|---|-------------|--|--|--|--|--|----|----|--|
|    |    |   |   |   | (A) | (A) | (X) | (X) | (Y) | (D) |    |    |  |
| (V–I) |  | vi | I | vi/vi | (V–i) bVI | i | III | | bvi(VI) | | (V–I) | I (Vped) | I |
| 1  | 9  | 17 | 25 | 33 | 49 | 53 | 56 | 60 | 63 | 79 | 91 | 99  119 | 131 |

DIAGRAM 3.2.  Hensel, Op. 5, No. 5

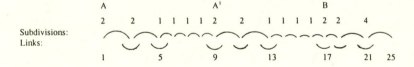

DIAGRAM 3.3.  Hensel, Op. 5, No. 5, mm. 1–25 only

| Intro | A | A¹ | | | B | Int | B¹ | | Int | B² | A² | | Coda |
|-------|---|----|--|--|---|-----|----|--|-----|----|----|--|------|
| x | a¹ | a² | a¹ | a² | a¹ | x | a² | a¹ | x | a¹ | a¹ | a² | a² |
| I |   |    |   |   |   | dim⁷ V/V_pedal | | V dim⁷ | | V/V/V_pedal | I |  |  |
| 1 | 7 | 10 | 15 | 18 | 22 | 30 | 34 | 40 | 44 | 46 | 54 | 57 | 63 |

DIAGRAM 3.4.  Mendelssohn, Op. 38, No. 3

Mendelssohn's interruption, however, is different; it uses his introductory material, the frame of his piece that contained the purest 3/4 meter. As material separate and different from the main body of the piece, it calls attention to itself in this new position by acting as a reminder of the first boundary of the piece, and, as such, it acts as a limiting force on the piece's expansiveness. Hensel's brief return to her opening melody at measures 49–50, brings back her central, most integral melodic material, and the remembrance turns the piece inward onto itself. This difference is significant: Mendelssohn calls attention to the boundaries of his form by focusing on an exterior supporting pillar, while Hensel calls attention to the core of the piece, as if returning to the center within an expanding spiral.

In 2/2 (from 1841) Hensel uses a B section, but her A–B–A form is not clearly delineated. There is little cadential definition to prepare the B section; measures 20–22 hardly give melodic closure, and the harmonies only momentarily rest on the minor dominant. The melodic upbeat from measure 22 to measure 23 barely has a sense of new beginning, and the melody, as it continues in measure 23, gives the impression of having been ongoing for a long time. The return of the A section (m. 47) is quite clear, but the listener is left with the puzzle of determining just when one left the A section in the first place. There was no such ambiguity in Mendelssohn's 38/3 even though he continued with A material in the B section. Balanced phrases, clear cadences, and the interludes defined his sections.

In 8/1 (from 1846) Hensel uses the same free approach to form exhibited in 5/5 and 2/2. By their very sameness, the coupling of the continuous texture with the continuously flowing melody obscures section breaks. Spinning a melody is the strongest force of the piece, and as the melody evolves it moves the piece forward. Ex. 8 gives this piece complete. This piece (in B minor) has one hint of sonata rhetoric in that its first cadential point (D major, m. 46) is combined with a new beginning that might suggest a second theme, but other sonata elements are absent. Rather, the form A–B–C–A$^1$–B$^1$–C$^1$–Coda (each section beginning, respectively, at mm. 1, 23, 46, 76, 98, 122, 149) suggests itself, but extensions of A and B material obscure this form by their melodic and textural force, and the sequential, unstable nature of C makes it a weak companion to the other two. This piece is, therefore, also primarily melodic and textural.

These four pieces — Hensel's 5/5, Mendelssohn's 38/5, Hensel's 2/2 and 8/1 using similar texture — highlight the siblings' individual approaches to composition. For Hensel, ideals of melody with a strong supporting complex of texture and rhythm are primary, while her formal structures are ambiguous, and her phrases grow amorphously in wave shapes. For Mendelssohn, ideals of form and phrase balance are most important; his melody is shaped, one might even say, constricted, by the principle of balancing and planning, and his neat phrases build a clear and regular form. The siblings may not have used these differing approaches consciously, but these pieces demonstrate that an expanding idea was primary to Hensel; and balanced structure, to Mendelssohn. Both, of course, exhibit features of the other.


# VII
# Summary

In all, Hensel uses less contrapuntal treatment in three-part texture, more blurring of the linear aspects within that texture, and a more pianistic texture. Mendelssohn's texture has strong contrapuntal aspects and distinct linear progress. Hensel uses the wider range, makes phrases through successive waves, and constructs longer-breathed melodies; Mendelssohn employs the smaller range and builds shorter, more regular, and more balanced phrases. In connecting texture and rhythm Hensel chooses an active approach with conflict in No. 7 to Mendelssohn's passive one with relaxation in Op. 117. Finally, Hensel's formal structures are more irregular and organic because she has the freer and more expansive approach to form, building it either on developing texture and rhythm (No. 7) or on an expanding melody in conjunction with texture and rhythm (5/5, 2/2, 8/1). Mendelssohn's forms are more prominent, closed, and balanced (117, 38/3), and his texture lies more in the background.

The attributes above have been described in terms of "more or less," and such description can imply value judgment. If we dismiss the premise that the amount or type of an attribute determines its worth, we can examine without prejudice the possibility that a composer's choices of these attributes might be gender related. This is not to suggest that gender alone creates a need or reason for these choices, but rather that these choices are made as outgrowths of who the composer became, as a gendered adult in a society that assigned men and women specific places and roles.

In this nineteenth-century culture, private gatherings like Hensel's salon were settings in which the feminine was not only accepted, but even celebrated. The corollary is that since the feminine included emotion, displays of emotion would have been encouraged both as behavior and as a characteristic of musical composition. Since emotion, sensuousness, and texture are all feminized in this context and therefore appropriate for this intimate setting, it is entirely possible that Hensel chose texture as an important compositional tool largely because her music was intended for her own use in her salon.

Hensel's comparative compositional freedom within the confines of this salon environment was a privilege belonging to the feminine, private sphere; Mendelssohn's search for control in his life and mastery in his field was the privilege of the masculine and public sphere. This exterior difference of gender roles seems to manifest itself in their piano composition not only in the differing ways they balance the importance of texture (the feminine) and form (the masculine) but also in the ways they treat range within the same texture type. Hensel's wider melodic range and her wider range from top to bottom of the texture suggest a freer treatment of musical environment. Mendelssohn's greater control of the musical environment is rooted in more traditionally masculine concerns. He controls his range to suit stricter contrapuntal requirements, the need for balanced phrases, and ultimately the requirements of an external form.

Hensel's heightened sense of pianism, as compared to Mendelssohn's slightly more restrained piano style, also suggests the feminine, although the argument has been advanced above that this difference can also derive from different performance settings — Hensel writing for herself; Mendelssohn, for the anonymous amateur. However, since sense of touch is a core attribute of texture, I suggest that Hensel's piano touch crafted for her own playing is another display of her feminine interest in texture — intimate and relevant touch is used as the reinforcer of the emotional and sensuous side of texture.

Additionally, melody, so closely related to texture for Hensel, has two feminine images associated with it that can help to explain why Hensel's formulations of melody evolved as they did. The first is the image of spinning (*spinnen*). Spinning was women's work in the early nineteenth century, and even today the phrase "to spin a melody" is common in both English and German. Spinning suggests not just a thread or musical line, but also the sense of having no beginning or end. Hensel's melodies have just this quality of endlessness because they are expanded additively, as best demonstrated in 5/5. Spinning also suggests singleness, a single melody line as separate from the rest of the texture, and Hensel's melodies lie in just that fashion, alone and distinctive, unlike her bass parts or her wide-ranging filler parts.

Yet another image that Hensel's wave-like, additive melodies suggest is a feminine type of discourse that she and her sister, Rebekka, engage in when they interrupt each other within the same sentence to write a letter. A good example of this technique is found in their letter of October 1828 to Mendelssohn.[65] Phrases interrupt, yet overlap one another, carrying on the same thought, as if breathless to clarify and expand the conversation, as if going on with one more aspect, one more interpretation, one more angle of the issue.[66] This pattern of feminine verbal discourse resembles greatly Hensel's musical discourse of additive, wavelike motion in her melodies. This is not to say that Mendelssohn does not expand melodies, but he does so more often in the context of motivic development, or by having separate and distinct phrases build larger melodic arches.

Another overtone of the feminine lies in the sheer expansiveness of Hensel's concept of a textless song or *Song for Pianoforte.* "Genuine music . . . fills the soul with a thousand things better than words," Mendelssohn's comment about his own *Songs without Words* suggests that such piano pieces express a content beyond the power of words.[67] Since the deeper content of music, and of Hensel's pieces in particular, is in its emotive and/or sensuous capacity, then texture can convey these qualities particularly well. Hensel, writing not only the more expansive melodies but also surrounding them with the more prominently textured and more openly sensuous accompaniments, shows the appeal of these feminine-gendered attributes for her.

The feminine image of spinning a musical thread will be invoked one last time to illuminate Hensel's general avoidance of formal, stand-alone introductions, a device quite common among Mendelssohn's *Songs without Words.* The image of a thread already in the process of being spun out describes well Hensel's restless openings to many of her pieces, for example, 6/1 and 5/5. Introductions such as Mendelssohn's, on the other hand, act as separating and delineating forces and are appropriate for him, because, as a man within his culture, he leaned to formal delineators and form sections. His introductions serve to balance form and stabilize the opening key in, for example, 53/1 and 38/3.

No one of these tendencies or devices is a feminine compositional technique. But, finding a collection of attributes with feminine connotation suggests that these techniques appealed to Hensel in her role as a woman. This subtle difference of pattern is best, and perhaps only, to be observed within this comparison of Hensel and Mendelssohn where they are restricted to similar situations. Whether such complexes of attributes are found in other male-female pairs of composers, whether they are employed to the same ends, and whether they stem from gender role expectations is a subject for further investigation.[68]

# Notes

I thank Paul McAndrew for his patient and generous support in generating this article, and John Daverio, Ruth Solie, and Herbert Lin for reading early drafts and offering insightful suggestions. I take full responsibility for the conclusions and inevitable errors.

1. Texture is most often discussed in twentieth-century or classical period essays. William Dale Dustin, "Two-Voiced Textures in the Mikrokosmos of Bela Bartók" (Ph.D. diss., Cornell University, 1959), provides a summary of the problems of defining the term, stating "many assume a common under-standing of the meaning of the term, an assumption that is not exactly justified" (p. 8). He supports his statement that, of the subdivisions of texture, counterpoint and polyphony have been considered "worthier" of analysis than homophony (p. 18), and he defines texture as "the character of the music in terms of its density and level of activity in continuity" (p. 33). Anne Carothers Hall, "Texture in Violin Concertos of Stravinsky, Berg, Schoen-berg, and Bartók" (Ph.D. diss., University of Michigan, 1971) considers the analogy of threads in a fabric to apply mainly to musical contrapuntal lines (p. 1). She does not consider timbre and dynamics elements of texture (p. 4). Wallace Berry, "Texture," in *Structural Functions in Music* (New York: Dover Publications, 1987), 184–300, constructs an analytical language for texture. Other studies are Orin Moe, Jr., "Texture in the String Quartets of Haydn to 1787" (Ph.D. diss., University of California at Santa Barbara, 1970); Jane R. Stevens, "Theme, Harmony, and Texture in Classic-Romantic Descriptions of Concerto First-Movement Form," *Journal of the American Musicological Society* 27 (1974): 25–60; Leonard G. Ratner, "Texture, A Rhetorical Element in Beethoven's Quartets," in *Israel Studies in Musicology* 2 (Jerusalem: Israel Musicological Society, 1980): 51–62; Janet M. Levy, "Texture as a Sign in Classic and Early Romantic Music," *Journal of the American Musicological Society* 35 (1982): 482–531.

2. The article concludes without author's name or bibliography. "Texture," *The New Grove Dictionary of Music and Musicians*, ed. Stanley Sadie (London: Macmillan, 1980), 18:709. Don Michael Randel's definition of texture in *The New Harvard Dictionary of Music* (Cambridge, MA: The Belknap Press of Harvard University Press, 1986), 843, focuses mainly on twentieth-century practices. These incomplete treatments may have evolved because texture is difficult to quantify and lacks the full analytical vocabulary of other musical elements. More likely, the apparent bias may stem from the fact that texture is often considered relatively unimportant. It has been referred to as a "surface" element, confusing a technical property of texture (the surface in art), with a negative connotation of the same word.

3. No piano studio is complete without phrases such as "Pull that soprano line out of the texture," or "Your texture is too heavy and thick."

4. Berry, *Structural Functions*, 185.

5. *The American Heritage Dictionary of the English Language*, ed. William Morris (Boston: American Heritage Publishing Co. and Houghton Mifflin Co., 1969), 1332. Musicians generally equate structure and form, but in this definition the word *structure* has a separate meaning. A further caveat concerns the word *surface*. The connotation of surface as shallow or unimportant — "This is a surface issue and without depth" — is not in this definition. Surface here is a concrete, technical term.

6. *American Heritage Dictionary*, 1332.

7. If the listener is also a pianist, the connection is the most direct, but nonpianists also invoke their sense of touch in order to imagine the feel of the piano. The accuracy of their perception is not at issue here. Audiences demonstrate this need when they choose their seating in concert halls. Even though the sound is usually better on the right side of the hall where the sound reflects off the open piano lid, audiences generally bunch up on the left to watch the pianist's hands. This suggests that the audience seeks not just an experience in sound, but an intensified visual image which may project them more completely into the physical, and finally emotional, sensations of the player.

8. In impressionist music, texture is the most immediately noticeable aspect; form, harmonic progress, and melody are more concealed. In minimalist music, the shifting of texture is usually primary, while harmony, melody, form, and sometimes rhythm are reduced to their simplest components. In aleatory music, changing texture may be the only thing the listener follows.

9. Examples are James Richard Bersano, *Formalized Aspect Analysis of Sound Texture* (Ph.D. diss., Indiana University, 1979; Ann Arbor: University Microfilms International, 1980); Dana Richard Wilson, "The Role of Texture in Selected Works of Toru Takemitsu" (Ph.D. diss., University of Rochester, 1982).

10. Rolf Hartung, *More Creative Textile Design: Color and Texture* (New York: Van Nostrand Reinhold Co., 1964); Ned Harris, *Form and Texture: A Photographic Portfolio* (New York: Van Nostrand Reinhold Co., 1974). Harris compares form and texture as follows, "Looking for form is a drive towards simplification, unity, and order; while texture counterpoints the need for complexity and embellishment" (p. 6).

11. John A. Nist, *The Structure and Texture of Beowulf* (São Paulo, 1959; reprint, Folcroft, PA: Folcroft Press, 1970); Michael Fishbane, *Text and Texture: Close Readings of Selected Biblical Texts* (New York: Schocken Books, 1979).

12. Thomas A. Sebeok, *Structure and Texture; Selected Essays in Cheremis Verbal Art* (The Hague: Mouton, 1974).

13. Richard P. Delone, "Timbre and Texture in Twentieth-Century Music," in *Aspects of Twentieth-Century Music*, ed. Gary E. Wittlich (Englewood Cliffs, NJ: Prentice-Hall, 1975), 66–207; David Lee Ott, "The

Role of Texture and Timbre in the Music of George Crumb" (D.M.A. thesis, University of Kentucky, 1982); Maud Alice Trimmer, *Texture and Sonata Form in the Late String Chamber Music of Haydn and Mozart* (Ph.D. diss., City University of New York, 1981; Ann Arbor: University Microfilms International, 1981).

14. For further discussion of the relationship of women, cloth, and myth, see Elizabeth Wayland Barber, *Women's Work: The First Twenty Thousand Years: Women, Cloth, and Society in Early Times* (New York: W. W. Norton, 1994).

15. As shown in the *Volsunga Saga*. James V. McMahon, "Valkyries, Midwives, Weavers, and Shape-Changers: Atli's Mother the Snake," *Scandinavian Studies* 66 (1994): 480.

16. Robert P. Morgan on Debussy, *Twentieth-Century Music* (New York: W. W. Norton, 1991), 50.

17. These terms are used casually in musicological and theoretical conversation. "Auxiliary" is in Levy, "Texture as a Sign," 482.

18. In spite of the feminine gendering of texture as fabric, it is a useful image with which to explore texture's properties. To use this metaphor might be seen as denigrating the importance and value of texture, but the feminine imagery actually enriches analytical language. To relieve negative connotations one might remember that fabric can also be created, touched, and worn by men.

19. Their lives are illuminated through their extensive correspondence and diaries, both published and unpublished. See especially Sebastian Hensel, *The Mendelssohn Family (1729–1847) from Letters and Journals*, trans. Carl Klingemann and an American collaborator, 2nd rev. ed., 2 vols. (1882; reprint, New York: Haskell House Publishers Ltd, 1969); Fanny Hensel, *The Letters of Fanny Hensel to Felix Mendelssohn*, ed. and trans. Marcia J. Citron (Stuyvesant, New York: Pendragon Press, 1987). See also Camilla Cai, "Fanny Mendelssohn Hensel as Composer and Pianist," *Piano Quarterly* 35, no. 139 (1987): 46–53; Marcia Citron, "Felix Mendelssohn's Influence on Fanny Mendelssohn Hensel as a Professional Composer," *Current Musicology* 37/38 (1984): 9–17; Victoria Sirota, *The Life and Works of Fanny Mendelssohn Hensel* (D.M.A. diss., Boston University, 1981).

20. Aunt Henriette Mendelssohn reinforced gender-role patterning with her gifts from Paris (August 1819). Fanny received a dress, a necklace, and a red and white belt, while Felix got an inkstand, specifically, Henriette said, to be used for writing his first opera or for composing a song dedicated to her. Christian Lambour, "Quellen zur Biographie von Fanny Hensel, geb. Mendelssohn Bartholdy," *Mendelssohn Studien* 6 (1986): 51–52.

21. Abraham Mendelssohn constantly advised and corrected all his children. When Hensel was twenty-three and of marriageable age, he reminded her that the first duty of a woman was as a housewife. Sebastian Hensel, *The Mendelssohn Family* 1:82, 84.

22. Mendelssohn's early visits to Goethe and Hummel (1821) prompted such comments. Fanny Hensel, *Letters*, 1, 4.

23. Mendelssohn was supported with family help in the production of his early *Singspiele* (first written when he was eleven) and his early operas (first written when he was fourteen). Karl-Heinz Köhler, "Mendelssohn (-Bartholdy), (Jakob Ludwig) Felix," *The New Grove Dictionary* 12:136, and Sebastian Hensel, *The Mendelssohn Family* 1:121.

24. The importance of salons as a creative outlet for women is discussed in Marcia Citron, *Gender and the Musical Canon* (Cambridge: Cambridge University Press, 1993), 104–6.

25. Letter to Mendelssohn, 1 July 1829. Fanny Hensel, *Letters*, 60. Similar sentiments are expressed throughout her life. Fanny Hensel, *Letters*, 106, 174, 201, 214, 229, 268, 288, 327, 352, 353, and 363.

26. In completing his first collection of *Songs without Words* for publication Mendelssohn used irony to express his impatience, "I have to get the damned [eternal] piano songs finished" (June 1832, from London to his father). "Die ewigen Clavierlieder muß ich fertig machen." Felix Mendelssohn, *Reisebriefe aus den Jahren 1830 bis 1832 von Felix Mendelssohn Bartholdy*, ed. Paul Mendelssohn-Bartholdy, 9th ed. (Leipzig: Hermann Mendelssohn, 1882), 366.

In a letter to his mother: "Nothing but annoyance is to be looked for from publishing." Felix Mendelssohn, *Letters of Felix Mendelssohn Bartholdy from 1833 to 1847*, ed. Paul Mendelssohn Bartholdy and Carl Mendelssohn Bartholdy, trans. Lady Wallace (Boston: O. Ditson and Co., 1864; reprint, Freeport, NY: Books for Libraries Press, 1970), 113.

In a letter to Ferdinand David: "He [Liszt] has forfeited a large degree of my respect for him through the ridiculous pranks that he plays . . . That may be all well and good for the public at large, but not for me, and that it was good enough for Liszt himself, that lowers my respect for him by a very great deal." As quoted in Wm. A. Little, "Mendelssohn and Liszt," in *Mendelssohn Studies*, ed. R. Larry Todd (Cambridge: Cambridge University Press, 1992), 122.

In 1834 on a visit to Cassel, Moritz Hauptmann relates Mendelssohn's deprecatory attitude toward women: "At first he did not want to play the 'Songs without Words' for me saying that [playing such pieces] is only for women." "Die Lieder ohne Text wollte er mir zuerst nicht spielen und sagte, das sei nur für Damen." As quoted in Christa Jost, *Mendelssohns Lieder ohne Worte* (Tutzing: Hans Schneider, 1988), 27.

27. "I have no intention of publishing any more of that kind. . . . If there are too many such worms between heaven and earth, then finally no one will like them." "Ich habe auch nicht die Absicht, mehr der Art herausgeben . . . Wenn's gar zu viel solches Gewürm zwischen Himmel und Erde gäbe, so möchte es am Ende keinem Menschen lieb sein." 4 March 1839, to his publisher Simrock, in Felix Mendelssohn, *Briefe aus den Jahren 1833 bis*

*1847 von Felix Mendelssohn Bartholdy,* ed. Paul Mendelssohn Bartholdy and Carl Mendelssohn Bartholdy, 6th ed. (Leipzig: Hermann Mendelssohn, 1875), 188.

28. The English publisher urged haste for the sixth book of *Songs without Words.* "Make me up another book — do it at once. I know you have got plenty ready. You need not be afraid of the people getting tired of them, they are the very things which have made you so many friends." Peter Ward Jones, "Mendelssohn and His English Publishers," in *Mendelssohn Studies,* 253.

29. "[G]ewisse Wendungen, Wiederholungen scheinen sogar Manier zu werden." Robert Schumann, *Gesammelte Schriften über Musik und Musiker,* 2nd ed. (Leipzig: Georg Wigand's Verlag, 1871), 2:228. In the *Neue Zeitschrift für Musik,* Schumann criticized *Schöne Melusine* because it "reminds us of things we have often heard before." As quoted in Leon Plantinga, "Schumann's Critical Reaction to Mendelssohn," in *Mendelssohn and Schumann: Essays on their Music and its Context,* ed. Jon W. Finson and R. Larry Todd (Durham, NC: Duke University Press, 1984), 15. Schumann also found originality lacking in the setting of *Psalm 114* (Op. 51) from 1839 and in the incidental music to *Midsummer Night's Dream* (Op. 61) from 1842. Schumann, *Gesammelte Schriften* 2: 188, 357–358.

30. Sebastian Hensel, *The Mendelssohn Family* 2:31.

31. Sebastian Hensel, *The Mendelssohn Family* 2:38.

32. Hensel to Mendelssohn, "Although I'm busy arranging festive events, I must sit down and write you . . ." Included in the description of her recent *musicale* for one hundred people is its physical appearance, "the garden was splendid, the rosebushes were in full bloom, and the place never looked better" (n.d., probably 11 June 1834). Fanny Hensel, *Letters,* 144, 146. Her correspondence is full of references to smaller social gatherings that included the extended Mendelssohn family and others, many of whom stayed at her home as house guests. Music was important to these events. "We started a Tuesday circle here recently, which will alternate among us three siblings. . . . It was arranged that at 9 o'clock, with the tea, instructions are laid out as people dive into the refreshments. . . . We performed music, danced, etc. until midnight. Incidentally, no one was there besides parents and siblings, Hauser, a few students, and Franz Woringen" [probably about thirteen people]. (Letter to Mendelssohn, 29 October 1835). Fanny Hensel, *Letters,* 187.

33. Citron, *Gender and the Musical Canon,* 90, calls Hensel's locus a "redefinition of professionalism."

Arthur Loesser, *Men, Women and Pianos* (New York: Simon and Schuster, 1954), cites examples from nineteenth-century literature that portray piano playing and singing as important social accomplishments for women (pp. 268–83). The piano, as opposed to the flute or violin, allowed well-bred women to maintain a physical stasis that reflected modesty and proper decorum (pp. 64–67).

For an excellent discussion of the genre nocturne as it relates to women, see Jeffrey Kallberg's "The Harmony of the Tea Table: Gender and Ideology in the Piano Nocturne," *Representations* 39 (1992): 102–33. Kallberg's statement concerning Hensel's *Notturno,* which, he says, "she withheld from publication" (p. 117), should not be interpreted to mean that she actively chose this route as a satisfying direction for her. Rather, her ambivalence about publishing — a condition that embodied her wanting it as much as not wanting — was nailed into inaction by Mendelssohn's strong opposition, vociferously expressed in a letter of June 1837. Kallberg mentions Hensel's discouragement, but only as an afterthought (p. 133, n. 75). Kallberg further suggests that Hensel may not have published the *Notturno* because it challenged tradition (p. 126). This suggestion, as it stands, overemphasizes the singularity of the *Notturno* since most of her piano pieces went unpublished in her lifetime. Rather, Kallberg's idea can be more usefully applied to all her unpublished works with unusual features: "for a woman there lurked unstated dangers in publicly confronting the orthodoxy" (p. 126).

34. Hensel objects to Mendelssohn's four-voice texture for his *Volkslieder* (pp. 128–29), comments favorably on his clarinet, viola, and flute writing in *Melusine* (p. 129), and complains that his F-minor fugue (Op. 35, No. 5) becomes too thin at the end (pp. 166, 170). She criticizes Marx's "murky, rattling" sound in his six-part men's chorus, *Wende dich Herr* (p. 142) and takes Cherubini to task for too thick textures in *Ali Baba* (p. 179). Fanny Hensel, *Letters.*

35. The importance of physical appearance at her *musicales* is shown in her criticism of a female guest's hair. "When the music was over, Rebecka [Fanny's sister] and I took over and expressed our opinion that it should be somewhat different. So she [Frau Wangen] had to sit down, I took a comb and dustcoat, and we fixed her hair" (Letter to Mendelssohn, 25 January 1834). Fanny Hensel, *Letters,* 122.

36. For the most extensive, though not complete, list of her works, see Sirota, *Life and Works,* 307–32.

37. A collection of twelve pieces in a copyist's hand was a gift to Mendelssohn in 1843 (Ms. M. D. Mendelssohn c. 85, Bodleian Library, Oxford). Published in her lifetime were *Vier Lieder für das Pianoforte,* Heft 1, Op. 2 (Berlin: Bote & Bock, 1846) and *Vier Lieder für das Pianoforte,* Heft 2, Op. 6 (Berlin: Bote & Bock, 1847) (in all, eight pieces); *Six Mélodies pour le Piano,* Heft 1, Op. 4 (Berlin: A. M. Schlesinger, 1847) and Heft 2, Op. 5 (Berlin: A. M. Schlesinger, 1847) (in all, six pieces).

38. Jost, *Lieder ohne Worte,* 56.

39. For ease of naming, all works with opus numbers will be referred to in the following manner: Op. 53, No. 1 = 53/1. All Mendelssohn pieces discussed are to be found in Felix Mendelssohn, *Complete Works for*

*Pianoforte Solo*, ed. Julius Rietz (Leipzig: Breitkopf & Härtel, 1874–77; reprint, New York: Dover Publications, Inc., 1975), vol. 2.

40. Fanny Hensel, *Lieder für das Pianoforte,* Heft 2 (Berlin: Bote & Bock, 1847; reprint, Berlin: Bote and Bock, 1983).

41. Rudolf Elvers and Ernst Herttrich, "Kritischer Bericht," in Felix Mendelssohn, *Lieder ohne Worte* (Munich: G. Henle Verlag, 1981), 169.

42. Mendelssohn Archive, MAMs 49, pp. 119–20, in *Haus* 2, Staatsbibliothek Preußischer Kulturbesitz, Berlin.

43. Jost, *Lieder ohne Worte,* 69, discusses their similar tempo markings.

44. Hensel's piece is called unnumbered because its autograph is embedded among other autograph pieces that are consecutively numbered. Mendelssohn Archive, MAMs 44, pp. 9–15, in *Haus* 2, Staatsbibliothek Preußischer Kulturbesitz, Berlin. It is published for the first time in the Appendix to Fanny Hensel, *Songs for Pianoforte, 1836–1837,* ed. Camilla Cai (Madison, Wisconsin: A-R Editions, Inc., 1993).

45. Camilla Cai, "Fanny Hensel's 'Songs for Pianoforte' of 1836–37: Stylistic Interaction with Felix Mendelssohn," *Journal of Musicological Research* 14 (1994): 55–76.

46. The tempo marking in Mendelssohn's first autograph of 38/5 is the same as Hensel's: *Allegro agitato.* His *Stichvorlage* has *Molto agitato,* and he published the piece as simply *Agitato* (Jost, *Lieder ohne Worte,* 133). Jost notes a resemblance to Schubert's *Erlkönig* (Jost, *Lieder ohne Worte,* 133, n. 337), but though valid, the resemblance to Hensel's unnumbered piece is far more extensive. (Jost's note 337 contains a typographical error: "5 April 1837" should be "6 April 1837" to conform to her page 67.)

47. In 19/3 and 30/4, octaves briefly intensifying a line. In 53/5 and *Reiterlied,* octave passages are somewhat longer.

48. This is one possible way of describing the progress of the melody. Because the melody is constantly undulating, it could also be described as having further subdivisions. The melody's overall rising shape, with the climax in measures 30–31, is another important aspect of its construction.

49. R. Larry Todd, *Mendelssohn's Musical Education: A Study and Edition of His Exercises in Composition: Oxford, Bodleian MS Margaret Deneke Mendelssohn C. 43* (Cambridge: Cambridge University Press, 1983), 12, 14.

50. George R. Marek, *Gentle Genius: The Story of Felix Mendelssohn* (New York: Funk and Wagnalls, 1972), 124.

51. Zelter had strong ideas, a sharp tongue, and he concerned himself with female decorum. Sebastian Hensel reports that after Zelter had insulted a shy young girl who was auditioning before him as a singer, he said, "Now don't cry, dear child; I really meant no harm, but with your personal appearance you ought not to open your mouth like that." Sebastian Hensel, *The Mendelssohn Family* 1:74.

52. Hensel tells of her anger that a guest would ask her to read out loud the number 10,430 just to see if she, an educated woman, really could comprehend big numbers. Sebastian Hensel, *The Mendelssohn Family* 1:160.

53. Carol Gilligan, "Women's Psychological Development: Implications for Psychotherapy," *Women and Therapy* 11, nos. 3/4 (1991): 12–14.

54. In 1832 she wrote and then abandoned a clumsy fugue theme and countersubject ("Pocket Album," 1828–33). Phyllis Benjamin, "A Diary-Album for Fanny Mendelssohn Bartholdy," *Mendelssohn Studien* 7 (1990): 211.

55. Mendelssohn Archive, MAMs 44, pp. 53–58, in *Haus* 2, Staatsbibliothek Preußischer Kulturbesitz, Berlin. For further source information and the first edition of the music, see Fanny Hensel, *Songs for Pianoforte, 1836–1837*, ed. Camilla Cai.

56. Eveline Bartlitz, "Works" for Felix Mendelssohn article, *The New Grove Dictionary* 12:154.

57. See Walter Frisch, *Brahms and the Principle of Developing Variation* (Berkeley: University of California Press, 1984).

58. *Six Mélodies pour le Piano*, Opp. 4 and 5 (Berlin: Schlesinger, 1847; reprint, Berlin-Lichterfelde: Robert Lienau, 1982).

59. Jost, *Lieder ohne Worte*, 52.

60. Mendelssohn Archive, MAMs 47, pp. 78–81, in *Haus* 2, Staatsbibliothek Preußischer Kulturbesitz, Berlin.

61. Heft 1 (Berlin: Bote & Bock, 1846; reprinted with minor changes, Berlin: Bote & Bock, 1983).

62. Mendelssohn Archive, MAMs 49, pp. 34–37, in *Haus* 2, Staatsbibliothek Preußischer Kulturbesitz, Berlin.

63. *Vier Lieder für das Pianoforte,* Op. 8 (No. 1 of the posthumous works) (Leipzig: Breitkopf & Härtel, 1850). Modern edition, *Vier Lieder ohne Worte, Op. 8*, ed. Eva Rieger (Kassel: Furore, 1989).

64. She subsequently crossed out *quasi Allegro.*

65. Fanny Hensel, *Letters,* 21–22.

66. This sentence is an example of the resulting style without actually demonstrating the principle of interruption. Deborah James and Sandra Clarke, "Women, Men, and Interruptions: A Critical Review," in *Gender and Conversational Interaction,* ed. Deborah Tannen (New York: Oxford University Press, 1993), 258–60. For verbal examples that demonstrate interruption, see Deborah Tannen, "Women as Cooperative Overlappers," in *You Just Don't Understand* (New York: Ballantine Books, 1990), 203–5.

67. Letter to Marc-André Souchay, 15 October 1842, in Felix Mendelssohn, *Letters,* 269–70. For further discussion of the relation of text and music in Mendelssohn's circle, see R. Larry Todd, "'Gerade das Lied wie es dasteht': On Text and Meaning in Mendelssohn's *Lieder ohne Worte,*" in *Musical Humanism and Its Legacy: Essays in Honor of Claude V. Palisca,*

eds. Nancy Kovaleff Baker and Barbara Russano Hanning (Stuyvesant, NY: Pendragon Press, 1992), 355–79.

68. Many of the questions necessary to such study are posed by Citron in her chapter "Music as Gendered Discourse" in *Gender and the Musical Canon,* 120–64.

# CHAPTER FOUR

# Chopin's "Concluding Expansions"

## Charles Burkhart

## I

THIS ESSAY is about an aspect of Chopin's music that, as far as I know, has not been heretofore described. It has to do with what theorists of today call "phrase expansion" — making a phrase longer than expected by puffing it out in the middle. For those readers who want or feel they need it, I am going to start with a short discussion of what phrase expansion is. But if you are not such a reader, I invite you to omit this part and skip to the sixth paragraph, where the essay really begins.

For a phrase to be perceived as "expanded," it has to be heard with reference to a previous shorter phrase, which is called the "prototype" (or, more precisely, "prototype phrase"), after Schenker's term *Vorbild*. In the most common situation, the prototype phrase occurs immediately before the expanded phrase. The prototype's length is taken as a norm that the expanded phrase then exceeds. The more often the prototype's length has been previously used in the composition, the stronger the effect of the expanded phrase when it occurs. In the terminology I shall use here, the "additional" measures in an expanded phrase must occur in the phrase's interior — before its cadence is concluded. (Additional measures occurring after the cadence are called by the familiar term *extension*.) For a phrase to qualify as expanded, the additional measures must be removable without damage to the essential pitch structure of the phrase. Such a removal reduces the expanded phrase to the same length as the prototype, that is, to its "basic length."

If the prototype does no more than provide a length against which the expanded phrase is measured, it is called a "purely metric prototype." But in many cases the prototype's melody and harmony will be repeated, either entirely or in part, in the expanded phrase. A common pattern is for the expanded phrase to begin by literally repeating the beginning of the prototype phrase, then "stretch out" its later measures. The term *prototype* is sometimes used to refer to just that portion of the prototype phrase that is subjected to the stretching-out process in the expanded phrase. Similarly, in the expanded phrase, the stretched-out portion is the expansion proper.

Expansion requires that a given phrase length (say, four measures) be first established as a norm, for without a clear norm there can be no departure from it — that is, without a clear prototype, expansion cannot come into existence at all. Therefore, the concept of expansion is most meaningfully applied to those styles in which regular periodicity of phrasing is common, that is, the Classic and later styles. In Baroque music, where regular periodicity is less common, the concept of expansion is more problematic.

Expansion is a rich compositional resource, not only for its expressive possibilities, which are infinitely various, but also because it promotes a sense of growth, development, and sometimes of climax. Many of the great tonal composers have exploited it, and in many different ways. (I shall be discussing only one type of expansion — and a fairly simple one — below.) Since the mid-eighteenth century, expansion has also been described by various theorists, notably Koch, Reicha, Riemann, and, most significantly, Schenker (see *Free Composition,* par. 297[1] ), whose theory of structural levels has made possible a deeper understanding of it. It has received much attention in connection with the resurgence of interest in rhythm theory in the past several decades, the most important recent work on it being that of William Rothstein, whose terminology I largely follow here.[2]

# II

In his excellent treatise on rhythmic technique and style, "Phrase Rhythm in Tonal Music,"[3] Rothstein shows that the music of Chopin makes relatively little use of phrase expansion. He suggests this may have been due to the nature of Chopin's early musical training and influences, which led him to rely very heavily on phrases of four-measure and eight-measure length, and he shows how Chopin, rather than employing the technique of expansion to counteract the monotony of too much regular periodicity, employs instead a strikingly original type of surface articulation that "capriciously" contradicts the basic phrase structure. He goes on to show how, in some later works, Chopin achieves the same end by more radical means — a kind of "endless melody" comparable to the late rhythmic style of Wagner.

I have no quarrel with this insightful thesis. Phrase expansion is certainly not as important for Chopin as it was for the Classic masters, or for the Classically oriented Mendelssohn. But there is, I submit, one type of expansion that Chopin does write so frequently that it calls for special mention. It goes like this: the phrase that concludes the main body of the composition (or a large closed section of a composition) is an expanded form of a phrase stated earlier (sometimes the one just preceding, sometimes an earlier one). This "concluding expansion" is not to be confused with a coda. On the contrary, it occurs just before the coda (if there is one) and overlaps into it. Such an expansion nearly always embodies an important — often the main — climax of the piece. Newcomers to the idea of expansion must understand that there are many kinds of expansion and that as a general phenomenon it can occur anywhere in a composition. I am discussing here just one very specific manifestation of it, dubbing it "concluding expansion," and showing it only in the music of Chopin, who wrote this kind of expansion so often that it may be considered an element of his style.

Consider the conclusion of the main body of the "Aeolian Harp" Etude, Op. 25, No. 1 (Ex. 4.1a). The prototype phrase is a four-measure group (and there have been many four-measure groups up to this point). We might reasonably expect another, but instead Chopin concludes with a seven-measure phrase — measures 30–36. The example shows measures 32–34 as the "extra" measures — the expansion proper — by means of parentheses. The omission of these measures would leave intact a four-measure basic structure that could have been composed something like Ex. 4.1b. Ex. 4.1b makes clear that it is the dominant $\frac{6}{4}$ chord begun in measure 31 that is stretched out for three more measures.

Though Ex. 4.1b shows the basic length of measures 30–36, Chopin, needless to say, would never have concluded his etude in so trite a manner. Various compositional forces require an expansion here. The expansion's gradual ascent not only achieves an expressive climax; it is also motivated by the need to fill the "gap" created by the falling 6th ($c^3$–$eb^2$) in measures 27 and 31. Notice that measure 28's four-note figure, Eb–E♮–F–Eb, provides the expansion's melodic seed. Also, the sequential repetition of this figure causes us to hear a kind of subordinate four-measure group in measures 32–35 (see the parenthesized 1 2 3 4 in Ex. 4.1a).

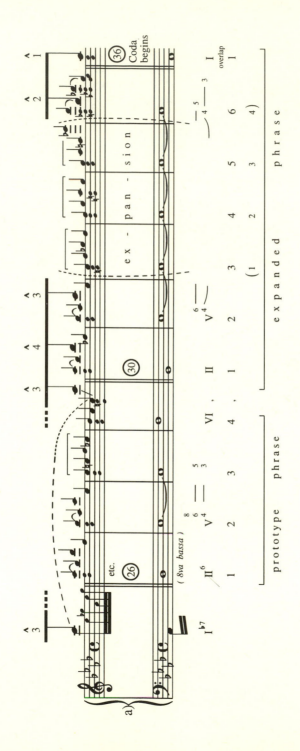

EXAMPLE 4.1a. "Aeolian Harp" Etude, Op. 25, No. 1 (1836)

EXAMPLE 4.1b. "Aeolian Harp" Etude, Op. 25, No 1 (1836). Hypothetical four-measure version of expanded phrase (mm. 30–36)

In Schenkerian terms, an expansion is of "lower" structural rank than the basic phrase structure — a departure from the norm, so to speak — and for that very reason is a source of expressiveness. To achieve still further expressiveness, expansions also frequently employ — as in the present case — more chromaticism than does the prototype (though they do not have to). It is as though the "extra" time (the expansion) is expressed via extra notes in the sense that the chromatics are extra to the more fundamental diatonicism. An eruption of chromaticism, often realized in the form of sequences — again as here — is typical of Chopin's concluding expansions. We will encounter more richly chromatic examples as we proceed.

I have said that Chopin's concluding expanded phrases usually "overlap" into a coda.[4] This is to say that the ending of one phrase (here the last phrase of the main body) occurs simultaneously with the beginning of the next (here the first phrase of the coda). The exact point of overlap in this case is measure 36.[5] Look again at Ex. 4.1b, which, because it consists only of basic measures, not only lacks the expansion but likewise is not followed by a coda — that is, its fourth measure represents the end of the piece and there is no coda. Note too that this measure is weak, 1–2–3–4 being strong–weak–strong–weak. Now when Chopin composes a concluding expanded phrase that is to be followed by a coda, he typically designs it so that it reaches its concluding tonic on a *strong* measure — again as here — and thus invites continuation. This way of initiating a coda was not original with Chopin; it was a time-honored Classical rhythmic technique that he early learned.[6] The "Aeolian Harp" is not unique among the etudes in having a concluding expansion. The phenomenon occurs in nearly half of the twenty-four etudes in Opp. 10 and 25.[7]

My second example, the Mazurka in A♭, Op. 59, No. 2, displays some different procedures. An A–B–A plus coda, its concluding expansion comes at the end of the A² section. Ex. 4.2a shows this entire section (which begins with the melody in the left hand). Notice that it is a "double parallel period," with its four segments marked W, X, Y, and Z in the example. W, X, and Y are all clear four-measure phrases, while Z, the expanded phrase, is twice as long. Because Z can be heard as a kind of 4 + 4, it may seem less obviously

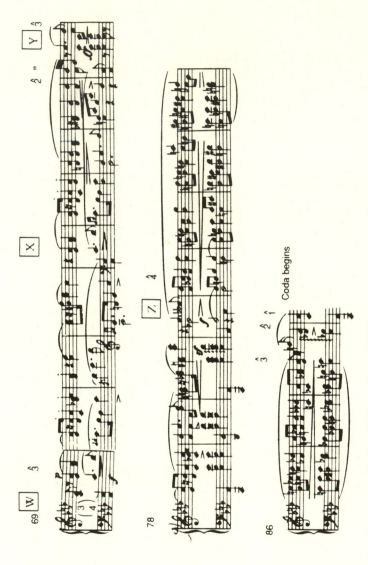

EXAMPLE 4.2a. Mazurka in Ab, Op. 59, No. 2 (mm. 69–89)

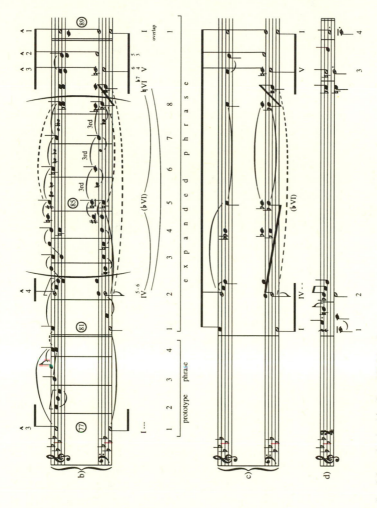

EXAMPLE 4.2(b–d).  Mazurka in A♭, Op. 59, No. 2

"expanded" than did the expanded phrase in "Aeolian Harp." But
since it has no closure of any kind until measure 89 (which again
brings the typical overlap), it is clearly a single expanded phrase.

Also unlike "Aeolian Harp," Phrase Y bears little melodic
resemblance to Z. Therefore Y is said to constitute a "purely metric
prototype" against which the longer length of Z is experienced. X is
even more of a metric prototype for Z for the following reason: since
W–X groups as 4 + 4, we expect Y–Z to be another 4 + 4, but
instead hear 4 + 8. And therefore, on a larger level, W–X as a whole
is a metric prototype for Y–Z.

The explosion of chromaticism in Phrase Z (especially in
mm. 85–88) is so astonishing that it seems almost *de trop* — more than
the style of this otherwise only conventionally chromatic piece can
bear. Such seemingly willful surprises are typical of Chopin. (An even
wilder chromatic expansion ends the C♯-Minor Mazurka, Op. 30,
No. 4.) I am reminded of the colorful remark by, I believe, Huneker:
"Chopin is the freest of spirits, unhinged from all moorings" — an
exaggeration, of course, but with a kernel of truth. I suggest that the
extreme chromatics here are just bearable only because they are
smuggled in as part of an expansion. Using them as basic phrase
material *would* have been too much.

Compared to the chromaticism in the "Aeolian Harp's" expansion, the chromaticism here is decidedly "farther out." A closer look
at Ex. 4.2a, measures 85–88 — particularly the first chord in each
measure — will reveal that this chromatic progression is founded on a
complete subdivision of the octave E–F♭ into major thirds: E–C–A♭–
F♭. The context of these measures shows them to be a prolongation of
the ♭VI of the A♭ tonality, as shown in Exx. 4.2b and 4.2c. Notice that
in measures 82–84 a series of rising sequences gradually removes the
flats by wheeling around the circle of fifths, as it were, to the four
sharps of E major. The subsequent sequence in falling thirds (mm. 85–
88) restores the flats. The E major of measure 85, beat 1, then, is
*locally* a true E♮, but in the large — that is, within the A♭-major
tonality — it is heard as ♭VI. Exx. 4.2b and 4.2c show also that this
♭VI is in turn an "upper 3rd" of a still larger prolonged IV. It is
precisely the prolongation (enclosed by parentheses in Ex. 4.2b) of
this IV that constitutes the expansion proper. Ex. 4.2d removes the
expansion, leaving just the four-measure "basic length."[8]

The next two examples show a new paradigm: prototype and expansion are not contiguous but far apart. Though the compositions I will discuss here happen to be quite long (for Chopin), this paradigm is common in his shorter pieces as well (see note 6).

The polonaise of the Andante Spianato and Grande Polonaise Brillante, Op. 22, is a large A–B–A–Coda in which A$^1$ is itself composed of a smaller a–b–a. Ex. 4.3a represents this smaller a–b–a and shows how prototype and expansion are here disposed such that the former concludes the a$^1$ and the latter a$^2$.$^9$

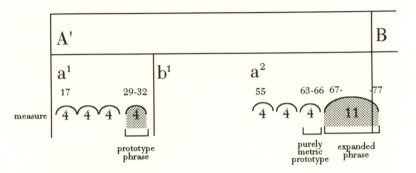

EXAMPLE 4.3a. Location of prototype and expansion in Grande Polonaise Brillante, Op. 22

In this new situation, there are actually two different prototypes: First, the four-measure group immediately before the expansion — that is, measures 63–66 — still is a "purely metric prototype" that alone would make us hear 67–77 as an expansion. The other is the much earlier phrase (29–32), which we might call the "pitch-structural prototype" because it is identical to the expansion in pitch structure. The more interesting of these is, of course, the pitch prototype. Exx. 4.3b and 4.3c make clear its relationship to the expansion.

In this expansion (Ex. 4.3c), rather as in "Aeolian Harp," the harmonies of the prototype's third and fourth measures — the cadential $^6_4$ — $^5_3$ — are stretched out (1–2–3---4---) so that both the $^6_4$ and the $^5_3$ now occupy four measures each. Since they are generated by the expansion, the resulting new four-measure hypermeasures (see the bottom of Ex. 4.3c) rank lower than the basic measures and are therefore parenthesized. Chopin gives this stretching out an ingenious motivic form: the rising fifth Bb–C–D–F near the end of the prototype (mm. 31–32) is expressed two times in elongated form in the expansion (see the brackets ⌐⌐ in Exx. 4.3b and 4.3c).

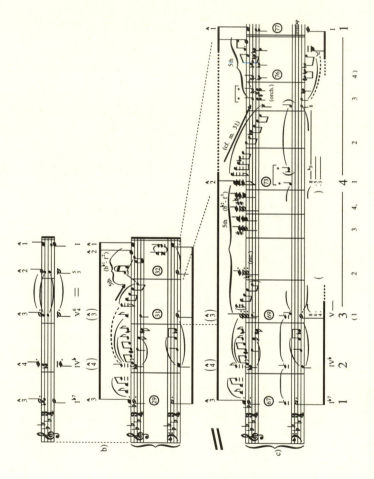

EXAMPLE 4.3(b and c). Prototype (b) and expansion (c) in Grande Polonaise Brillante, Op. 22 (1830–35).

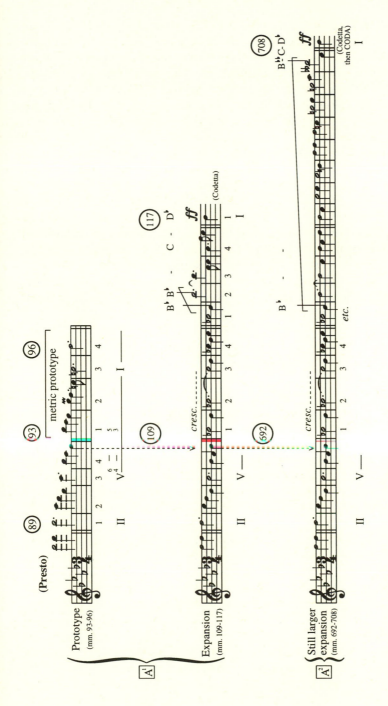

EXAMPLE 4.4. Scherzo No. 2, Op. 31 (1837)

The form of Scherzo No. 2 in "B♭ Minor," Op. 31, like that of all four scherzos, derives from the Classical Scherzo–Trio–Scherzo tradition. This huge A–B–A gives Chopin the opportunity for another expansion of the noncontiguous type we have just seen. In the Polonaise's A² section, he simply repeats A¹, but in the Scherzo he goes the Polonaise one better, as shown in Ex. 4.4. First, in the Scherzo's A¹, the prototype's length is doubled in the expansion, thus bringing the section to a climactic conclusion. But in A² (the *scherzo da capo*) Chopin further expands the expansion, now quadrupling the prototype's length. In a motivic sense, it is the right hand's octave leap b♭²–b♭² at the turn of measures 113–14 that is now stretched out for twelve measures (696–707) as b♭²–b♭♭³, thus bringing A² to an even more ringing conclusion. See Ex. 4.4 and compare the second and third lines. Notice also that in both A¹ and A² the precise length of the expansion is bounded by the dynamic marking *crescendo — ff*.

Though measure 708 marks the structural close of the composition, it is interesting that the ensuing coda contains still another, though materially different, expansion (compare 736–39 with 744–55), which raises the mood to a still more frenzied pitch.

## III

Since I am describing "concluding expansion" not merely as a technique, but as a style element in Chopin, it seems relevant to ask: Does this style element appear in other music, and if so, what music did the young Chopin know that might have taught it to him?[10] While it is obvious that no one can determine exactly where and how a great composer learns his techniques, an attempt to answer this question may at least tell us something about the history of rhythmic style. The question may at first seem too general, since some sort of lengthening at the end of a piece is found in so many earlier periods and styles. But "concluding expansion," as defined here, is a specific technique by no means found in all times and places. Is it found in any music the young Chopin would have known?

I propose that Classical movements in sonata form provide at least the beginning of an answer. It is well known that in the first movement of the Classical concerto, the first and last solo sections typically end with an extended progression that culminates in the conventional cadential trill. In sonata-form terms, the first such progression occurs in the "second exposition" at the structural close of the second thematic group, just before the second orchestral ritornello. In many concertos there is a two-phrase scheme at this point that is quite similar to our Chopin examples: the first phrase establishes a given length; the following phrase is an expanded repetition of the first, and, by means of the expansion, achieves a very emphatic close. A good example is in the first movement of Mozart's D-Major Piano Concerto ("Coronation"), K. 537 (Ex. 4.5). Notice how the $I^6$–IV–V progression in the two-measure prototype (196–97) is expanded from measures 201 to 215 (with ten of those measures devoted to a particularly imaginative prolongation of the IV).[11] Clearly this fits the definition of concluding expansion.

It is not so well known that concluding expansion is also frequently found in sonata-form movements in all the other Classic instrumental genres — and in exactly the same place as in the concerto, that is, at the structural conclusion of the second thematic group in the exposition (and repeated in the recapitulation with occasionally a still larger expansion).[12] Exactly as in our Chopin examples, the concluding expansion will occur here just before, and overlap into, the codetta. I have found fourteen instances, realized in a variety of ways, in the eighteen Mozart piano sonatas.[13] The one in the first movement of the C-Major Sonata, K. 309, is typical (see Ex. 4.6).[14] Many other examples from sonata-form movements in sonatas, chamber works, and symphonies of Haydn, Mozart, and Beethoven could be cited.[15]

Since Chopin was schooled in the German masters by both his teachers, Zywny and Elsner, and early formed a particular affinity for Mozart, it is pertinent to ask: Does he use concluding expansion in his sonata forms? To be sure, sonata form did not come easily to him, and the few examples of it he wrote are often structurally quite peculiar. But he did write seven of them, and — most pertinent here — four of these were written between the ages of seventeen and twenty, that is, before he left Poland. These four are the first movements of the following:

> Sonata No. 1 in C Minor, Op. 4, 1827–28[16]
> Trio in G Minor, Op. 8, 1828–29
> Concerto No. 2 in F Minor, Op. 20, 1829[17]
> Concerto No. 1 in E Minor, Op. 11, 1830

The first two of these are ineffective student works and the second two are masterpieces. Together they show that by 1830 Chopin had not only grown as a composer but also had learned a good deal about concluding expansion, even if he did not always handle it with complete mastery. In the stiff, Bach–influenced Sonata, both exposition and recapitulation conclude with the conventional elongation of

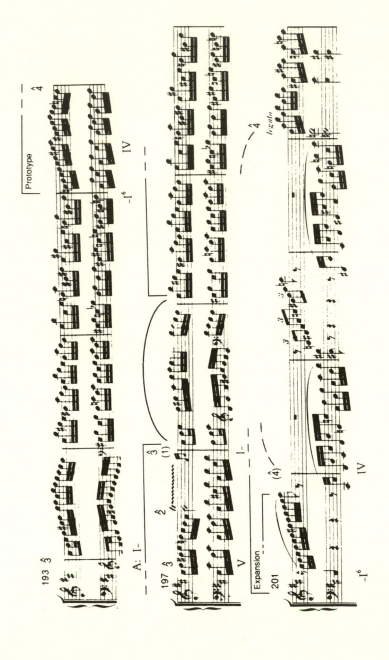

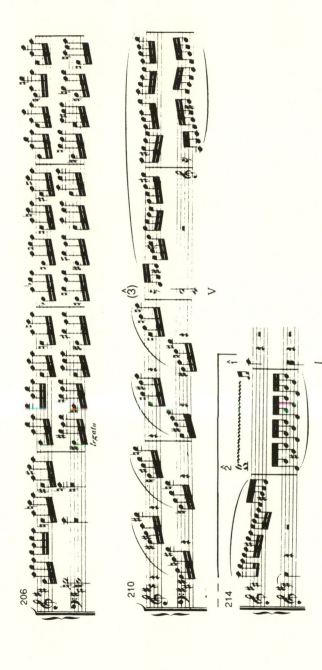

EXAMPLE 4.5. Mozart "Coronation" Concerto, K. 537, I (piano part only).
Conclusion of "second exposition"

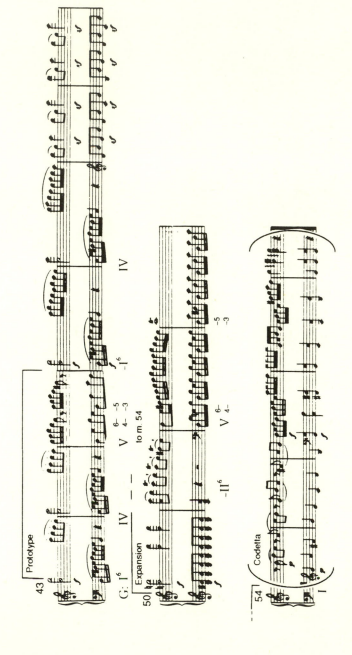

EXAMPLE 4.6.  Mozart Piano Sonata in C Major, K. 309, first movement. Close of exposition

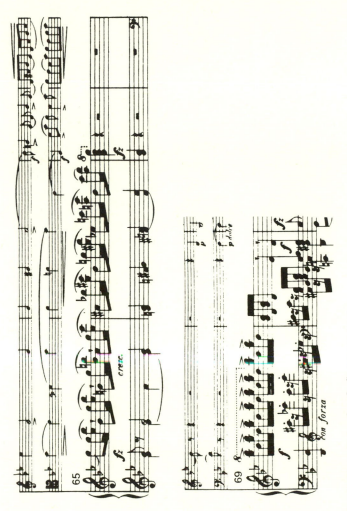

EXAMPLE 4.7a. Chopin Piano Trio, Op. 8, first movement. Prototype phrase (mm. 65–70)

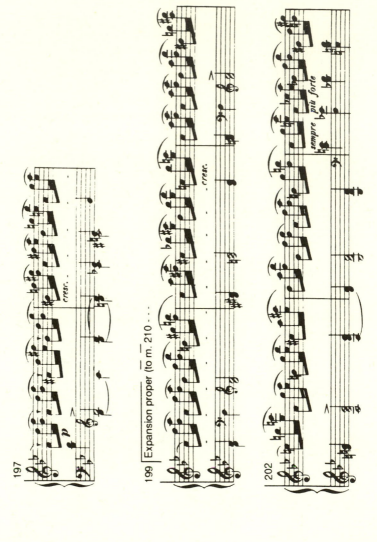

197

199 | Expansion proper (to m. 210 · · ·

202

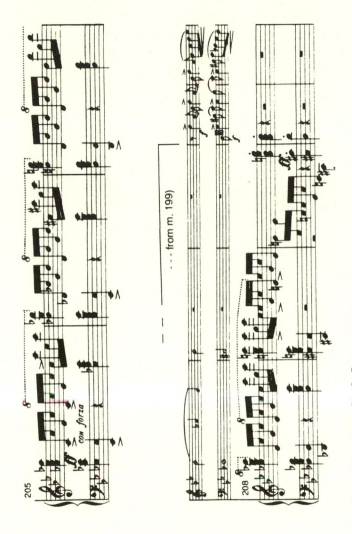

EXAMPLE 4.7b.  Chopin Piano Trio, Op. 8, first movement.
Expanded phrase (mm. 197–215) [string parts mostly omitted]

the cadential harmonies, but no prototype is present. In the Trio, on the other hand, there are two quite clear cases of prototype–cum–expansion spanning measures 29–53 (a passage one would like to call the transition except that it never leaves the home key of G minor, and also ends with a full cadence in that key). More significantly, the second theme, measures 53–71 (also entirely in G minor!), concludes the main body of the exposition with a passage that is greatly expanded in the recapitulation. Ex. 4.7 shows just the prototype phrase and its later expansion. In the recapitulation the second theme has started in D minor and now modulates back to G minor in the course of the expansion. (Is it possible Chopin learned to use expansion before he learned about the harmonic structure of sonata form?)

The two wonderful concertos are quite another story, both showing a great advance in every way — including the handling of phrase rhythm — over everything Chopin had so far composed. In the F minor, as in the Trio, the end of the exposition is expanded in the recapitulation, but now with far greater effectiveness. In the E minor, each of the second theme's two large sections, A (starting at m. 222) and B (starting at *Risoluto,* m. 283), end with huge expansions beginning, respectively, at measures 252 and 315.[18]

Sonata form is more complex rhythmically than the part forms typical of Chopin's work as a whole. My examples of expansions from Chopin's part forms (Exx. 1–4) are relatively simple: all have four-measure hypermeter, and the majority expand the cadential domi-nant $^6_4$. Though there is a long stylistic distance between these expansions and the Mozart examples given here, it nevertheless seems likely that Chopin learned the technique of concluding expansion from its use in the classical sonata genres, especially so considering that he used it, as I have shown, in his own early sonata forms. I suggest that he subsequently adapted the technique to the simpler forms that came more naturally to him. It is one way that his music, for all its startling originality, is related to an older tradition.

# Notes

1. Heinrich Schenker, *Free Composition*, trans. and ed. Ernst Oster (New York: Longman, 1979), 1:par. 297.

2. William Rothstein, *Rhythm and the Theory of Structural Levels* (Ann Arbor, MI: University Microfilms 8125672, 1981), chap. 7, and Rothstein, *Phrase Rhythm in Tonal Music* (New York: Schirmer Books, 1989), chap. 3. See also the important discussion by Carl Schachter in "Rhythm and Linear Analysis: Aspects of Meter" in *The Music Forum* (New York: Columbia University Press, 1987), 6:40ff.

3. Rothstein, *Rhythm and the Theory,* chap. 7.

4. I am using "coda" in the traditional sense, that is, to denote a section that is structurally subordinate to the main body — an extension of the main body's closing tonic chord.

5. But *overlap* is not synonymous with *elision*. Elision is a special (and more drastic) kind of overlap in which an entire measure is "omitted," or better, in which what could be two adjacent measures are compressed into one — elided, thus causing the listener to *reinterpret* that measure's hypermetrical position. Measure 28 of Mozart's 40th (beginning of the bridge) is an elision; compare measure 9.

6. The technique of overlap is by no means confined to the starts of codas. It occurs throughout tonal composition between phrases of *equal* rank.

7. The eleven etudes having concluding expansions are here listed. (Most are A–B–A forms in which the prototype phrase occurs at the end of $A^1$ and the expansion at the end of $A^2$ — a paradigm to be discussed later.) For each etude in the list, the location of the prototype is given in measure numbers before the stroke, the expansion after: Op.10: No. 4 (15–16 / 65–70), No. 6 (15 / 47–50), No. 7 (36–37 / 40–43), No. 9 (13–16 / 49–56), No. 10 (13–16 / 59–68), No. 11 (7–8 / 39–44). Op. 25 (in addition to No. 1): No. 8 (5–8 / 21–28), No. 9 (5–8 / 29–37), No. 11 (13–22 / 77–89), No. 12 (9–15 / 55–71).

8. A few details of Ex. 4.2b are from an unpublished analysis by Ernst Oster.

9. In Ex. 4.3, measure numbers apply to the polonaise only. Since the polonaise begins with a sixteen-measure orchestral introduction, the $a^2$ section starts in measure 17.

10. The use of concluding expansion by Chopin's contemporaries and followers lies outside the scope of this essay. Suffice it to note that it is used variously by some other nineteenth-century composers, perhaps most "classically" by Mendelssohn, who employs it frequently in the *Songs without Words.*

11. Rothstein (*Phrase Rhythm,* 83) cites a similar expansion in the C-Major Concerto, K. 467, measures 171–94, in his discussion of "expansion by composed-out deceleration or fermata," by which he means a slowing up of the harmonic rhythm — what I have been calling "stretching out" the harmonies.

12. In an excellent article, "The 'Expanded Cadential Progression': A Category for the Analysis of Classical Form," *Journal of Musicological Research* 7 (1987): 215, William E. Caplin describes the elongated harmonies I⁶–II(IV)–V–I that often appear at this and other points in the typical sonata form. Though he focuses only on the bass, some of his examples are what I have called "concluding expansions."

13. They are: K. 279 I and II, K. 281 II, K. 283 II and III, K. 309 I, K. 330 III, K. 332 I and II, K. 333 I, K. 457 I, K. 533 I, K. 570 I, and K. 576 I. In K. 333 and K. 533, prototype and expansion are noncontiguous, lying respectively in exposition and recapitulation.

14. Notice in K. 309 how the expansion of the IV is enclosed by the use of a higher left-hand register spanning measures 48–51. The left hand's return to the lower octave at measure 52 forms a registral connection with measure 47.

15. It would seem possible that the repertoire of eighteenth- and early-nineteenth-century Italian opera also might yield relevant examples of concluding expansion. The young Chopin had many opportunities to hear opera in Warsaw, and we know that it influenced his style in other ways. One immediately thinks of the long drawn-out endings of many operatic arias and finales, but these are, much more often than not, codas, and, I repeat, we are not concerned with codas, but with the end of the main body. Though concluding expansion occasionally does occur, like the following one in "Che faro senza Eurydice?" from Gluck's *Orfeo ed Eurydice* [Italian version, 1762; French version, 1774] (for which I am indebted to Dr. Henry Burnett), my investigations so far suggest that a connection between concluding expansions in opera and those in Chopin is tenuous at best.

Je — suc - com - be à — ma — dou⁻ - leur!

End of first strophe

Je — suc - com - be à — ma . dou - leur,       à — ma — dou - leur, ___       à — ma — dou - leur!

End of aria

16. Dates are from Jim Samson, *The Music of Chopin* (1985; reprint, Oxford: Clarendon Press, 1994).

17. So numbered because published *after* the E-Minor Concerto.

18. But harmonic structure in the E-Minor Concerto's first movement is still idiosyncratic — second theme in E major in the exposition, then in G major in the recapitulation. While the similarity of this plan to that of the Trio's first movement is noteworthy, the important thing is that Chopin makes it work beautifully in the concerto. Surely he knew he was not following traditional harmonic structure here. At any rate, he had followed it fairly closely in the earlier F-Minor Concerto.

# CHAPTER FIVE

# The Coda Wagging the Dog: Tails and Wedges in the Chopin Ballades

## David Witten

*There is the tall lily in the fountain that nods to the sun. It drips in cadenced monotone and its song is repeated on the lips of the slender-hipped girl with the eyes of midnight . . .*

James Huneker, imagining a
descriptive narrative for the
G-Minor Ballade (1900)[1]

*The age of description is over.*

Hans Keller (1956)[2]

## I

CHOPIN'S Waltzes, Mazurkas, Etudes, and Preludes have been universally acclaimed as "perfect miniatures,"[3] the representatives *par excellence* of their respective genres. His works in larger forms, however, have not always received such unrestrained praise. Though the Sonatas, Ballades, and Concerti certainly have never lost their popularity with the public, analysts of the past have felt obliged to preface their discussions of these more extended works with defensive remarks apologizing for Chopin's so-called weakness of form.

Most Ballade discussions at the turn of the century praised Chopin for his dramatic, heroic moments that succeed *in spite of* a lack of formal structure. William Hadow went so far as to accuse Chopin of "indifference to the requirements of key-relationship."

> Not only in his efforts at sonata form does he show himself unusu-
> ally unable to hold together a complex scheme of keys, but in works
> of a more loose structure, his choice seems to be regulated rather by
> hazard than by any preconceived plan.[4]

Hadow was expressing the misconceptions of his day, opinions that
had become widely accepted. Not everyone agreed; James Huneker
intuitively recognized the danger of these rash statements and came
forth with his own evaluation:

> Not loosely-joined, but compact structures glowing with genius and
> presenting definite unity of form and expression, are the Ballades.[5]

Huneker unfortunately lacked the analytical insight with which to
explain his intuition, and he is remembered today more for his skill
with prose than with analysis:

> [Chopin] sonnets to perfection, but the epical air does not fill his
> nostrils.[6]

In recent years, more meaningful analyses have appeared that
probe beneath the surface of Chopin's larger works to reveal their
sturdy, rock-solid foundations. Standing on the shoulders of giants
such as Heinrich Schenker and Rudolph Réti, analysts Alan Walker,
Carl Schachter, Edward T. Cone, John Rink, and Jim Samson have
written perceptively about works that previous generations had praised
only superficially.[7]

# II

The formal integrity of the four Ballades remains a mystery only if
one tries to dissect them using blunt descriptive tools of the past.
Imposing strict sonata or rondo forms onto the Ballades will leave
those very forms twisted, hopelessly bent out of shape. Chopin's
innovative art includes the ability to hide his well-crafted and innovative structure behind its beauty — *Ars est celare artem*. Not unlike
Debussy's assessment of the genius of Musorgskii,

> It is like the art of an *inquisitive savage* who discovers music at
> every step made by his emotions. . . . The form is so manifold that
> it cannot possibly be likened to the recognized or orthodox forms. It
> is achieved by little consecutive touches linked by a mysterious bond
> and by his gift of luminous intuition.[8]

Though Chopin could hardly be called a "savage," his Ballades prove him "inquisitive" in the extreme; he has discovered hidden sideroads branching off the traditional instrumental forms.

Without a doubt, the temptation to examine the Ballades through the lens of sonata form is strong — each Ballade contains contrasting themes and developmental sections, which are both primary ingredients of sonata style. As Samson has pointed out, "far from ignoring sonata form, we need to recognize it as the essential reference point for all four Ballades."[9] Chopin does not merely use sonata form as a point of departure — he carries the principle of statement-intensification-reconciliation to new heights not forseen in the works of his predecessors. One might say that he leaves sonata form behind in a Schenkerian cloud of dust.

The form of the Ballades remains problematical only as long as the themes are given greater consideration than the overall tonal plan. Specifically, we must consider the location of the structural dominant — in Schenkerian terms, the V of the *Bassbrechung*. In textbook sonata form, classical composers commonly used the dominant as a tonal area for the contrasting theme. Beethoven and Schubert subsequently experimented with mediant and submediant key areas for their contrasting themes; they often delayed the structural dominant until the *end* of the development section, at which point the arrival of the tonic coincided with the recapitulation (e.g., Beethoven's "Waldstein" Sonata).[10] Chopin extends this evolutionary trend even further — he postpones the structural dominant until the end of the piece, *after* the themes have gloriously exhausted themselves.

An overview of the tonalities used in the Ballades will bear this out. In each Ballade, the dominant is never used as a key area, nor does it appear as a $V^7$ leading to a recapitulation. The G-Minor Ballade employs its submediant (VI) for the second theme. The F-Major Ballade (if you believe F major to be its tonality!) appears to use its mediant (III), the key in which the piece ultimately ends. The Ab Ballade contains large sections in the major and minor submediant (VI, vi) and the subdominant (IV) as well. The first theme of the F-Minor Ballade bends toward the subdominant (iv), and its second theme arrives in the major subdominant and later in the submediant (VI). In each of the four Ballades, Chopin creates an "accelerating intensity curve"[11] by deliberately delaying the dominant and the subsequent tonic reconciliation until after all the themes have been stated and metamorphosized.

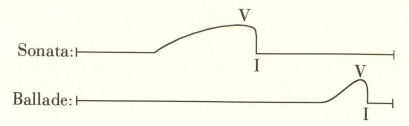

EXAMPLE 5.1. Chopin's extremely delayed structural V in the Ballades, compared with earlier sonata-style movements

In every Ballade, Chopin's favorite tactic for delaying the structural V is the deployment and prolongation of its upper neighbor, VI. Chopin's inclination for VI–V should come as no surprise to the discerning listener familiar with his melodies. Indeed, his predilection for melodic motion from the sixth to the fifth degree of the scale ($\hat{6}$–$\hat{5}$) is so pervasive in his music on the foreground level that it may be termed a musical "thumbprint" (Ex. 5.2).

In the Ballades, motion from the sixth to the fifth degree is an essential element not only melodically, but on *every* structural level; it occurs in the melodic contour of the themes, it strengthens various secondary dominants, and it plays the major role in preparing the structural dominant. Heinrich Schenker and his disciples have identified this type of compositional device — the small detail being reflected out into the larger picture. It is sometimes referred to as a "hidden repetition" or "motivic parallelism." To quote Carl Schachter, "Chopin's ability to connect large structure with detail through the enlargement of basic melodic figures is one of the most striking aspects of his compositional genius."[12] Far from being a detail of limited significance in the Ballades, the ubiquitous $\hat{6}$–$\hat{5}$ serves as a unifying force — it is a *motivic metaphor* for the larger tonal structure of each work.

It is this feature, Chopin's use of $\hat{6}$–$\hat{5}$ on every structural level, that provides unity within, and even among, the four Ballades. Like scientists who can track an animal implanted with an electronic tracking device, we can follow the peregrinations of the sixth and fifth degrees ($\hat{6}$–$\hat{5}$ as well as VI–V) throughout each Ballade and learn a great deal about Chopin the musical strategist.

(a) Prelude in E Minor, Op. 28, No. 4

(b) Polonaise in A♭ Major, Op. 53

(c) Nocturne in E Minor, Op. posth. 72, No. 1

(d) Waltz in A Minor, Op. 34, No. 2

EXAMPLE 5.2. Four examples of Chopin's predilection for $\hat{6}$–$\hat{5}$ in his melodies

In addition to his tonal deployment of the submediant, VI, Chopin engages several thematic techniques to delay the arrival of the structural dominant. Most of his Ballade melodies are purposely open-ended, curiously incomplete. To borrow a phrase used both by linguists and geneticists, Chopin applies "chiasmic reversal" and avoids the conventional "Question?–Answer!" phrase pattern. He favors "Answer!–Question?" phrases; at times, he even invents "Question?–Question??" phrases. (See Exx. 5.10–12.)

Related to chiasmic reversal is Chopin's purposeful tonal ambiguity. Often, a four-measure phrase can be interpreted as cadencing either *on* V or *in* V, rather than I. In his excellent article, "Ambiguity and Reinterpretation in Chopin," Edward T. Cone points out two Ballade moments that share identical tonal ambiguities: the introductory phrase of the F-Minor Ballade (see Ex. 5.66), and the second theme of the A♭ Ballade (Ex. 5.3). Regarding the latter, he asks, "Do we hear its first phrase as F:V$^7$–I–vi$^7$–V$^7$/V–V, or as C:V$^7$/IV–IV–ii$^7$–V$^7$–I?"[13]

EXAMPLE 5.3. Second theme of A♭ Ballade (mm. 54–57). Two ways of hearing Chopin's ambiguous phrase structure

It is interesting to note that this ambiguous harmonic scheme *also* appears in the second theme of the G-Minor Ballade (Ex. 5.4), a second time in the A♭ Ballade (mm. 189–192, shown in Ex. 5.52), and again in the F-Minor Ballade, during a dancelike segment (mm. 112–121) whose harmonic rhythm, though not its mood, is reminiscent of that Ballade's introduction. Cone suggests that in cases such as these, Chopin was being "deliberately ambiguous, and that a convincing analysis of the passage must reveal that intention."[14]

EXAMPLE 5.4. Second theme of G-Minor Ballade (mm. 54–57). Two harmonic interpretations of Chopin's ambiguous phrase structure

Finally, Chopin frequently undermines our sense of security with wildly deceptive tonal splices. He will properly prepare a new key, only to substitute another at the final moment. The listener would be well advised to watch the well-crafted V$^7$ signposts rather than the last-minute feint to the *un*prepared key. As any experienced basketball coach would tell you, "Don't watch his eyes, watch his belt-buckle."

What is Chopin's motivation for chiasmic reversals, for open-ended, incomplete themes, for last-minute key splices and interruptions? It is to raise more questions than answers, to add another dimension to the accumulating tension, and to delay the desired structural dominant and its sweet promise of release.

When the dominant finally arrives, Chopin resolves the enormous tension and concludes the musical discourse. The commonly designated term "coda" for these strikingly dramatic conclusions is, in fact, pale and insufficient. These final pages are not simply vestigial "tails" or cosmetic appendages added to smooth out the endings; rather, they are very much an integral part of each Ballade. They are the long-awaited arrival of the structural tonic. For these final dazzling pages that affirm the tonic, the themes are no longer available — the themes have already undergone an irreversible metamorphosis. Instead, Chopin deploys the most elemental building blocks of music — half steps. He uses these half steps to form powerful wedges around the notes that define tonality: the dominant and the tonic (Ex. 5.8).

## III

Chopin does not send us on our journey completely blindfolded. In the early measures of each Ballade, he plants clues to the unusual events that will later unfold. Whereas Musorgskii used "little consecutive touches," Chopin uses what we might term "prescient forebodings." The careful listener will notice them early on in the journey, like a hiker who discovers mysteriously glowing rocks whose molecular structure defies chemical analysis. As any science-fiction fan knows, the rocks arrived on this planet *from the future.* And Chopin's prescient forebodings are indeed clues from the future, prophetic moments that foretell the outcome of the piece.

Before looking at each Ballade separately, it would be appropriate to look at an extraordinary Chopin Nocturne in which repeated ♭6̂s trigger a ♯4̂ and create a powerful wedge, from above and below, into V. I am referring to the Nocturne in B Major, Op. 32, No. 1.

The opening theme is so sweet and gentle that no one would suspect the enigmatic, stormy ending of the piece. But a sharp listener would be placed on alert by the oddness of measures 6–7. The phrase

EXAMPLE 5.5. Chopin Nocturne in B Major, Op. 32, No. 1, mm. 6–7

unexpectedly stops in its tracks; a low G♮ (♭6̂) sets the melody in motion again. To impose a conventional Question–Answer phrase analysis would be naïve: this consequent phrase offers more Questions than Answers. Was the tension-filled fermata really necessary? And wouldn't a low F♯ instead of G♮ have functioned just as well?

EXAMPLE 5.6. Hypothetical version of Nocturne, Op. 32, No. 1, mm. 6–7, that bypasses the mysterious interruption and G♮ (♭6̂)

Chopin repeats this foreboding moment in three more versions of the theme. As we will see in the Ballades, when Chopin dwells on ♭6̂, the pitch a half step *above* the dominant, his sense of symmetry demands an eventual ♯4̂, the pitch one half step *below* the dominant.[15] Predictably yet nevertheless disturbingly, a bass E♯ (♯IV) begins to throb in measure 62 of the Nocturne — we are experiencing *the dark side* of the dominant.

The struggle that ensues between the half steps surrounding the dominant needs no further comment — it is ferocious and unprecedented, but not unprovoked. The performer-analyst can now turn to it, and, with heightened awareness of those half steps, make sense of the battle.[16]

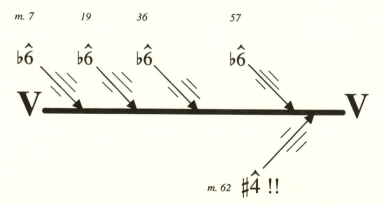

EXAMPLE 5.7. Nocturne, Op. 32, No. 1. The four bass-note G♮s (♭6̂), which sound a half step *above* the dominant F♯, eventually demand, for the sake of equilibrium, an E♯ (♯4̂) *below* the dominant

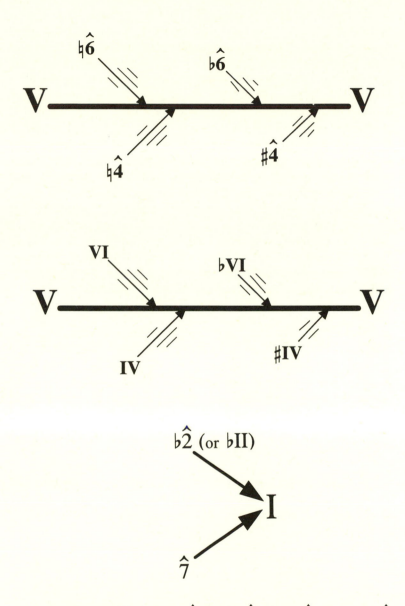

EXAMPLE 5.8. Illustrations of $\hat{6}$ and VI, $\hat{4}$ and IV, $\hat{2}$ and II, and $\hat{7}$, represented as wedges closing in on the dominant (V) and the tonic (I)

IV
## *Première Ballade*

The opening of the G-Minor Ballade presents the listener with a dilemma rarely found in music prior to 1831. Rather than clarifying the tonality of the piece in the opening measures, Chopin creates an ambiguous first-inversion Ab sonority, which we recognize only in retrospect as a Neapolitan-sixth chord in G minor. Certainly, there were well-known precedents for such a beginning, but those precedents all seem to have occurred in pieces with disturbing titles such as "The Dissonant Quartet," or "The Representation of Chaos"![17]

Toward the end of the introductory measures, we realize that Chopin's strategy was to structurally outline the pitches above and below the dominant — in other words, to present his first Ballade "wedge" (See Ex. 5.9). Chopin has achieved extraordinary poignancy with extreme economy of notes and provided a "prescient foreboding" of the importance of Eb (b6, and later bVI) in this Ballade.

EXAMPLE 5.9. First instance of converging wedge motion above and below V: Cs and Ebs wedging into D (mm. 3–8)

In one of the great ironies of analytical history, it is Huneker and Niecks, usually the writers of outdated flowery prose, who defend the Eb of measure 7, and Schenker who denies it!

> This dissonant Eb may be said to be the emotional keynote of the whole poem. It is a questioning thought that, like a sudden pain, shoots through mind and body. (Niecks)[18]

> Until this very day, many editions insist upon this ninth, and yet it can have been only Chopin himself who finally substituted for Eb the octave D. (Schenker)[19]

When the first theme begins in measure 8, we recognize its chiasmic nature; Chopin has reversed the more usual antecedent-consequent phrase structure:

EXAMPLE 5.10. Chopin's    "Answer!-Question?"    phrase    structure, mm. 8-10

Imagine how short and simple-minded the entire piece might have become had Chopin "properly" asked and answered this question (Ex. 5.11). In Chopin's startling "Answer!-Question?" version, the phrases never come to a resting point. In fact, as shown in Ex. 5.12, they create incomplete vectors, wedge motion that will not be fulfilled until the final pages of the Ballade.

EXAMPLE 5.11. Hypothetical, more conventional "Question?-Answer!" version, mm. 8-9

EXAMPLE 5.12. Frustrated, incomplete wedge motion in the opening page

The open-ended structure of this first theme, with very little adjustment, later becomes the launching pad for the apotheosis of the second theme (mm. 94-106), and still later, for the powerful conclusion of the work (mm. 194-206).

As a "hidden repetition," the $\hat{6}$-$\hat{5}$ motif in measure 7 (E♭ as the upper neighbor to D) proceeds to generate what many analysts have perceived as a tripartite, "arch" form. And indeed, if both feet of the arch were equally solid and well-prepared, this would certainly be the case. E♭ does indeed span the large middle area from measures 69 to 189. The large arch even supports a smaller, mini-arch (the section built on E♮) — a digression from the digression. The reversed order of the themes after measure 166 further strengthens the arch construction theory, illustrated in Ex. 5.13.

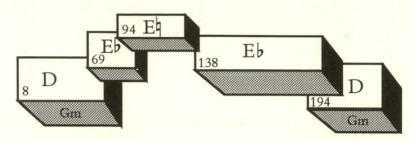

EXAMPLE 5.13 G-Minor Ballade: Arch construction analysis (drawn to scale!)

Schenker himself used the Ballade as an example of tripartite structure (Ex. 5.14).

EXAMPLE 5.14. Schenker's graph of G-Minor Ballade[20]

Schenker's graph, concerned primarily with tonal shifts, does not notate the return of the second theme at measure 166; the return of E♭ in the bass clef of his graph at measure 138 corresponds *not* to the second theme, but to the developmental material in E♭, preceded by its dominant, B♭. Schenker's notational difference between the two B♭s is extremely significant; the first is an eighth-note B♭ (m. 68), the second is a quarter-note B♭ (m. 126). It is these areas of $V^7$ of E♭ that need to be reexamined. They are the points that will illuminate the tonal structure.

Schenker, always scrupulous and precise in his graphic presentations and their implications of structural hierarchy, was certainly aware of the different mechanics involved in Chopin's *approach* to the various sections in Eb, but he apparently did not think them distinctive enough to disrupt the larger illustration of tripartite form. It seems to me that Schenker missed an opportunity to discuss the differing preparations to the same tonal area.

To establish a tonality, a composer must stress the dominant of that tonality. The history of tonal music, in fact, illustrates the increased "taking-for-granted"-ness of the tonic. Early on, it was necessary, in fact enjoyable, to dwell on the tonic. Later, a composition could merely arrive on the tonic and then bounce away, and still later, a piece could simply *suggest* the tonic. Eventually, a composer needed merely to suggest the dominant, or simply allude to the *pitches* of the dominant.[21] Any decision regarding a composer's formal structure must involve a close look at the passages *on the way* to the next theme — those are the passages that are the most telling. In the case of this Ballade, a comparison of measures 56–67 with measures 158–65 will disclose surviving vestiges of sonata principle and weaken the more popular arch-form analysis.

Indeed, the first approach to Eb is actually a preparation *not* for Eb (VI), but for Bb major (III), the more conventional second-theme area in a minor-key piece. In other words, we were expecting the version shown in Ex. 5.15.

EXAMPLE 5.15. Hypothetical version with second theme beginning in the expected Bb major (III)

But when the properly prepared tonality of Bb becomes a dominant of its own subdominant, Eb, we hear it as a last-minute replacement — VI pinch-hits for III.

On the other hand, what if Chopin had really wanted to prepare Eb properly? The hypothetical version shown in Ex. 5.16, complete with a strong measure of Eb$^6_4$ at measure 65, would more "properly" introduce Chopin's actual Eb setting of the second theme.

In fact, Chopin actually created a hybrid version: Bb (III) *is* properly prepared, only to be replaced at the last moment by Eb (VI). (See Ex. 5.17.)

EXAMPLE 5.16. Hypothetical version that would have fully prepared E♭ (VI) as the second theme

EXAMPLE 5.17. Bass motion with I $^6_4$ — V preparing B♭ (III) — although it is prepared, it never arrives

The second theme finally begins, then, in Eb. But a new element of ambiguity enters: the "Answer!–Question?" construction discussed above (Exx. 5.10 and 5.11). Its consequent phrase ends in V of Eb, which happens to be Bb, and may sound, momentarily, as if it were the key of the second theme (Ex. 5.4). As the theme proceeds, however, Eb finally becomes established as the tonic. The cadences in measures 68–69 and measures 76–77, which involve Bb$^7$–Eb, are too strong to be pulled by subsequent secondary dominants.

To summarize Chopin's startling preparation of the second theme and its tonality: we *expect* Bb major because it has been prepared by its dominant. But Chopin shifts the tonality one harmonic notch forward in the circle of fifths without really endangering our perception of the *prepared* tonality. His purpose? To hitch his wagon for the long haul to VI, the half-step wedge note above V, the structural dominant.

A lengthy and dramatic intensification follows (mm. 94–125), featuring an apotheosis of the second theme built on an E♮ pedal (*the upper neighbor* to the upper neighbor of the true dominant!). A long retransition ensues. Chopin's long-range sense of perspective is flawless here — as if to "atone" for his unprepared submediant the first time around, his preparation this time (mm. 150–66) reinforces V of Eb with considerable emphasis and repetition. We even hear a bass line that includes every possible version of the sixth degree of the scale: #6̂, ♮6̂, and b6̂!

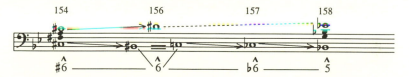

EXAMPLE 5.18. Three forms of 6̂ wedging downward into 5̂ (mm. 154–58)

The half steps above the dominants create parallel situations; the upper half step Gb leads to F as a dominant in the exposition, and the upper half step Cb emphasizes Bb as a dominant. Whereas Eb was ambiguous as a tonality in the exposition (mm. 68–82), it is now firmly ensconced as the key area at the beginning of the recapitulation (mm. 166–80).

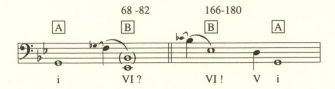

EXAMPLE 5.19. Comparison of unprepared key area VI, versus thoroughly prepared VI

The descending scale of measures 162–66 deserves close attention. On casual hearing, and in too many performances, it sounds like a cadenza, starting at the top of the keyboard on F and traveling down to a low Bb in the bass. It is important to note, however, that Chopin maintains the eighth-note pulse throughout this "cadenza." Although he certainly possessed the notational tools to indicate free rhythm (e.g., penultimate measure of the Barcarolle, Op. 61), he chose not to do so here. If the pianist resists the pianistic temptation to speed, the downbeats of the descending scale form, surprisingly, an *a*scending scale. Chopin's counterpoint here is flawless; a slower-moving ascending line in contrary motion, disguised through octave transpositions, forms a wedge with the more obvious descending line (Ex. 5.20).

EXAMPLE 5.20. Ascending line "hidden" within the descending scale (mm. 164–66), forming a converging wedge motion into V of VI

The arrival of Eb for the second theme, therefore, could not possibly be stronger. The antecedent phrase of this theme, although melodically and harmonically identical to its first appearance, receives a decidedly different emphasis. The Bb-major chord is convincingly the dominant in measure 169, and continues as a dominant pedal through the next three measures. This time, Eb major is properly prepared and quite believable as the intended tonal area.

Perhaps now would be the moment to point out the important hidden relationship of fifths between, to borrow from sonata terminology, the exposition and the recapitulation. The relations between the first and second themes are always by thirds, but between the second-theme areas themselves, specifically their dominant preparations, there exists the strong fifth relation:

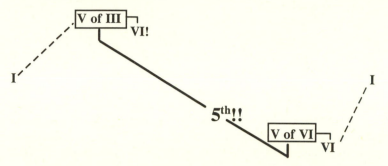

EXAMPLE 5.21. Internal relation of fifths between V of III and V of VI

The notes of measure 193 beautifully mask their true mission: to remind us of the early hidden clue of measure 7, and get us back to the task at hand — the approach to the structural dominant. Unsupported by any harmony or bass line, this unaccompanied line recalls the introduction. The broken chords of G minor pass through every inversion before an E♭ slips in (sixth eighth note of m. 193). Because G minor has not firmly established itself with a D⁷ chord, Chopin could flip back into E♭ major at any moment. This eighth–note E♭ should have slipped down to D — instead, it leaps down a fourth to B♭. The avoidance of its resolution is a direct reference to the famous E♭ in measure 7, which we now recognize as a presentiment of the entire harmonic scheme of the Ballade; i.e., the tonicization and extensive digression on the upper auxiliary of the dominant. Measures 7 and 193, then, are both microcosms of the entire Ballade (Ex. 5.22).

EXAMPLE 5.22. Illustration of the underlying unity of mm. 7–8 and 193–94, showing the pitches that converge and wedge into V

The D in the bass (m. 194) sets the stage for the long-awaited return of G minor. The parallel D of the opening stood alone on a downbeat in the bass during the entire statement of the opening theme (mm. 8–35). In other words, the D of measure 194 picks up where the earlier D of measure 8 left off.

The procedures of measures 94–105 reappear, with one vital difference: where measures 90–94 led from E♭ to its *upper* auxiliary, E♮ (V of A), measures 189–194 lead from E♭ to its *lower* auxiliary, D♮ (V of G).

The pedal tone on D generates a pedal-chord, I$^6_4$, and any further attempts at melody are abandoned against the gravitational force of this Gm $^6_4$ situation. The outcome of this struggle is the cadential climax of measures 206–7. The wailing sixths of the right hand can trace their contour back to the introduction. The penultimate A of this dramatic passage, which was so vital in the delayed cadence of measures 31–36, now is scrambled into a double *cambiata,* creating a dramatic leap, rather than a cautious step, into the turbulence that follows.

Measure 208 not only heralds the arrival of the hard-won tonic G minor, it also secures B♭, the structural continuation of D–C that was left incomplete in the first theme. As if making up for lost time, Chopin presents B♭s repeatedly and emphatically.

Although this essay focuses on the issues of form and tonality, I cannot resist a few words at this point concerning the special metric situation in the ensuing *Presto con fuoco* (mm. 208ff.). The most arresting feature of the *Presto* is the rhythmic interplay between the metric accents of the left hand and the cross-accents in the right; unfortunately, this feature is all too often lost in performances of this piece. Chopin's tempo indication, *Presto con fuoco,* is usually approached as if it meant "as fast as possible," or worse, "faster than possible." Despite the left-hand chords on the strong beats of each measure, and the single staccato quarter notes on the weak beats, pianists persist in stressing the cross-accents of the right hand at the expense of the metric pulse articulated in the left hand. Such faulty performances would defy even the most gifted student of rhythmic dictation to correctly perceive the true metric situation.

All too often, musicians ignore bar lines and look only at the syncopations and cross-accents. For Chopin, as for his immediate predecessors, the bar line served as an organizing force *against which* events of rhythmic interest could take place. Beethoven's *sforzandi* on weak beats, for example, cause every generation of conductors to invent new elbow contortions. Schumann often wrote long successions of accented offbeats, obscuring the true downbeat for long stretches, as in the "Paganini" of *Carnaval*. (In his very late pieces, Schumann carried this device to excessive proportions, going beyond any hope of ever getting the listener back to the true downbeat.) But in the Chopin passage under discussion, there is no question as to the rhythmic and metric priorities. The left hand *must* maintain the basic pulse, against which the right hand jabs and spars with weak-beat accents.

It is all too tempting to shift the bar line to make it occur one quarter note late, to ignore the *fz* indications on the first beats of measures 208 and 212, and to employ a "fudge factor" to compensate for a loss or gain in time at the beginning and end of the eight measures. In spite of expedient pianists who neglect the bar lines as the governing force in the metric scheme of things, these bar lines remain stubbornly on the page, issuing a silent reproach to those who do not bother to acknowledge their existence.

The motion of the moving parts in measures 208–16 describes a giant wedge. The notes which form this wedge appear on the offbeats; the Gs within the lines of the wedge sound on the downbeats. The following diagram splits the music onto three staves, in order to illustrate more clearly the motion of the individual lines (Ex. 5.23).

For the first time in the piece, every voice functions to define G minor as tonic. In measures 208–9, the only notes foreign to the G-minor sonority can be explained as accented passing tones or incomplete neighbors. Through a skillful use of register transfer and rhythmic displacement, Chopin creates the impression of unresolved dissonance, which in turn generates an impetuous galloping rhythm.

EXAMPLE 5.23. Inner notes in mm. 208–12 form wedges around I (G) as well as V (D)

In measures 210–11, the right hand adds a spearhead figure aimed towards B♭, consisting of a four-note chromatic line:

This adds a whirlpool effect to the right hand part and creates the impression of great agitation in contrast to the stable harmonic motion of ii⁷–V⁷–i. If the performer has maintained the proper metric pulse up to this point, the Neapolitan-sixth (A♭⁶) chord in measure 216 will properly sound as a syncopation. Once the octave leaps and transpositions are cleared away, another structural wedge emerges. Its strong contrary motion by step serves once again to confirm the G-minor tonality, this time by means of a very strong harmonic progression:

EXAMPLE 5.24. As an upper wedge into I, the pitch ♭2̂ is strengthened by the chord ♭II! (mm. 216–24)

With A♭, the wedge around the tonic has begun. A♭, the upper half-step to G, balances F♯, its lower half step. In a similar situation, Gerald Abraham has described Chopin's use of flattened notes as an intensification:

> The melody strains down, as it were . . . the leading-note principle here makes itself felt in the "downward sharpening" (which we are paradoxically obliged to call flattening) of the second degree of the scale, just as centuries before it had made itself felt in the sharpening of the seventh degree of the modes.[22]

Of course, now we have a better explanation for the Neapolitan-sixth harmony of the introduction. Just as E♭ as an upper auxiliary was vital in defining the dominant, now A♭ has a parallel function as an upper auxiliary to G minor, the tonic.

Since measure 216, the bass has been:

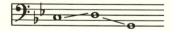

On the fourth repetition, however, Chopin throws in an embellishment of this figure (mm. 226–7):

This is, note for note, the bass movement of the introduction (see Ex. 5.9). The intermediate D is now made explicit, unlike its first appearance as a "phantom" bass note. Chopin is summing up, recapitulating the important structural events that began early in the piece and controlled the tonal events on the way to the *Presto*.

From Ex. 5.24, it is clear that the right-hand line has reached a G through an octave descent, a descent that matches the left hand's ascending scale. Both meet on G at the point of the wedge. Beginning with measure 228, Chopin starts a repetition of the eight-measure wedge, but he interrupts its motion in the sixth measure (m. 229). The bass remains on its ascending path, but becomes increasingly chromatic and climbs beyond the destination of G. The new goal becomes B♭, the third of G minor. Over this elongated line, the right hand also reaches B♭, but by a roundabout route. The interval of a second from C to B♭ is inverted to a seventh, and filled in by minor thirds.

EXAMPLE 5.25. B♭ (3̂) as a temporary goal of wedge motion, in mm. 228–38

E♮ instead of E♭ in measures 240–41 is startlingly dramatic. It presages the completion of an ascending tetrachord toward G. The total effect of this raised sixth is that of an energized D, champing at the bit, eager to complete a motion that had proved so difficult throughout the Ballade — an ascent to G. More importantly, this E♮ negates E♭ as a tonality, the submediant key that had dominated such a large portion of the work.

With the D firmly entrenched in the bass in measure 242, the ascending version of the two-note idea reappears in its struggle to climb rather than descend, recalling measures 101–4 and 201–4. The motion this time culminates in an expansive 4–3 struck suspension ranging over four measures. The right hand, with a four-octave chromatic scale followed by scale passages dropping down through six octaves, adds enormous drive and impetus to the left-hand activity. All sorts of thematic fragments are revisited and reassembled, including those first heard in the introduction (Ex. 5.26).

EXAMPLE 5.26. Reminiscences of the wedges of the introductory measures (mm. 4–5) are found imbedded in the cascade of notes of mm. 246–49

This volatile passage ends in measure 250 on the whole note G. Although G resolves the $V^{4-3}$ harmonic progression, by no means does it suffice as an outlet for the dramatic tension. From the isolated G bursts forth a three-octave G-minor scale in octaves.

In yet another capsule summary of the tonal plan of the entire work, a sextuplet figure crests up and over Eb–D — a clear indication of the now subservient position of the dissonant nonchord tone Eb. And to conclude the Ballade, Chopin writes a series of octaves that howl in contrary chromatic motion. Of course, the two lines are calculated to converge on G, but also the choice of the starting notes is significant: the right hand reaches *beyond* Eb to begin on E♮, the dissonant double upper-auxiliary tone, which, as $V^7$ of A major, supported the triumphant statement of the second theme in measures 94–124. This octave wedge, then, screeching to a halt in the final measures, produces the ultimate microcosm of the Ballade:

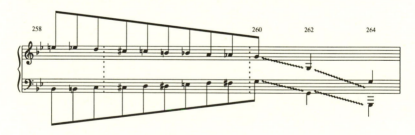

EXAMPLE 5.27. Final, ultimate, explicit wedge of the G-Minor Ballade, in octaves (mm. 258–60)

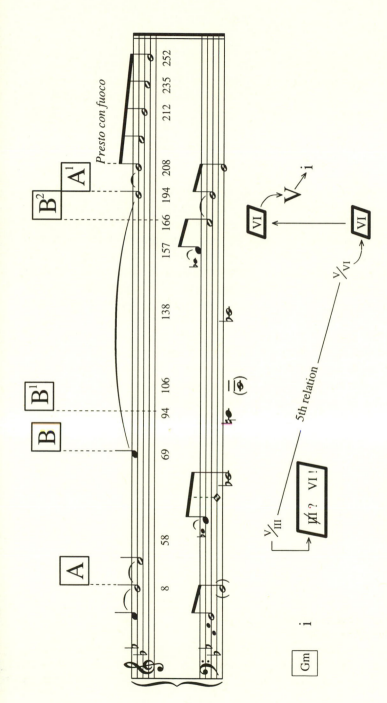

EXAMPLE 5.28. Graph of *Première Ballade*

## V
## *Deuxième Ballade*

While preparing the Chopin Ballades for the Breitkopf & Härtel edition, one of the editors, whose name was Johannes Brahms, wrote the following in a letter to his co-editor:

> In the A-Minor Ballade, I would also leave the ♩ ♩ ♩ ♩ ♩ ♩ , although they seem inexplicable to me.[23]

The quarter-note triplets to which Brahms refers are an editorial issue that need not concern us here. What is vitally significant, however, is Brahms' casual designation of the piece, not as the F-Major Ballade, but as the A-Minor Ballade. Clearly, Brahms the composer understood the A-minor destiny of this piece. More than the drama, more than the startling textural contrasts, the most striking feature of this Ballade is that Chopin abandons his original key of F major and proceeds inexorably and convincingly to a conclusion in A minor. How does he do it?

The distance between the roots of F major and A minor is, of course, a major third, but Chopin was apparently intrigued with an alternate perception of these sonorities as nearly identical chords. Two of the chord tones, A and C, are common to both; the third tone is either F or E, separated by only a half-step. In terms of the scale degrees of the A-minor scale, this F–E "toggle switch" is $\hat{6}$–$\hat{5}$.

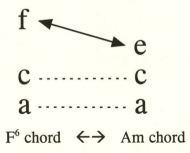

F⁶ chord  ←→  Am chord

Example 5.29. F–E as a "toggle switch" between F-major and A-minor sonorities

Chopin creates Jekyll and Hyde personalities for these sibling chords, obviously enjoying the irony of that half-step distance between them — so small, yet so great. It is the same irony, no doubt, that a chemist enjoys when contemplating the close molecular similarity of $CO_2$, a vital nutrient for plant life, with $CO$, a dangerous, noxious gas. Chopin works with this half step throughout the piece, usually in the inner texture, treating it melodically only in the final *agitato* section of the Ballade.

I am convinced of Chopin's conscious fascination with the F–E interval because he also exploited it in a mazurka he had written some years earlier — the Mazurka in A Minor, Op. 17, No. 4.[24]

EXAMPLE 5.30.  Chopin Mazurka in A Minor, Op. 17, No. 4, mm. 1–14

The most interesting thing about this A-Minor Mazurka is the scarcity of A-minor chords. Chopin uses what a tedious chord-labeler might call a first-inversion F-major chord, but our ears tell us that it is an A-minor chord with an unresolved F.

The Mazurka begins (and ends) with four introductory measures. The note F (6) prevails throughout the four-measure introduction, and persists a few measures after the theme begins. By the time F slides down to E (m. 8), it is too late to form the A-minor sonority — the other components of A minor have long since dissipated. Pitches in the other voices begin to mimic this delayed-resolution technique, generating a feeling of *saudades,* of nostalgic longing. In Ex. 5.31, I include both a mundane, predictable harmonization, and Chopin's own version.

Chopin takes this same principle of withholding E by prolonging F and works with it on a grand scale in the Second Ballade. The opening two pages of the Ballade are filled with hints of the changes to take place. While the first E that we hear is, properly, a leading tone (m. 3), it is practically the only time E will resolve to F within $V^7$–I in F major.

EXAMPLE 5.31. Melody of Mazurka, Op. 17, No. 4, with overly-predictable voice-leading, and Chopin's own voice-leading

Progressing through the pastoral theme, Chopin avoids any substantial $V^7$ of F. An alternative version (Ex. 5.32) offers a more banal but "correct" realization. With this version, Chopin would have had a much more difficult task abandoning the tonality of F major.

EXAMPLE 5.32. Hypothetical version of mm. 5–9 with numerous $V^7$–I's in F major

Chopin's actual phrase, by comparison, is beautifully delicate and fragile, but his prolonged use of I$^6_4$ renders it as unstable as a penny balanced on its edge. Only the IV$^6$ chords that alternate with I$^6_4$ keep them from toppling over (mm. 5–8).

Measure 17 offers the first clue that Chopin is inventing a new type of deceptive cadence — rather than the traditional $V^7$–VI, Chopin writes $V^7$–(I)–III$^6$. The mediant (A minor!) of F major is being introduced as a legitimate tonic-substitution chord. By the time this cadence recurs (mm. 32–33), Chopin no longer uses I as an intermediary — III$^6$ now stands on its own somewhat questionable merits. A minor now has a chance to precariously balance itself on its own $^6_4$ edge before slipping into the F♯-diminished chord in measure 37. Another clue concerning the instability of F major — Chopin avoids a perfect cadence at measure 45 by insisting on A ($\hat{3}$) rather than F ($\hat{1}$) in the soprano voice.

The *Presto con fuoco* that follows (m. 46) is one of Chopin's most dramatic and compelling, but this is false bravado, the kind often heard in the music of Haydn. If one temporarily ignores the bombast, the octaves, and the cascades, the F–E "toggle switch" floats to the surface (Ex. 5.33). This, by the way, is the first appearance of F as an accented upper neighbor to E.

EXAMPLE 5.33. Highly magnified view of the first two sixteenth notes of *Presto con fuoco* (m. 46). The pitches F–E, buried beneath the bravado, are here revealed as the true structural event of this section

Through various sequences and diminished chords, Chopin arrives at a pedal point on E♭ (mm. 66–78). Since his goal is to eventually wedge into V of A, this must be perceived as a prolepsis of the eventual lower wedge (E♭=D♯ → E). Ironically, one of the strongest "V$^7$" sonorities of the Ballade occurs in measure 69, but of course its function is completely different: it is its enharmonic brother, an F♭-German-sixth chord (F♭–A♭–C♭–D♮).

The sequences between measures 78 and 82 sound abrupt and unworthy of a true retransition, no matter how liberally the pianist applies *ritardando* to these measures. The die is cast — no listener could possibly believe the bluff of the return of the opening theme at measure 82. And Chopin shamelessly interrupts the F$^6_4$ chords and splices in Am$^6_4$ chords (mm. 88–90).

A minor is at last a strong candidate for the concluding tonality of the Ballade; the return of the second *Presto con fuoco* (mm. 140ff) is, in fact, in that key. However, even here Chopin seems to be saving the structural dominant until after the second theme has been repeated; avoiding V$^7$ of A minor, he begins this *Presto* on IV$^6_4$. This leads to a V$^6_4$ — the bluster and bravado are present, but not the structural V. In other words, the *thematic* recapitulation arrives before the *tonal* recapitulation.[25] The effect is not unlike the cinematic technique when the sound and dialogue of a new scene begin a few seconds before the visual image can catch up. Measures 156–67 provide a long retransition into the A-minor *agitato* ending. The left hand plays melodic excerpts of the opening theme that are now completely subsumed, both tonally and texturally, within the rhetoric of the second theme.

The use of iv$^6_4$ at the beginning of the recapitulation now can be understood as particularly appropriate. It emphasizes the new function of F as the dissonant upper neighbor to E by adding a partner note, D, to move in tandem with it. Creating a double dissonance, they both demand a double resolution (Ex. 5.34).

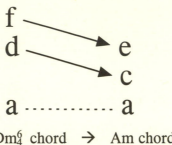

Dm$^6_4$ chord  →  Am chord

EXAMPLE 5.34. Double upper-neighbor-note resolution (iv$^6_4$–I) in mm. 140–48, Chopin's unique strategy for avoiding a strong dominant and increasing the urgency of F wedging downward to E

The A in the bass is clearly strong enough to remain consonant against the F and D notes that would have liked to retain their own integrity within the context of D minor. By the end of the period (mm. 146–47), A minor easily regains control. Only at measures 153–56 do we hear, at last, a strong chromatic descent into E, which finally triggers a dramatic E–F tremolo in the right hand.

For the next eight measures, the left hand emphasizes the dotted-rhythm motive (first heard in measure 3!) in *marcato* octaves, which mainly outline A-minor $^6_4$. All the while, the right hand sustains a complex double-note tremolo, which can be examined and divided into its component parts:

EXAMPLE 5.35. Double-note measured trill in right hand (mm. 157–59 shown here), embedded with F–E wedge, intensified by its own F♯–D♯ wedge!

The top notes consist of a measured trill between E and F. By measure 158, this vibrating wedge, through centripetal force, has expanded outward to its *own* upper and lower neighbors, F♯ and D♯ — a wedge *surrounding* the wedge!

The last four measures before the coda form the final inevitable push toward A minor. The dominant trill in the left hand begins with a V*orschlag* in which Chopin specifies that the pianist begin with D♯; this will strengthen the lower wedge below the dominant, just as the upper trill note strengthens the upper wedge. The ii[7] tremolo in the right hand finally collapses and joins the left for octave trills on each note from E down to A, and the so-called "coda" begins.

EXAMPLE 5.36. Mm. 160–68. The left-hand trill creates a vibrant wedge around V, especially if the D♯ (of the *Vorschlag*, m. 164) is prominently placed *on* the beat

The remainder of the Ballade (*agitato*, mm. 169ff.) is so compelling that I hesitate to submit it to an analytical dissection. Nevertheless, there are clear points to be made to understand Chopin's achievement.

First, the texture changes from a tremolo of alternating sixteenth notes to repeated sixteenth notes. If the passage had continued as before, the section would have lost some of the extra impetus and might have sounded as in Ex. 5.37. Chopin clearly understood that when *repetition* replaces *alternation* within a measure, the music takes on a more frenzied character.[26] In addition, the musical "gasp" on the downbeat makes this coda resemble a triple-meter version of the *Presto con fuoco* of the First Ballade. The left hand retains a simplified version of the melodic events of the energetic right hand. Most important are the pitches involved. As in measure 158, Chopin relies on the upper and lower neighbor notes of E — that is, F and D♯.

EXAMPLE 5.37. Hypothetical version of m. 169 with alternating rather than repeating figuration in the right hand

The pitches involved at the very outset of the *agitato*, F and E, have finally and irreversibly exchanged their roles. F as a dissonant upper auxiliary is clearly subservient to the E, which is in the position of resolution and consonance. The slower moving bass line relays this message through "hidden repetition" — measures 168–69 themselves contain bass-note motion F–E:

EXAMPLE 5.38. Bass line that continues to emphasize F–E interval (mm. 168–69)

At measure 176, the right hand begins a series of descending chromatic slides into E, followed by a turn figure that creates wedges into E from above and below. Chopin reproduces this same chromatic line in the bass, but in extreme augmentation — an ingenious touch that strengthens the passage yet remains hidden (mm. 176–79).

Above this powerful bass motion, the right hand freely explores chromatic nooks and crannies. It is like the empowerment a leashed dog feels when he boldly barks and snarls at bigger dogs whom he would otherwise shy away from. The upper voices at last turn back to the notes of A minor, and, with still another F–E as a "sigh"-motive resolution, measure 179 cadences into A minor. The bass, which until now had vacillated between registers, marking time, now proceeds to rise through the chromatic scale. Measures 186–187 retain the textural pattern of the previous measures, but the voice-leading is completely obscured. This arrangement clarifies a strong wedge that subtly takes shape in the outer voices. By stripping away further layers of the basic outline, we can observe the emergence of a strong approach by contrary motion toward E. If we return to measure 183 and sketch the basic melodic structure of the bass and the treble, it becomes apparent that most of the *agitato* is based on a two-note wedge that converges onto E (Ex. 5.39).

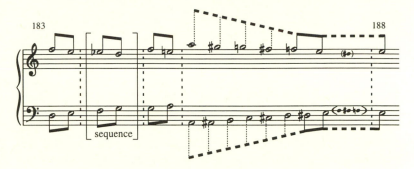

EXAMPLE 5.39. Strong contrary motion in mm. 183–88, creating converging wedges onto the dominant E

The strength of measures 186–87 is that they cross voices and go *beyond* E; the E emerges at measure 188, stronger than ever.

The right-hand part at measure 188 is unique in all of Chopin's output; although basically an A-minor scale, with punctuating chords added, it really is a string of two-note resolutions, mimicking the two-note F–E motive. Theoretically, this right-hand part might be written as follows, in order to clarify the true function of the first of each pair as an accented upper neighbor (Ex. 5.40).

EXAMPLE 5.40. An alternative notation for m. 189 that highlights the two-note "sigh" motives and F–E motives in both hands

While these harmonic events are taking place, certain key melodic notes are closing in on the A minor tonality; the wedge action now shifts to a convergence around the tonic note, A.

The disposition of the hands beginning with measure 190 causes certain notes played by the thumbs to become prominent. Although the right hand plays a descending scale-with-chords pattern in measures 188–89 and 192–93, we hear a two-note *ascending* line on the strong beats. A sketch of these events is shown in Ex. 5.41.

EXAMPLE 5.41. Metrically stressed *ascending* scale created out of descending and oscillating figures (Compare with Ex. 5.20, which illustrates similar motion in the First Ballade)

As the final cadential progression ensues (V/V–vii°⁷/V–i$^6_4$–V), Chopin stops on vii°⁷ and begins an ascending sequence by half-step. But when he reaches F in the bass, the last vii°⁷ chord becomes a French sixth in A minor. The outer notes of this chord are, of course, the upper and lower wedge notes into E. This French-sixth chord announces in yet another way just how dissonant and irreversible the note F has become, both as a scale tone and a tonality!

French
Sixth Chord

EXAMPLE 5.42. Motion toward the French-sixth chord of m. 196

In measure 196, Chopin dramatically suspends all voice-leading motion while the seven unaccompanied notes of the introduction emerge, but heard now as an A instead of C. The D♯, which insists on moving up to E in contrary motion to the bass F–E motion (m. 198) is delayed until measure 200.

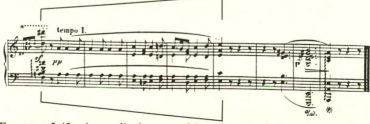

EXAMPLE 5.43. A startlingly powerful and unusual inversion of the wedge into V. This wedge moves *out,* rather than *in,* toward its target, due to the special propensities of Augmented-sixth chords (Compare with French-sixth chord in Fourth Ballade, m. 194, Ex. 5.77)

Having satiated us with the exploration of paths to E, Chopin allows a deep musical breath, and writes the simple, unadorned wedge of G♯ and B, both of which resolve to the tonic note, A (Ex. 5.44).

EXAMPLE 5.44. Final upper and lower wedge around A, the true structural tonic

From the time we heard E descend five notes to A in measure 166, it was highly unlikely that E would return to its function as the leading tone to F. F is now as dissonant within the context of A minor as was E in the context of F major in measure 3. Every measure of the *agitato* hammers home the idea that F is dissonant and E consonant. The link between F major and A minor, which originally had been used for mildly interesting harmonic details (e.g., mm. 17ff.), becomes, in the *agitato,* the melodic center of attention; F is the dissonant upper neighbor to E, the dominant of A minor.

No discussion of the Second Ballade would be complete without a consideration of the alleged F-major ending that Chopin is said to have originally composed. The initial statement that sparked the chain reaction of speculation is found in Robert Schumann's 1841 review of this Ballade:

> I recollect very well that when Chopin played the Ballade here, it ended in F major; now it closes in A minor.[27]

The performance to which Schumann was referring had taken place five years prior to this review, so it is probable that Chopin had not completed the Ballade at that time; he may have played only the opening *Andantino* for Schumann. Gerald Abraham, however, conjectures that the F-major ending may have been a repetition of the *Andantino* section where the *agitato* section is presently, thus rounding off the Ballade with identical A and B sections:

> Imagine, then, that, instead of the coda, heralded and rounded off by fragments of the first subject, Chopin had here simply written out the first subject in full and in F major; we should have a form almost exactly like that of the G-Minor Ballade. And it seems to me highly probable that this or something like it was the original form of the piece that Schumann heard.[28]

If Abraham's conjecture is correct, the Ballade would have used a transition of the kind that I fatuously suggest in Example 5.45:

EXAMPLE 5.45. Preposterous, hypothetical version of mm. 164–171, if indeed Schumann heard the *entire* Ballade with an ending in F major

This would enable a complete restatement of the opening *Andantino* and an ending in the initial tonality of F major. The musical evidence throughout the Ballade, however, denies any such retransition or ending; A minor becomes imbedded gradually and irreversibly as the piece progresses. An ending in any key other than A minor would be anticlimactic and negate the drama that Chopin so skillfully created.

Does this Ballade bear any resemblance at all to sonata form? In conventional sonata movements, the initial theme establishes a tonal center, against which the second theme introduces a state of tension by arriving in a contrasting key area. In the Second Ballade, these contrasting themes are present, but their functions are reversed. A minor, the key of the second theme, turns out to be the true tonic of the piece, the key to which the first theme must be reconciled. The recapitulation, then, does serve the conventional function of resolving the tension created in the exposition, with the important difference that the tonality of the first theme is subordinate to that of the second theme.

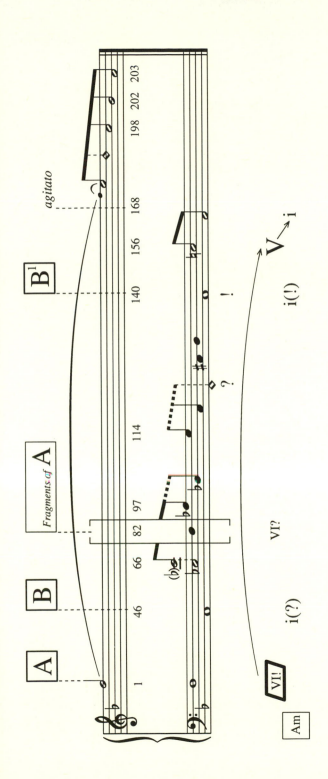

EXAMPLE 5.46. Graph of *Deuxième Ballade*

# VI
## *Troisième Ballade*

Unlike the first two Ballades, the A♭ Ballade begins immediately with its opening theme. There are two unusual features to note in the first eight measures: thematically, the melody jumps to a different voice for every two-bar phrase; harmonically, the unstable $^6_4$ position of the tonic A♭ is in abundance, even where a V$^7$ chord would have strengthened the cadence. These two anomalies create elaborate registral shifts and an open-ended, incomplete feeling within an otherwise regular periodicity.

The antecedent phrase highlights $\hat{6}$-$\hat{5}$ (m. 2 and m. 6), which subsequently appears in the treble in measures 10–11, and after measure 21 as part of the bass line; $\hat{6}$-$\hat{5}$ has quickly established itself in this Ballade as an important motivic kernel, ripe for "hidden repetitions."

EXAMPLE 5.47.  Recurrences of F-E♭ ( $\hat{6}$-$\hat{5}$ ) in various voices of the A♭ Ballade (mm. 17–25)

By measure 29, C in the bass is destined to become a dominant — it is just waiting for the right moment. By eventually minimizing the melodic motion and stabilizing the harmonic motion around C in measures 33–35, Chopin encourages our perception of C as the dominant of F.

It is well known that, in tonal music, isolation and repetition of a pitch causes it to sound like a dominant — the ubiquitous E♭ in the opening eight measures illustrated this. After so many Cs (mm. 29–36), the abrupt return at measure 37 to A♭$^6_4$ is confusing. Chopin isolates the octave bass C and chromatically slides up a third to E♭. C and E♭, already so important to the Ballade as pivotal notes of the *melodic* contour, are now making contact with each other on a *harmonic* level. As dominants, they cause a transition between their respective tonics, not unlike foreign ministers sent out to further the interests of their respective governments.

The second theme (m. 54) is introduced by broken-octave Cs, which adopt the rhythm of the F–E♭ motif of measure 2. If we look beyond the interesting rocking-horse rhythm, the contour of this theme clearly emerges — the basic line is a six-note descending scale (Ex. 5.48a). If this sounds familiar, a quick comparison with the contour of the opening theme will explain why:

(a) Extracted thematic notes of second theme (mm. 54–57)

(b) Notes of first theme

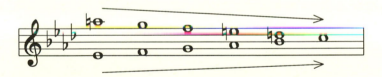

(c) Alignment of first theme (a) and second theme (b)

EXAMPLE 5.48. The latent unity underlying the manifest variety (à la Hans Keller) of the two main themes of the A♭ Ballade. When the notes are freed from their rhythmic moorings, the themes clearly reveal their identical but inverted nature

"Transposed inversion" and "retrograde motion" are hardly terms that spring to mind when discussing Chopin, but their appropriateness here is irrefutable. Not only is the intervallic inversion exact, but the lines form a contrary-motion wedge into C — a compositional coup of which even Bartók would have been proud.

By measure 58, Chopin begins to emphasize F *minor* — vi rather than VI — of Ab. Of the six-note scale identified above, he breaks it into three-note fragments to use in mix-and-match combinations.

The second theme is another instance in which Chopin emphasizes the dominant rather than the tonic of the phrase (See Ex. 5.3, and also Exx. 5.4, 5.52, and 5.66). It is this ambiguity which causes us to hear measure 116, the momentary reentry of Ab major, as a third relation. This new so-called contrasting section is derived from the opening theme. Furthermore, it is impacted with endless half-step and whole-step wedges around the dominant (6̂–5̂, b6̂–5̂, and even ♯4̂–5̂), all "prescient forebodings" that we have come to expect from Chopin (Ex. 5.49).

Ex 5.49. Comparison of mm. 1–2 with mm. 116–17, highlighting similar contour and wedge notes above and below the dominant, Eb

Measures 134–42 celebrate the dominant Eb as a *melodic* note, not only with a staircase of trills approaching from below (mm. 134–35), but also with variants of the F–Eb motive from above. This is one of the glorious moments of the Ballade, and it is reassuring to have a wedge explanation to go along with it.

When the second theme returns for the third time (m. 146) Chopin uses its ambiguous nature to dip down to the subdominant key, spelled at first as Db major. Enharmonically, this becomes C♯ (now minor) at measure 157. Although the subsequent melody remains unaltered from its original version, its aggrandizement by means of broken octaves and thickened chords raises the intensity to new heights. It spins out of control and spirals into a vortex of falling fifths. It slips through all the diatonic keys of C♯ minor, and then one beyond it — B♮, which, handily, is V of bVI:

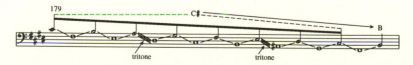

Ex 5.50. A spiral of falling fifths, which end on B, the dominant of bVI (mm. 179–83)

Since C♯ minor had been heard earlier for so many measures as a temporary key area, we are not surprised that its new function, in retrospect, is VI — a Ballade-style preparation for V of E major. For a moment, the extended circle of fifths blindfolded us and spun us around until we lost any sense of a tonal center; the tremolo on B put us back on the track. Chopin is preparing to emphasize E, the upper wedge note above the dominant. The quarter-note Bs sound ominous in the tenor range above a grumbling left-hand tremolo; they represent a single-note variant of the familiar broken octaves that have always preceded statements of the second theme.

In the bass, the metrically accented lower auxiliary, A♯, creates a "brooding omnipresence"[29] to an otherwise bland dominant pedal tremolo on B, preventing any complacent or relaxed perception of this section. Chopin favors a measured tremolo over a free one to maintain the momentum provided by continuous sixteenth notes. The right hand begins the second theme in E major, disturbed only by the G♮ instead of F♯ in measures 187–88. The G♮ against A♯ in the left hand, forming a diminished seventh, promotes an uneasy restlessness and sounds a prescient warning that we are leaving familiar ground. The harmonies simple and direct, the rhythm intact, the first theme emerges from the second theme.

In the remote key of E major, Chopin reveals the true unity between the two themes, rendering explicit what we already knew and felt implicitly. Chopin's juxtaposition removes any shred of doubt that these two melodies are cast from the same intervallic mold (Ex. 5.51). And, of course, E major is not really remote — it is ♭VI, the half step between VI (F) and V (E♭).

Chopin delays the resolution of the $\hat{6}$–$\hat{5}$ motive (appearing here as "C♯–B") by two measures. The intervening diminished chord suspends the expanded resolution that changes from $\hat{6}$–$\hat{5}$ to $\hat{2}$–$\hat{1}$ as the phrase gravitates to the dominant. Chopin cannot resist the opportunity to lead to a cadence in V, a procedure quite familiar to us by now from other Ballade themes (Ex. 5.52; cf. Exx. 5.3 and 5.4). The compound second-theme/first-theme structure occurs several times in sequence, until even the most skeptical listener is convinced that these themes are two sides of the same coin.

(a) Mm. 183–93

(b) Thematic notes extracted from mm. 183–91

EXAMPLE 5.51. Developmental section (a), from which the contours of both themes have been extracted (b) to reveal their mirror-like nature (Cf. Ex. 5.48)

EXAMPLE 5.52. Another Ballade example of Chopin's predilection for four-measure phrases cadencing on V

In the fourth sequence, Gm $^6_4$ is a propitious choice; the D can wedge outward to D♭ and E♭ to create V$^7$ of A♭ (Ex. 5.53).

EXAMPLE 5.53. Approach to E♭ (V$^7$ of A♭) via unusual dominant-preparation chord of Gm $^6_4$

Because the harmonic structure of the second theme emphasizes its own dominant, the sequences through four keys cannot simply be discussed as a sequence in the keys of E, F, Gm, and A♭; they are heard more as a succession on their dominants; none of those dominant chords asserts itself long enough to take control. The accented lower auxiliary in the bass is a primary factor in the temporal quality of each visiting key. Not until measure 209, when E♭ finally occurs on the downbeat, is the restless motion dispelled by a bass that

EXAMPLE 5.54. Comparison of pedal tones in First and Third Ballades, against which soprano line chromatically rises

has anchored down the sixteenth-note texture. This, at last, is the final ascent to the structural dominant. Only now can the melodic line free itself from sequences and repetitions, and discover its true path.

But rather than playing a freely diatonic version of the theme, the right hand can only manage a chromatic scale — it is dragged back by the gravitational pull of the double pedal tones in the left hand (mm. 209–12). Only in the G-Minor Ballade have we seen such an intense situation. The harmonic details of these two places are startlingly similar (Ex. 5.54).

For the important arrival of the structural dominant at measure 213, Chopin adds one small, special detail — a D♮ in the left-hand ostinato. The D♮ is of course ♯IV, the *lower* wedge into the dominant. The soprano line catapults up and over the E♭ goal (Ex. 5.55).

Example 5.55. Final chromatic climb, aided by ♯4̂ and 6̂, into the apotheosis of the theme (mm. 212–13)

As the theme repeats (m. 217), Chopin cannot resist spelling out for us, one more time, the mirrorlike nature of the two themes. This time the lines are not just back-to-back — they are simultaneous:

EXAMPLE 5.56. Simultaneous occurrence of the two themes (m. 217)
(Cf. Ex. 5.48)

This statement of the opening theme completely avoids the
unstable I⁶₄ that plagued the opening of the Ballade. By slightly altering
the left hand at measure 219, Chopin now begins to explore the half-
steps between E♭ and F. A fragmented melodic line takes over, a
dotted rhythmic structure that, like so many lines in Bach, suggests
two melodic voices within one (Cf. Exx. 5.57 and 5.58).

EXAMPLE 5.57. Bach, Cantata No. 140, "Wachet auf"; No. 4.
Chorale

EXAMPLE 5.58. Chopin, A♭ Ballade, mm. 222–24

The following strong series of chords in measures 221–25 creates
a descending sequence that, in the larger picture, answers the ascending sequence of measures 183–206:

EXAMPLE 5.59. Comparison of ascending and descending sequences that
create a hidden symmetry within the Ballade (mm. 183–208 and
221-25)

Measures 225–26 represent a parenthetical harmonic V–I cadence on
an augmented-sixth chord, a preparation for I⁶₄ in A♭. Melodically, it
is the continuation of the aborted line that began at measure 221.

Structurally, it is a 4–3 struck suspension from D♭ to a C that was enormously delayed. In measures 225–26, using the fragments created by the Bachian interplay of the melody, Chopin finally reaches C, a point of arrival that we enjoy all the more because of its delay (Ex. 5.60).

EXAMPLE 5.60. Illustration of the harmonic parenthesis Chopin creates using Bachian inner voices between mm. 221 and 227

The return to A♭ $^6_4$ at measure 227 sets up still another delaying tactic. Full chords in both hands, marked *stretto* and *crescendo,* tug against an insistent E♭ pedal, which does not resolve to A♭ until measure 231. In these measures, Chopin's thematic use of the first-theme motive is masterful. The first theme, beginning as six notes spanning a major sixth, had always led to the fifth or the third, never to the first degree of A♭ major. In these final moments of the Ballade, Chopin takes this opportunity to present a compressed, altered arrangement of those opening six notes that lead to the first degree, A♭. The six notes travel through half-steps, a chromatic rather than a diatonic ascent, and then, continuing the thematic contour, leap a third to the descending two-note motive of the scale degrees 3̂–2̂ — only the final 1̂ (A♭) is missing (Ex. 5.61).

EXAMPLE 5.61. Compressed version of opening theme, bringing the Ballade closer to a completion of its *Urlinie* (mm. 227–31)

A codetta, *più mosso,* follows, using material from measures 116ff. E♭ is not employed at the beginning of the small-note arpeggio — it has been sufficiently stated up until this point. Instead, C usurps its position (Ex. 5.62). But Chopin continues to avoid A♭, while he hammers home C and E♭ at every opportunity. Measure 235 places the small-note arpeggio figure in a rhythmic context, emphasizing the tenth between C and E♭ (Ex. 5.63).

EXAMPLE 5.62. Two versions of "ornamental" arpeggio. Earlier ones began with 5 (Eb) but the arpeggios at mm. 231 and 233 begin with 3 (C)

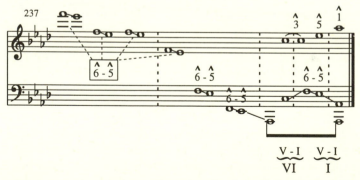

EXAMPLE 5.63. Formerly written only as an ornamental little-note figure, this arpeggio becomes structurally significant in m. 235

The final pianistic flourish down the keyboard in measures 237–38 is not a pure Ab arpeggio — rather it includes F that resolves to Eb, that is to say, 6̂–5̂. And, as Chopin's final parting shot, the cadential formula gives us V–I in F minor (VI), followed by V–I in Ab major (I). Any intervening V/V is omitted, having had no prominent harmonic role in the Ballade. Not until the last measure are we given a melodic Ab, the note we have waited for since the first theme returned at measure 207. The last F–Eb motive, in these final moments, is given extra meaning. Clearly accented in the bass in octaves, Eb now assumes its proper function as the dominant, and resolves directly to Ab in the bass (Ex. 5.64).

EXAMPLE 5.64. Final keyboard flourish, featuring 6̂–5̂ (mm. 236–41)

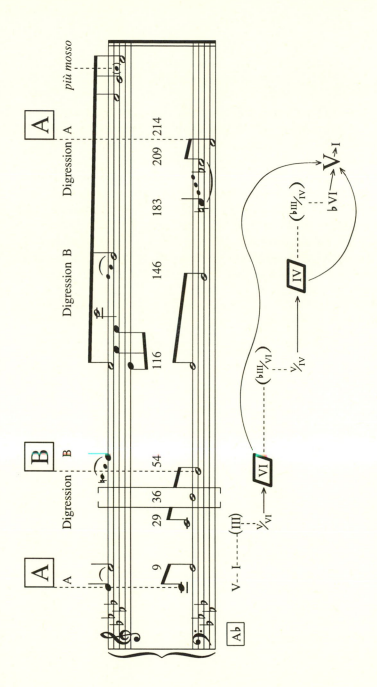

EXAMPLE 5.65. Graph of *Troisième Ballade*

# VII
## *Quatrième Ballade*

The year 1842 witnessed the thirty-two-year-old Chopin writing his final Scherzo, Polonaise, Impromptu, and his fourth and final Ballade.[30] Most people consider the F-Minor Ballade to be the greatest of the four Ballades, an opinion with which I agree.

Poetically, this Ballade describes a hero who suffers many setbacks but struggles to overcome them and emerge victorious. Analytically, it narrates the story of a tonality (I) that continually slips down a fifth to its subdominant (IV), but ultimately discovers the path home (V–I) via the submediant (VI).

The open-ended introductory phrase has been cited earlier as an example of the open-ended quality that Chopin builds into the phrase to create ambiguity (See Ex. 5.3 and Ex. 5.66. Cf. Exx. 5.3, 5.4, and 5.52).

EXAMPLE 5.66. Harmonically ambiguous opening phrase of F-Minor Ballade

Is this phrase in the key of C or F? On the one hand, the repetitions of C major continue until measure 7. But the 9–8 struck suspension in measures 2 and 4 are an expressively persuasive argument for F major; also, tiny plagal cadences act as "filler" after each phrase, and keep the sonority of F in our ears. To decide what key we are in, however, is not the most interesting point here — it is more illuminating to focus on the pitches themselves. The gentle introduction presents several versions of E and G, the notes above and below F. By the end of the Ballade, the alert listener will realize that the powerful wedges around F in the final pages were foretold in the most gentle manner in these opening measures — the wedge notes are introduced one by one.

EXAMPLE 5.67. Gentle introduction of lower wedge (E♮) and upper wedge (G) around F

One notational detail in the introduction clamors for attention. Chopin has carefully added a third beam to certain sixteenth notes in the treble that connect unaccented inner voices to give them eighth-note status in measures 2 and 4. (These beams have mysteriously vanished in some editions.[31]) Chopin would not have bothered with this awkward notation if he did not think it important. It adds thickening and overlapping to the texture of the right hand, a texture that progressed from the initial two voices (octave Gs), to three voices, to four voices, and finally to four *overlapping* voices. The point to be made is that the thickness emphasizes the F-major sonority.

The closer we examine the opening phrases, the more we perceive its contrapuntal features. Inner voices weave more than just two-note wedges around F major, the key hiding behind the harmonic curtain of C major. The important contrapuntal fragments imbedded in the texture owe their contour to the descending melodic line, G–C (Ex. 5.68).

EXAMPLE 5.68. Gentle wedges above and below C (V) and F (I) in mm. 1–3, 4–7

At measure 7, we hear an unaccompanied C survive the introduction, but a chromatic turn figure breaks the diatonic mood. This, we realize in retrospect, is an absolutely clean, chromatic Ballade wedge into the dominant — again, a prescient foreboding of the outcome.

EXAMPLE 5.69. Pure, half-step Ballade wedge into the dominant, C (mm. 7–8)

The hauntingly beautiful opening theme in F minor begins with two antecedent phrases that linger on D♭, the sixth degree of the F-minor scale. The consequent phrase rescues these incomplete D♭s by heading toward the relative major, A♭ (III). The progression sequences to IV; and one additional sequence (Ex. 5.70) would have provided a conventional affirmation of F minor.

EXAMPLE 5.70. Hypothetical version of mm. 16–18, showing how an additional sequence might have cadenced in F minor

It comes as a surprise, then, that measure 17 and the ensuing phrases reinforce IV and divert the motion away from V as a goal. Chopin prolongs IV (B♭ minor) as a key area and even creates a "false return" by reiterating the opening theme in V of IV! (See mm. 18–22.) The cadence into B♭ minor is so strong at measure 22 that the last-minute addition of C[7] (V of F!) sounds like an afterthought: "Oh yes, we need to return to F minor!"

It is interesting to note that the excessive bending toward B♭ minor, a fifth *below* F, somehow balances the excessive time spent initially on C major a fifth *above* F. Was the introduction on C a harmonic cantilever, balancing what was to follow?

The entire first theme is repeated in measures 23–36, and this time it succumbs to the downward pull of the subdominant. Still pretending that we are *in* rather than *on* the key of B♭ minor, Chopin skates on the glassy surface of G♭, which is ♭VI of B♭ (m. 38).[32] It is so unstable, of course, that the subsequent tumble into the circle of fifths (mm. 49ff.) comes as a welcome relief. But the braking action, provided of course by ♭6̂–5̂ is in the key of the subdominant, not the tonic (mm. 55–57). Everything since measure 36 has been a digression from the "proper" goal of C⁷. And the *tenuto* Gb, unaccompanied, makes us even more nostalgic for a cadence into Bb minor, not F minor.

Reluctantly, C⁷ does occur on the weak half of measure 57, and we hear a third statement of the theme, this time beautifully ornamented. But the lengthy sections on the subdominant have taken their toll — with left-hand octave runs (which, by the way, always commence with b6̂–5̂), the outcome of the theme this third time is to a true arrival in IV —now *major* IV (Bb major). The listener enjoys a tantalizing moment in measures 74–75 as Chopin waffles between Gb and G♮ (b6̂ and 6̂) before choosing G♮. If Chopin had really wanted to return to iv–V⁷–i in F minor, he might have written the version shown in Ex. 5.71.

EXAMPLE 5.71. Hypothetical version of mm. 70–72 that returns to a cadence in F minor

But Chopin has now created sufficient tonal stability on IV (Bb) to present new thematic material without the distraction of worrying about a return to F minor. With this freedom, he presents the second theme (mm. 84–99) — a stately chorale theme that bends down toward its own subdominant!

The subsequent developmental material abandons the serious nature of the Ballade, and as a diversion, employs Polish dance rhythms. Chopin uses this diversion to create quick harmonic sequences below Bb major; he visits its relative minor, G minor, and then dances among the keys above and below G minor. Not incidentally, the key *below* G minor is F. Measure 111, indeed, cadences on F minor, but we do not hear it as an arrival. Chopin drops to its lower-third relation, Db major (mm. 111–13).

The harmonic progression is yet another of the ambiguous phrases that cadence on its dominant rather than its tonic (See Exx. 5.3, 5.4, 5.52, and 5.66). It even repeats its consequent phrase, as did the introduction of the Ballade. Creating an alternate reality in the next measures (mm. 121ff.), Chopin creates simultaneous phrases on Ab and A, creating parallel winding phrases that want to cadence on Db and D, respectively — a musical "double helix"! Both Db and D are, of course, VI!

The canonic return of the opening theme presents an imitative texture rare for Chopin, but harmonically he is cadencing on keys familiar from the original version of the theme: I, III, and IV. Of course, the I on F has no structural significance because it was not properly prepared by a structural dominant — it was, shall we say, "convenient." The key of IV, however, triggers a more familiar passage — at measure 145, Chopin splices into the original setting of the opening theme, and with it, returns to the now familiar dip into the subdominant.

Left-hand broken chords begin in measure 152 and generate a sweeping variation of the theme. This time, there is no waffling or hesitation about bending towards the subdominant. Beginning with measure 162, this strikingly beautiful aggrandizement of the first theme seems destined, as in earlier versions, to dip into the subdominant. The left hand controls the passage with $F^7$ chords. We are fully expecting the second theme to return in the subdominant, as in Ex. 5.72.

EXAMPLE 5.72. Hypothetical version of mm. 166–72 that would have swept the music into the now familiar subdominant key of Bb

Chopin instead interrupts the chromatic scale on the note Db, and from this vantage point of the submediant (bVI), presents a lustrous setting of the second theme (Ex. 5.73).

The Db tonality, though unexpected, is the deferred resolution of the ambiguous $Ab^7$–Db dancelike theme of measures 112–20. Ab major at that time had never gained the stature of a full-fledged tonic in the subsequent measures — now it is "fulfilled" as the dominant of Db. And Ab and Db polarize around F, the ultimate tonic target. It has

EXAMPLE 5.73. Chopin's own version of mm. 164–69

been Db (6̂) throughout the piece that stubbornly refused to resolve to
C (5̂). The continued presence of Db generated the various digressions, even in the guise of C♯, spawning the A-major episode
(mm. 129–34). Now, at measure 169, Chopin is on the verge of
confronting Db as a single pitch (6̂) as well as a key area (VI),
assessing its relationship with the notes of F minor. (See Ex. 5.94.)

The unusual feature of the second theme, it will be remembered,
is the intrusion of V of IV in its fourth measure, leading to a feint
toward IV. Chopin's handling of this peculiarity serves as the focal
point of this metamorphosis of the theme. The flattened seventh
(creating V⁷ of IV) now appears one measure early, and Db⁷ is
prolonged for an unusual three measures — the resolute arrival of Gb
in the low bass (m. 174) hints at solid subdominant motion this time.
But in measures 175–76, the measures that pianists love to play, the
Cb is gloriously negated by C♮ (Ex. 5.74). This moment is especially
significant — arriving as a first inversion, the bass line outlines Db–C,
the most important resolution of Db to appear thus far. The C♮ negates
any implications of IV of Db, and the complete absence of V of IV
signals the elimination of this Ballade's inherent peculiarity of bending
toward the subdominant.

EXAMPLE 5.74. mm. 179–80

The bass line, however, continues through C to Cb. Because Cb is the bottom note of Db⁷ (Db², to be more precise), the phrase is still in danger of falling down to its own subdominant, Gb.

As the harmonic progression strays further and further from the initial setting, Chopin alters the thematic content of the passage. And hidden among the octave transpositions, the opening theme traces its own contour, with the notable difference that the notes of the diminished chord resolve (Ex. 5.75).

The subsequent appearance of C♮, not Cb, as a struck suspension (4-3) in measure 185 signals the end of Gb major, as does the pedal point in measures 185–87. If Chopin had placed a Gb in the pedal, Gb major may have had a chance to regain control; without it, there is no chance of Gb becoming the tonic. Gb, once the important b6 of Bb minor, now loses its status and wedges down into F.

Chopin arrives on an F-minor ⁶₄ chord in measure 187, and if it were not for Chopin's faultless sense of proportion, he might have prematurely headed home at this point, as in the version shown in Ex. 5.76.

Instead, he uses a pivotal Ab in measure 189 to remain longer on Db major. By replacing Dbs with Cs, Chopin still might have resolved to F minor in measure 190. The decisive arrival of Db major in measure 191 is, however, not permanent. The subsequent measures undertake one more attempt to reach F minor — not through a Db–C (6̂ –5̂) resolution this time, but through Bb minor, an appropriate path considering Bb's role throughout the Ballade. Measures 191–94 describe chromatic alterations that would lead toward the sought-after dominant, as in Ex. 5.77.

EXAMPLE 5.75. Contour of opening theme returns unexpectedly, with various notes of diminished chord now resolved (mm. 181–84)

EXAMPLE 5.76. Hypothetical version of m. 190 that cadences prematurely in F minor

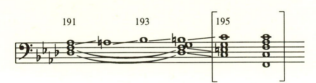

EXAMPLE 5.77. Hypothetical progression that bypasses I$^6_4$ and arrives in F minor too early. Compare the expressive power of the French-sixth chord (m. 194) with that of the Second Ballade (See Ex. 5.43)

The French-sixth chord in measure 194, a dominant-preparation chord that Chopin rarely uses but saves for dramatic moments such as this, results from carefully prepared chromatic motion, and leads to a tonic $^6_4$ chord. We sense that the bass C (mm. 195ff.) is *now* the true dominant pedal. It indeed persists as such; paradoxically, it is inaudible (not always captured by the pedal) yet remains stronger than ever. Staccato chords in measures 198–200, which provide micro-summaries of ♭VI, ♯IV, and ♭II, themselves delay yet again the desired structural dominant. The eighth-note bass line finally restores F minor (in its first inversion), followed by a chord so close to C$^7$ that it has no where else to go (m. 201). In the interests of thematic unity, an opening-theme fragment fittingly ushers in the long-sought dominant-seventh harmony (Ex. 5.78).

EXAMPLE 5.78. Dramatic arrival of V chord, including three-note fragment of opening theme as a launching pad (mm. 198–202)

Throughout the Ballade, Chopin has built harmonic tension and suspense by delaying C; as each statement of the opening theme leaned on its subdominant side, the subsequent digressions that delayed $V^7$ grew increasingly longer. The C-major chords in measure 202 signaled the end of the wildest and longest excursion yet; the final irony is that Chopin, after sustaining the suspense that postpones $V^7$, writes C major on the weakest beat of the measure and *without* the seventh (m. 202). A hypothetical passage in Ex. 5.79 retains the drama, but satisfies our craving for $C^7$ on a strong beat.

EXAMPLE 5.79. Hypothetical arrival of a full-fledged $V^7$ on the strong second half of m. 202

Chopin's choice is suspenseful in two ways; the seventh is avoided in favor of an internal I–$V^7$–I in V, and the metric center of the measure falls on a rest, producing the most disturbing "rest" imaginable. Together, these elements generate one of the most chilling moments of silence in all of Chopin's works. The following five *pianissimo* V and $V^7$ chords usher in, at last, the turbulent return of the true structural tonic, F minor.

The vigorous and turbulent nature of the section from measure 211 to the end of the Ballade is made especially effective by the abruptness of the resumption of triplet sixteenths that follow the sustained chords. The basic eighth-note pulse remains the same; the shift from dotted half notes to triplet sixteenths creates an explosive charge into F minor that carries through into the final measures.

The twisting lines in both hands in measures 211–14 give the illusion of four or five simultaneously running voices. The twists and turns are not random, however; as in the other Ballades, they complete unfinished structural lines. Especially significant are the many resolutions of Db to C, or $\hat{6}$–$\hat{5}$. Example 5.80a isolates the $\hat{6}$–$\hat{5}$'s, and Ex. 5.80b illustrates the longer wedges generated in these measures.

(a) Highlights of $\hat{6}$–$\hat{5}$

(b) Structural view

EXAMPLE 5.80a and b. Two views of mm. 211–12

The *crescendo,* indicated for *only* the left hand (m. 212), brings into relief the important long wedge gesture upward towards Db–C, a gesture that will be repeated in the treacherous right-hand "double-thirds" passage (mm. 215–17). These measures and their repetition stabilize the structural descent to the tonic only as far as Bb–Ab ($\hat{4}$ and $\hat{3}$); G and F ($\hat{2}$ and $\hat{1}$) have yet to be significantly presented.

The bass line in measures 215–17 explores a chromatic descending line from F, pausing along the way to outline various dominant and secondary-dominant chords, all within the larger context of F minor. Chopin carefully writes a slower moving right-hand line with upward stems, above the thirds, that recall the melodic descent in measures 38–46; he avoids G♮ and gives G♭ a metrically strong position (m. 215). This is the beginning of the ultimate downward wedge into I. The outer parts of the diminished-chord sonority in measure 216 set the stage for the final wedge that will drive home the tonality in the concluding moments of the Ballade — E♮ wanting to resolve up to the tonic, and D♭ pushing down toward the dominant.

EXAMPLE 5.81. Upper structural line including ♭2̂ and 7̂ as wedges around the tonic; lower structural line still emphasizing ♭6 (mm. 215–18)

Chopin's compositional technique of securing the tonality in this section is similar to the *agitato* of the Second Ballade — descending chromatic lines polarized around the tonic, followed by a few measures of ascending lines. Ex. 5.82 outlines the comparable measures of both Ballades.

(a)  Second Ballade, mm. 176–80

(b)  Fourth Ballade, mm. 215–18

EXAMPLE 5.82. Chromatically descending bass lines of Second and Fourth Ballades provide longer and more secure wedges than anything previously heard in either Ballade

Measures 215–27 are filled with various deceptive cadences and harmonic regressions, all designed to delay the eventual arrival of F minor in measure 227. For instance, the cadence across the bar line into measure 218 proves that the bass note D♭ still has some influence. This initiates a series of sequences that seamlessly slide through two octaves without ever fully cadencing on F minor.

In the second half of measure 218, the *marcato* indication leads us to expect, finally, a V–i cadence — we might have expected the version in Ex. 5.83.

EXAMPLE 5.83. Hypothetical version of mm. 218–19, cadencing prematurely in F minor

Instead, the lower voices twist into a V of IV to IV position, recalling Chopin's preoccupation with the major and minor subdominant areas throughout most of the Ballade. Attempting to regain tonal balance, the line hops diatonically through B♭, A♭, G, and F, only to slip into another V of IV situation in measure 220. Triplet sixteenths continue in the left hand, outlining an ascending harmonic-minor scale in F minor; the right hand plays in sixths parallel to the left hand, and then turns to produce a wedge in contrary motion. The descending tetrachord again appears, emphasizing the D♭–C resolution.

EXAMPLE 5.84. Various downward dips into the subdominant — vestigial remains of the power of IV

Measure 223 arrives powerfully on F minor, but Chopin's odd G♯ sparks an instant switch from I to V of IV, a last-ditch attempt to regain the subdominant.[33]

EXAMPLE 5.85. Chopin's deployment of G♯ (enharmonic equivalent of A♭) to regain F⁷, as a final dramatic attempt to regain the subdominant B♭ as ersatz tonic (mm. 223–24)

It is interesting to note that Chopin's Nocturne, Op. 55, No. 1, written one year later (1843) and in the same key of F minor, features a similar feint toward the subdominant in the closing pages, beginning with measure 77. The turbulence is absent, but the harmonic intent is the same (Ex. 5.86).

EXAMPLE 5.86. Chopin's Nocturne in F Minor, Op. 55, No. 1, whose closing pages lean toward subdominant (mm. 85–87)

With the aid of the $\hat{6}$–$\hat{5}$ intervals of *both* the subdominant and the tonic keys, the cadence reaches the expected IV–V⁷–I. But this time, Chopin is playing for keeps — compare the earlier diffident setting (m. 22) with the now wildly aggressive version of IV–V–I (Ex. 5.87).

EXAMPLE 5.87. Metamorphosis of V/IV–IV–V⁷ from its genesis in mm. 21–22 to the anguish of m. 224

In the original opening theme, we recall the incomplete nature of
E♮ and D♭ where these pitches were left with unsatisfactory resolutions; they did not directly resolve, nor did they seem related to each
other. In these final two pages, the pitches E♮ and D♭ are given a
more "proper" status within the scale of F minor: D♭ resolves to C,
and E♮ acts as the leading tone to F. These isolated resolutions are
highly profiled as the melody in measures 224 and 226, producing the
cleanest 6̂–5̂ and 7̂–1̂ wedges of the Ballade (Ex. 5.87; see mm. 224–
25).

The final definitive tonic arrives in measure 227. Lower and
upper wedge notes around I finally appear in equal numbers
(Ex. 5.88).

EXAMPLE 5.88.  Final wedges, now taking aim at I rather than V

The high point of this motion leads to F minor in measure 231,
and the line begins a scalar descent, punctuated by i and VI⁶ chords;
the VI⁶ chords recall the important function of D♭ in the Ballade, but
now indicate this chord's origin. It is rooted firmly within the context
of F minor; the raised fifth degree (5̂ raised to ♭6̂) produces the D♭
sonority.

EXAMPLE 5.89.  Final, desperate attempt of left hand to reinstate ♭VI!

The right-hand notes that are contiguous with these D♭ chords
themselves form the outline of a descent through D♭ and C:

EXAMPLE 5.90.  D♭ to C wedges, now aided by F and E♭, forming an
entire tetrachord wedge into C

The final flurry of triplet sixteenths outlines b̂6̂-5̂-3̂-1̂, a situation comparable to measures 237–38 of the A♭ Ballade. It is more extended, and the excitement is intensified by the metric rhythm in threes, which rub against the four-note groups (Ex. 5.91).

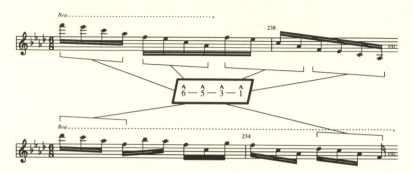

EXAMPLE 5.91. Similar cascades of b̂6̂-5̂-3̂-1̂ that appear in both the Third Ballade (shown in upper staff) and Fourth Ballade (lower staff)

At the bottom of the passage, the repetitions produce one final ascending outline of the four-note unit on the eighth-note beats. Finally, the last three measures represent a distillation of the entire Ballade; the hands alternate D♭s, followed by an authentic V⁷–i cadence (Ex. 5.92).

EXAMPLE 5.92. Final statement of b̂6̂-5̂-3̂-1̂ on the beats of m. 236, and final statement of VI-(ii⁶₅)-V7-I in the last measures of the Ballade

Unlike the earlier Ballades, the F-Minor Ballade succumbs to the subdominant, the easily accessible fifth *below* the tonic. The subdominant as a contrasting key area may have tempted Chopin because of its built-in sense of ambiguity — unlike V, IV does not imply a direct resolution. Furthermore, Chopin may have enjoyed the challenge of a key area that would reduce tension rather than increase it. Classical composers, certainly because of the relaxing "falling fifth" nature of the subdominant, frequently featured subdominant slow movements in their sonatas to calm down the listener. By placing the second theme of the Ballade in the subdominant, Chopin precluded any of the more conventional tonal paths back to the tonic, paths that sonata-form movements usually take. His challenge, then, was to regain the tension and sweep up to the dominant from *the other side* of the tonic.

The subdominant area of the Ballade, B♭, is itself easy to reach from the tonic; F minor, with no change of root, can easily become $F^7$ (V of IV). The predilection for IV was made evident as early as measures 18–22, when the opening theme strayed longer than expected on V of iv. In measure 22, the "correct" $C^7$ chord sounded wrong, as if B♭ minor had become the tonic. After every subsequent appearance of the opening theme, each digression becomes increasingly elaborate, threatening to take over the piece. In a sense, this does happen with the appearance of the second theme; V of iv becomes V of IV and the second theme appears in B♭ major.

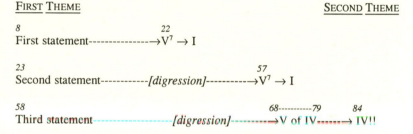

FIRST THEME                                                    SECOND THEME

8                                    22
First statement---------------→$V^7$ → I

23                                                         57
Second statement------------*[digression]*-----------→$V^7$ → I

58                                         68-----------79        84
Third statement-------------------*[digression]*---------→V of IV-------→ IV!!

EXAMPLE 5.93. Increasing lengths of digression after each statement of the theme until IV takes charge (m. 84) and becomes the new tonality for the second theme

The development section (mm. 100–128), after several wandering motions, settles into V of VI at measure 112, but never resolves to VI. The recapitulation may be said to begin when the introduction returns around D minor, measure 129, and finds its way to F minor and a full statement of the opening theme, then shifts to VI for the aggrandizement of the second theme at measures 169ff. This appearance of D♭ resolves the tension left over from V of D♭ in the development section. D♭, then, has several meanings: it acts as the delayed resolution to the developmental material, it serves as a substitute tonic during the return of the second theme, and, in measures 191–201, it takes on the characteristics of a dissonant upper neighbor to V of F minor (Ex. 5.94).

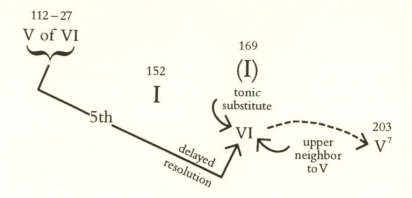

EXAMPLE 5.94.  Various multiple functions of VI (D♭) in m. 169

While standard, "textbook" sonatas follow a tonal plan that could be described by a *sine curve* (Ex. 5.95), the Ballade can be said to describe a *reverse sine curve* (Ex. 5.97). Classical composers usually moved to an area of tension a third or fifth above the tonic, and after regaining the tonic at the beginning of the recapitulation, restored the tonal equilibrium by dipping briefly into the subdominant side.

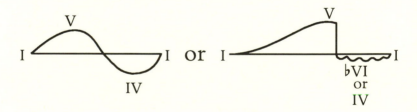

EXAMPLE 5.95.  Two graphs showing tonal plan of classical sonatas. Sine-curve metaphor clarifies that the prefix "sub" (*sub*dominant, *sub*mediant) refers to "below" the tonic

Early in the nineteenth century, a few composers occasionally inverted the sine curve by dipping a third or fifth *below* the tonic; they would balance this in the recapitulation with an opposite motion *above* the tonic. The first movement of Schubert's "Unfinished" Symphony is an example of this procedure (Ex. 5.96).

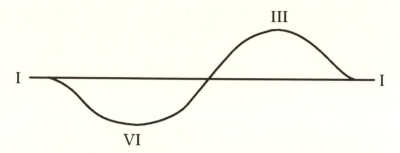

EXAMPLE 5.96. Schubert, "Unfinished" Symphony No. 8 in B Minor, D. 759 (1822), first movement

Chopin has inverted the sine curve in this Ballade. The subdominant area occurs early in the piece, requiring increased amounts of energy to regain the tonic and continue across into the dominant side to reach the $V^7$ chord.

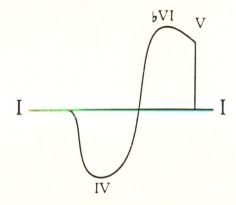

EXAMPLE 5.97. Graph illustrating F-Minor Ballade's *reverse sine curve.* To overcome the initial dip down to the subdominant, Chopin must summon considerable energy and passion to reverse direction, rise up, and arrive at ♭VI–V

Chopin has, for the fourth and final time, prepared the structural dominant of a Ballade with ♭VI. In this case, D♭ (♭VI) was itself prepared by its own dominant (A♭) in the developmental section (mm. 112–21). The enormous energy necessary to overcome the inertia of IV generates considerable excitement and passion, and Chopin's arrival at ♭VI, and ultimately V and I, produces one of his most beautiful and gratifying compositions.

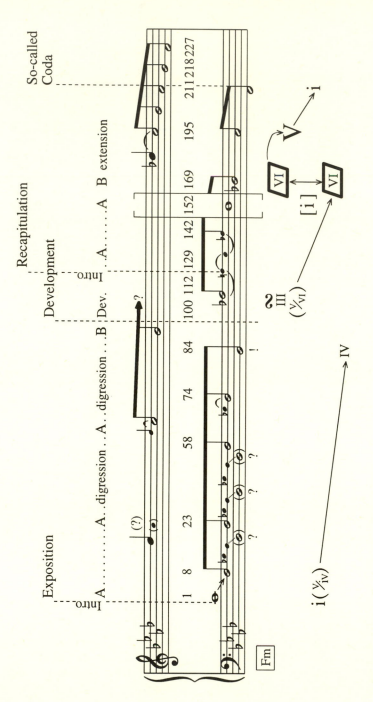

EXAMPLE 5.98. Graph of *Quatrième Ballade*

# VIII

In tonal music, any definitive statement of the structural dominant implies a commitment to resolve to its tension-releasing tonic. In each of the four Ballades, Chopin creatively blocks the well-worn path to the tonic by delaying access to its gatekeeper, the dominant. He manages to delay the dominant longer than any previous composer who had worked within the confines of sonata form. The bulk of the entire piece becomes, in a sense, one huge dominant preparation. In this way, tension builds up throughout the piece, and its release in the final pages, via the long-awaited V–I resolution, is all the more gratifying and exciting.

The structural dominant and tonic are not the only fundamental elements to be delayed until the end of each piece. In every Ballade, the fundamental *Urlinie* remains incomplete until the final measures. In the First, Third, and Fourth Ballades, this final section begins on 3̂. The Second Ballade is the exception; the interchange between 6̂ and 5̂ (F and E) is maintained not only throughout the piece, but also into the "coda," and 3̂–2̂–1̂ do not occur until measures 198–203.

(a) *Première Ballade*

(b) *Deuxième Ballade*

(c) *Troisième Ballade*

(d)  *Quatrième Ballade*

EXAMPLE 5.99.  Completion of the *Urlinie* in each Ballade

# IX

It is impossible to overstate the importance of the delayed structural dominant in the Ballades. It is certainly the most significant factor that hinders any forthright classification of the Ballades within conventional forms. While Chopin had available many methods and techniques for delaying the structural dominant, he seems to have favored one device in particular — the prolongation and deployment of the submediant (VI) to control the digressions on the way to the dominant. In the final pages of each Ballade, VI is represented by $\hat{6}$, the degree of the scale. Ultimately, $\hat{6}$ is joined by ♯$\hat{4}$ to form a wedge around $\hat{5}$, and in the *very* final pages, the half steps ♭$\hat{2}$ and $\hat{7}$ dramatically wedge around $\hat{1}$ to clinch the tonic. These wedges, which function as basic elemental building blocks, are absolutely fundamental to the tonal stability of each Ballade. Chopin's wedge technique, and his creative use of the submediant to postpone the structural dominant, are factors so basic to the tonal design of each Ballade that they may be considered the defining characteristics of Chopin's "Ballade style."

* * * * * *
* * * * *
*

# Notes

For a more comprehensive analysis of the Chopin Ballades, see my D.M.A. dissertation from Boston University: Neil David Witten, *The Chopin Ballades: An Analytical Study* (Ann Arbor, MI: University Microfilms No. 79-23960, 1979).

1. James Huneker, *Chopin, the Man and his Music* (1900; reprint, New York: Dover Publications, 1966), 156.

2. Hans Keller, "The Chamber Music," in *The Mozart Companion,* ed. H. C. R. Landon and D. Mitchell (New York: W. W. Norton, 1956), 91.

3. Peter Gould, "Sonatas and Concertos," in *The Chopin Companion,* ed. A. Walker (New York: W. W. Norton, 1973), 144.

4. William Henry Hadow, *Studies in Modern Music* (London: Seely, 1895), 2:154.

5. Huneker, *Chopin,* 155.

6. Huneker, *Chopin,* 169.

7. Alan Walker, "Chopin and Musical Structure: An Analytical Approach," in *The Chopin Companion,* ed. A. Walker (New York: W. W. Norton, 1973), 227–57; Carl Schachter, "The Prelude in E Minor, Op. 28, No. 4: Autograph Sources and Interpretation," in *Chopin Studies II,* ed. J. Rink and J. Samson (Cambridge: Cambridge University Press, 1994), 161–82; Edward T. Cone, "Ambiguity and Reinterpretation in Chopin," in *Chopin Studies II,* 140–60. John Rink, "The *Barcarolle: Auskomponierung* and Apotheosis," in *Chopin Studies,* ed. J. Samson (Cambridge: Cambridge University Press, 1988), 195–220; Rink, "Tonal Architecture in the Early Music," in *The Cambridge Companion to Chopin* (Cambridge: Cambridge University Press, 1992), 78–97; Jim Samson, *The Music of Chopin* (1985; reprint, Oxford: Clarendon Press, 1994); Samson, *Chopin: The Four Ballades* (Cambridge: Cambridge Music Handbooks, 1992).

8. Claude Debussy, from a review of *La Chambre d'enfants* of Musorgskii (1 April 1901), quoted by Leon Vallas, *The Theories of Claude Debussy* (1929; reprint, New York: Dover Publications, 1967), 152. Italics mine. See also Joel Sheveloff's comments about this quotation in chapter 9, n. 1.

9. Samson, *Chopin: The Four Ballades,* 45.

10. While Beethoven and Schubert certainly contributed to the entrance of third relations into the tonal "collective unconscious" of their contemporaries, they cannot be considered the direct predecessors of Chopin — Chopin, in fact, knew only a few works of Schubert. He was far more familiar with the works of Hummel and Spohr, composers whose themes slipped effortlessly in and out of nondominant key areas, yet who lacked the technique and control necessary to generate logical, solid works at the highest level. It was the music of these composers, whose works are seldom heard today, that Chopin learned from, emulated, and ultimately surpassed.

11. "There is, then, a calculated ambiguity in the formal design of the Ballade between a sonata-based structure, allied to an accelerating intensity

curve, and the more closed formal symmetry of an arch design." Samson, *Chopin: The Four Ballades,* 49.

12. Schachter, "Prelude in E Minor," 162.

13. Cone, "Ambiguity and Reinterpretation in Chopin," 142.

14. Cone, "Ambiguity and Reinterpretation," 141.

15. See also the bass line of Chopin's E-Minor Prelude, measures 18–24. Bach and Mozart (the composers whom Chopin most admired!) often added, in the last lines of their pieces, a feint toward the subdominant, a gesture toward the fifth *below* the tonic, which provided a "counterweight" to the time spent a fifth *above* it. Chopin adapted this principle for his own purposes, exploring the use of *half steps* above and below the dominant, and eventually above and below the tonic.

16. Charles Rosen remarks about this ending, "The increased passion is only a partial preparation for the astonishing operatic recitative that follows, which seems both unprovoked [*sic*] and satisfying, as it completes without resolving." Rosen, *The Romantic Generation* (New York: Schirmer, 1995), 82. Rosen seems unaware of the role of the four mysterious silences and their interruptions by G♮, which inevitably *provoke* the E♯.

Most available editions, unfortunately, now print F♮ instead of E♯ in the left hand of measures 62–63; only the Karl Klindworth (Jurgenson) and the Paderewski editions show E♯. I would hope that the E♯ is authentic — the implied upward nature of "sharp" $\hat{4}$ shores up the dominant. Furthermore, this more correct spelling helps us understand the true nature of this augmented-sixth chord as a dominant preparation. For those devoted to pinpoint precision in their chord labeling, the resulting vertical sonority is "♯IV$^{\natural 7}_{5}$".

17. Mozart's "Dissonant" Quartet, K. 465 (1785) and Haydn's *The Creation*: "Representation of Chaos" (1798).

18. Frederick Niecks, quoted by Huneker, *Chopin,* 157.

19. Heinrich Schenker, *Free Composition,* trans. T. Krueger (Ph.D. diss., University of Iowa, 1960), 171.

20. Heinrich Schenker, *Der Freie Satz* (Vienna: Universal, 1935), 215.

21. By 1857, for example, Wagner was able to imply the A minor of Tristan not by stating A minor, nor by stating its V⁷, but by presenting three opening phrases that end on V of A, V of C, and V of E.

22. Gerald Abraham, *Chopin's Musical Style* (London: Oxford University Press, 1968; 1st ed. 1939), 69.

23. Johannes Brahms, in a letter to his co-editor Ernst Rudorff (1 November 1877), quoted by Oswald Jonas, "On the Study of Chopin's Manuscripts," in *Chopin Jahrbuch,* ed. Franz Zagiba (Vienna: Amalthea, 1956), 143.

24. The A-Minor Mazurka was published in 1832, but Maurice Brown gives the probable date of composition as 1824.

25. Mendelssohn's "Italian" Symphony, No. 4 (first movement, mm. 345–50) shares a feature similar to this spot in the Ballade, but Mendelssohn is more conventional beginning with a I$^{6}_{4}$, not a IV$^{6}_{4}$.

26. *Répétiteurs* and editors of piano reductions, take note!

27. ". . . ich erinnere mich sehr gut, als Chopin die Ballade hier spielte und in F–Dur schloss; jetz schließt sie in A–Moll." Robert Schumann, "Kürzere Stücke für Pianoforte," *Neue Zeitschrift für Musik* 15 (1841): 36. English translation from Robert Schumann, *On Music and Musicians* (London: Dennis Dobson, 1956), 143.

28. Gerald Abraham, Chopin's Musical Style (1939; reprint, London: Oxford University Press, 1968), 56–57.

29. "The common law is not a brooding omnipresence in the sky, but the articulate voice of some sovereign or quasi-sovereign that can be identified . . ." Oliver Wendell Holmes, Jr., J. dissenting, *Southern Pacific Co. v. Jensen,* 244 U.S. 206, 222 (1917).

30. The following is a letter that Chopin sent to Breitkopf & Härtel, his publisher in Leipzig:

Paris. 15 December 1842

Gentlemen,

I should like to offer you a Scherzo for 600 francs, a Ballade for 600 francs, and a Polonaise for 500 francs. In addition, I have written an Impromptu of a few pages which I do not even put forward to you — I wish to oblige an old acquaintance who for the last two years has been urging me to give something to Mr. Hofmeister. I only mention it so that you may understand my intentions in the matter.

If my Scherzo, Ballade, and Polonaise are acceptable, please let me know by next post and suggest a time for their despatch.

Yours sincerely,
F. Chopin

Place d'Orléans,
Rue Saint-Lazare

Chopin correspondence, *Selected Correspondence of Fryderyk Chopin,* trans. and ed. by Arthur Hedley (New York: McGraw-Hill Book Company, 1963), 225–26.

31. For a solid discussion of editions, see Samson, *Chopin: The Four Ballades,* 26–33.

32. An appropriate metaphor of geography comes to mind here, for which I acknowledge my brother Sam Witten. While visiting the island of Guam, he learned that, because of its size, he was *on* Guam, not *in* Guam.

33. Rubinstein and Horowitz have both recorded a variant (mm. 223 and 225) that is found only in the Herrmann Scholtz edition (C. F. Peters): G♯ and E♭ in the right hand instead of G♯ and F. Unfortunately, neither the Paderewski edition nor the Jan Ekier edition (Wiener Urtext) mentions this alternate version. It is particularly disappointing not to know its origin because the E♭ (instead of F) adds extra crunch to this deceptive progression (V slipping to V/iv). In other words, E♭ signals V/iv ($F^7$) immediately on the downbeat, and the G♯ (as opposed to A♭!) is heard as the dissonant note. Without the Chopin/Scholtz E♭, the downbeat sounds momentarily like a minor tonic chord, which seems to be contrary to Chopin's intention.

# CHAPTER SIX

# Madness or Prophecy? Schumann's
# *Gesänge der Frühe,* Op. 133

## John Daverio

## I

WITH THE EXCEPTION of the ebullient "Rhenish" Symphony, Op. 97, the music of Robert Schumann's Düsseldorf years (1850–54) has yet to be admitted to the canon of works that figure regularly in our concert halls and conservatories. The lack of substantive references to either the *Drei Phantasiestücke,* Op. 111, or the *Gesänge der Frühe,* Op. 133 — the last and most puzzling of Schumann's collections of piano pieces — in the early biographies of Wilhelm Josef von Wasielewski (1906) and Frederick Niecks (1925) is perhaps understandable. The absence of these pieces from recent overviews of Schumann's piano music is more surprising.[1] Nor are we apt to hear either cycle regularly in performance. The products of Schumann's last years would thus seem to bear out Carl Dahlhaus's assumption that the after-history of "late works" is discontinuous, their assimilation temporally distant from their point of origin.[2]

Like the relative silence surrounding them, the negative valuations of Schumann's late works frequently encountered in the scholarly and critical literature are by and large motivated by the suspicion that during his last years the composer labored under the curse of impending madness. As Eduard Melkus has shown, this notion was in fact fostered by the select group gathered around Schumann during the final phase of his career: his wife, Clara (who went so far as to destroy his last completed chamber work, the *Romanzen* for 'cello and piano of November 1854, presumably because it evinced signs of mental decay), the young violin virtuoso Joseph Joachim, and the burgeoning compositional talent whose praises Schumann would sing in "Neue Bahnen" ("New Paths"), Johannes Brahms.[3] The dissipation of creative power in Schumann's later compositions was accepted as a matter of course by early biographers like Walter Dahms, whose metaphorically charged account of the *Gesänge der Frühe* (the last of Schumann's works to be published during his lifetime) speaks of "the hoar-frost of a resignation that can no more rejoice at the longed-for sun, but must rather dry the tears of night secretively and greet the daylight with forced composure."[4] Recent critics, even if their prose is less purple than Dahms's, have followed suit. Dieter Schnebel, for instance, hears a "droning impotence" in the Violin Concerto, and an outpouring of "depressive melancholy" in the Mass and Requiem.[5]

Nonetheless, the last decade or so has witnessed the growth of a sizeable body of literature aimed at debunking the myth that Schumann's late works were conceived in the shadow of his final mental breakdown. Michael Struck — one of a number of German scholars who have done significantly better by the late works than their anglophone colleagues — argues convincingly that Schumann's last illness hardly supplied the tragic backdrop against which the creative products of the Düsseldorf years should be interpreted. On the contrary, Struck makes an excellent case for the possibility that the composer's last illness brought an abrupt halt to his ongoing personal and professional plans.[6]

This reappraisal of the relationship between Schumann's illness and his artistic projects has had important ramifications for the critical evaluation of the late compositions themselves. Indeed, the work of Struck and other German writers including Gerhard Dietel, Helmuth Hopf, Reinhard Kapp, Irmgard Knechtges, and Norbert Nagler has led to a wholesale vindication of the aesthetic sense of what had previously been an intractable repertory.[7] Yet the "rehabilitation" (as Nagler calls it) of Schumann's late style has resulted in a kind of neutralization whose effects are most obvious in the many attempts to interpret the late works as harbingers of musical developments more readily associated with the late nineteenth and early twentieth centuries. Hopf, for instance, hears in the *Gesänge der Frühe* harmonies suggestive of Reger, while the opening movement of the Violin Concerto, in his view, displays an unmistakably Brucknerian tone.[8] Similarly, Nagler finds a remarkable premonition of the late Liszt (and even the Second Viennese School) in the thoroughgoing monomotivicism of the *Faust* Overture.[9] Kapp's virtuosic demonstration of Schumann's move toward a total integration of his materials (in an analysis of the orchestral opening of the Violin Concerto's first movement that relates practically every note to every other note) is aimed, by implication, at the same end.[10]

In short, the prevalent views of Schumann's late works have clustered around the opposing poles of madness or prophecy. Yet it would seem that the critical challenge posed by this music lies precisely in the preservation of a sense for its structural integration that, at the same time, allows for the recognition of its esoteric, enigmatic, yes, even its "mad" qualities. An ideal criticism, in other words, should aim at mediating the elements of madness *and* prophecy that crisscross in Schumann's late works.

By way of demonstration, we will focus on the cycle of five piano pieces that make up the *Gesänge der Frühe.*[11] Composed from 15–18 October 1853, the cycle thus fell within the incredibly productive spell that also saw the completion of the Violin Concerto (3 October), the *Märchenerzählungen,* Op. 132, for clarinet, viola, and piano (begun 9 October), the second and fourth movements of the "F.A.E." Sonata for Joachim (its first and third movements composed by Albert Dietrich and Brahms, respectively), the "Third" Sonata for violin and piano (completed 31 October, and made up of Schumann's contributions to the "F.A.E." Sonata plus newly composed first and third movements), and the *Romanzen* for 'cello and piano (completed 2 November).[12]

Roland Barthes, that irrepressible if idiosyncratic Schumann lover, is one of the few commentators to have sketched out a model for addressing the refractory side of Schumann's art. The French critic locates several areas in which a kind of "madness" can be said to inform this music: its embodiment of an extramusical reality whose outward signs take the form of descriptive titles, its stubborn adherence to intentionally fragmented (and hence "dizzying") structures, and the "obsessive" nature of its harmonies and rhythms, both of the latter elements cultivated, in Barthes's view, toward the end of registering "pain."[13] If the "painful" quality of Schumann's music emanates from the mute voice of the subject straining to speak itself, then we might detect the poetry of pain in the registral drop in the climactic phrase of the first of the *Gesänge der Frühe* (m. 30), or in the "breakthrough" and sublimation of the fanfare motive in the second piece (mm. 12–16), or in the fantastically extended dominant and bravura close — gestures that attempt to transfer the miniature into the realm of the grand concerto — in the third piece.

As suggestive as Barthes's model may be, we will nonetheless opt for a different means of balancing the claims of madness and prophecy in Schumann's last cycle of character pieces for piano. For the sake of clarity of presentation, I will address four interrelated enigmas, each suggested by an aspect of the cycle's reception: What is the character of the "completely individual tone" ("ganz eigne Stimmung") that, according to Clara, hindered an easy comprehension of the pieces? To what extent does the cycle reflect Schumann's encounter with the young Brahms and his music? Why did Schumann waver over the

number of pieces (four or five) that would ultimately constitute the
cycle? What, in other words, is the nature of the cycle's totality? Why
did Schumann suppress the reference to "Diotima" (a figure of ideality
probably culled from the life and work of the poet Friedrich Hölderlin)
that figured in the original title? And as a corollary to our fourth
question: What are the implications of the final title — *Gesänge der
Frühe* ("Morning Songs" or "Songs of Awakening") — for the poetic
message of the work? In that my aim is less to solve than to analyze
these enigmas, I will offer only tentative, and in some cases,
speculative observations. Indeed, if we proceed under the assumption
that each of our enigmas allows for a certain remainder, a blind spot
that resists explication, then it may just be that this remainder marks the
site of the whole critical enterprise.

## II

On 18 October 1853, the day on which Schumann completed the
*Gesänge der Frühe,* Clara noted in her diary: "R[obert] has just
composed five Morning Songs ['Frühgesänge'], completely original
pieces as always, but difficult to grasp, for a completely individual tone
resides therein."[14] What are we to make of the "tone" to which Clara
refers? Unfortunately, music criticism has yet to develop a clear idea of
musical "tones" or "moods"; it certainly has nothing on the order of the
fully elaborated but hermetic theory of "alternating" poetic tones
developed by Hölderlin (to whom we will return) — a theory that has
exercised the interpretive powers of more than a few critics in the
roughly two centuries since its conception. We might however suggest
as a working hypothesis that the distinctive tone of the *Gesänge der
Frühe* derives from three aspects of its harmonic language: archaicism,
dissociation, and attenuation.

The concept of the "late work," Dahlhaus maintains, plays on the
interaction of modern and deliberately archaic elements.[15] The latter
surface in the unmistakably modal flavor of the harmony at measure 13
in the first of the *Gesänge der Frühe,* where an F♯-minor chord
substitutes for the expected major dominant. Yet this harmonic turn
provides more than an isolated touch of color, for it complements the
choralelike quality of melody and texture alike. Similarly, the hieratic
character of the cycle as a whole is reinforced by the extended plagal
closes of its third, fourth, and fifth pieces. The archaic harmonic effects
(not unlike those employed by Ravel half a century later) thus lend to
the composition a patina of religiosity by marking out a distance

between receptor and artwork. They contribute, in short, to the imponderables best subsumed under the term "aura."

Another sort of distance is articulated in the fabric of the music itself. At several points during the first piece in the cycle (mm. 6–8, 15–17, 25–26), the bass and inner voices appear to become dissociated from the melody. The progression in measures 6–8 (See Ex. 6.1), for instance, is hardly justifiable in conventional tonal-harmonic or contrapuntal terms. Viewed as a tonal construct, the passage includes bass notes (F♯ in m. 6; E in m. 7) that come one beat "too soon" in anticipating the harmonies appropriate for the following downbeats. The parallel seconds in the upper voices (E–D, D–C♯, C♯–B), on the other hand, seem to result from a suspension pattern gone awry. Yet to write off the passage as harmonically ambiguous or contrapuntally deficient is to miss the point. The dislocation of melody and bass is rather a means of suggesting space, specifically, the immense space of a sonorous hall or cathedral whose reverberations might indeed alter the vertical dimension of the music for the listener far removed from the actual sounding source.

EXAMPLE 6.1. Robert Schumann, *Gesänge der Frühe*, Op. 133; No. 1, mm. 1–8

Something similar occurs in measures 39–42 of the third piece, where pandiatonic clashes arise from the combination of a plagal progression in the bass fanfares and a tonic-supertonic-dominant seventh sequence in the treble. In both cases, the suggestion of reverberatory space is composed into the music itself; in both cases, harmony contributes much to the work's distinctive aura.

Kathleen Dale, one of the less sanguine critics of Schumann's late style, has written disparagingly of the "intractable $^6_4$ chords" that obstruct the logical course of the tonal flow in the *Gesänge der Frühe*.[16] In fact, the disposition of the second-inversion tonics in the cycle is both systematic and logical: systematic, because the (sometimes climactic) tonal-thematic return in each piece is supported by $^6_4$ harmony (No. 1: m. 27, No. 2: mm. 29–30, No. 3: m. 43, No. 4: mm. 16, 29, No. 5: m. 18); and logical, because the attenuation of tonic harmony by way of the $^6_4$ voicing aptly complements the effects we have already described under the rubric of dissociation. The "intractable" $^6_4$'s result, as it were, from the reverberation of the preparatory dominant bass note into the succeeding tonic chord. The apparent deficiencies of Schumann's part-writing turn out to be a means of suggesting sonorous spaces.

It is important to recognize that in none of the harmonic effects considered above — archaicism, dissociation, attenuation — does Schumann make his point by recourse to chromatic writing. The "completely individual tone" of the music emanates from the site where diatonicism reaches its outer limits. In this, Schumann opts for the road less frequently taken in the nineteenth century, a period during which chromaticism generally served as an emblem of musical progress. Yet, as any student of the *Gesänge der Frühe* can attest, Schumann's reconfiguration of the *strenger Satz* (with its interdependence of melody and bass, counterpoint and harmony) represents a decidedly "modern" means of suggesting remarkable spatial effects through the medium of a single instrument. Schumann's anomalous harmonies (an unsympathetic critic would attribute them to his madness and leave it at that) call up the future under the sign of the past.

III

The composition of the *Gesänge der Frühe* coincided with the midpoint of Brahms' visit to Düsseldorf in the autumn of 1853. During the course of his month-long stay (30 September to 2 November), the "young eagle," as Schumann dubbed him,[17] was an almost daily presence in the home of the older composer, who was mightily impressed by Brahms' interpretive and creative powers. Indeed, Schumann's household account books, taken together with other pertinent documents, provide ample evidence of the breadth and depth of the young Brahms' compositional portfolio; among the works that Schumann heard, many of them subsequently lost or destroyed, were string quartets, Lieder, sonatas for violin and piano, piano sonatas (or "veiled symphonies")[18] including the Second in F♯ Minor, Op. 2,[19] and a host of shorter works for piano: character pieces, scherzos (the E♭-Minor Scherzo, Op. 4, probably among them),[20] and a *Phantasie*.[21]

While scholars have often credited Brahms with inspiring the renewal of Schumann's creative energies in the fall of 1853,[22] it is difficult to gauge the younger composer's influence in this regard. For although Schumann clearly welcomed the opportunity to commune with a much needed kindred spirit, he was far from idle in the weeks immediately preceding Brahms' visit: during September of 1853, Schumann in fact completed the *Fantasie* for violin and orchestra, Op. 131, the *Kinderball,* Op. 130, for piano four-hands, and did the principal work on the Violin Concerto — no mean achievement.[23]

More than any other work completed in October 1853, the *Gesänge der Frühe* has been viewed by critics as a prime example of Schumann's ability to absorb the elements of the young Brahms' style. According to Hans Köhler, who provides an analytically detailed rationale for his assertion, the cycle "without doubt represents [Schumann's] fascinated reflection of his encounter with the genius of Brahms."[24] Yet the purportedly Brahmsian characteristics invoked to support this claim — monomotivicism, tonal ambiguity, audacious dissonance treatment[25] — are just as much a part of Schumann's compositional style: a penchant for motivic limitation is detectable in his first mature essays in the larger forms (the Piano Sonatas in F♯ Minor and G Minor, Opp. 11 and 22 respectively; the *Concert sans Orchestre,* Op. 14; and the C-Major *Fantasie,* Op. 17 — all from the 1830s); the ambiguous blend of tonalities related by third is often encountered in the cycles of miniatures from the *Papillons,* Op. 2, forward; and lastly, the idiosyncratic handling of dissonance in the first of the *Gesänge der Frühe* (as described in the previous section) has no real counterpart in Brahms' earliest extant works. And even if the opening chorale theme of the first of the *Gesänge der Frühe* betrays the influence of the finale of Brahms' F♯-Minor Sonata[26] (whose motto it presents in free inversion; cf. Ex. 6.1, mm. 1–2, and Ex. 6.2), the two compositions are radically different in ethos: Schumann's is as understated and introspective as Brahms' is impassioned and exuberant.

EXAMPLE 6.2 Johannes Brahms, Piano Sonata in F♯ Minor, Op. 2, Finale, mm. 1–2

If anything, the *Gesänge der Frühe* are better interpreted as a premonition of Brahms' late style, as evinced in the keyboard works of 1892–93, than as a reaction to his earlier manner. The "evolving" form of the cycle's last piece, whose concluding section brings together the opening music and the dreamy accompanimental pattern of the middle section, bears comparison with the design of Brahms' Intermezzo, Op. 116, No. 4. The inseparability of melody and decorative arabesques in No. 4 of the *Gesänge der Frühe* is echoed in the similar texture of Brahms' Intermezzo, Op. 117, No. 2. The tonal duality evident in the third of Schumann's pieces, where A major is strongly colored by F♯ (in both minor and major forms), looks forward to the similar third-based dispositions in Brahms' Intermezzo, Op. 118, No. 1 (A minor or A Phrygian versus F major). Likewise, Schumann's emancipation of melody from bass and vice versa at several points throughout the cycle prefigures the tonal ambiguities occasioned by Brahms' melodic third chains in the Intermezzo, Op. 119, No. 1.

Still, it would be a mistake to ascribe the "late Brahmsian" features of Schumann's cycle to the divinatory force of prophecy alone. The idiosyncratic approach to form, texture, and tonality in the *Gesänge der Frühe* rather points up the reflectivity that Schumann's late works share with late works in general. The "New Paths" that Schumann discerned in Brahms' music were already being explored in his own.

## IV

At some point shortly after the completion of the *Gesänge der Frühe* in mid-October 1853, Schumann had second thoughts about the number of pieces that would ultimately make up his cycle. Over the opening piece in the *Stichvorlage* (engraver's copy), he wrote: "Diese erste Nummer bleibt aus" ["This first number should be left out"]. The second draft of Schumann's autograph title page correspondingly reads: "Gesänge der Frühe/Vier Stücke für das Pianoforte." But before sending off the *Stichvorlage* to his publisher, Friedrich Arnold, Schumann changed his mind again: the "Vier" of the title was altered to read "Fünf."[27] Nor was this the first time that the composer had registered his indecision over the constitution of a cycle, witness his experiments with order and number in the much earlier *Papillons,* Op. 2, *Davidsbündlertänze,* Op. 6, and *Dichterliebe,* Op. 48.

Before suggesting a possible rationale for Schumann's move to suppress the first piece of the *Gesänge der Frühe,* let us briefly consider its form. In the first place, there is nothing quite like it in all of Schumann's piano music. As if to complement the hymnic quality of the piece's main theme, Schumann casts the whole as a series of chorale variations. Hence the presentation of the main idea (modulating from D to the dominant of B minor) gives way to a series of four roughly parallel strophes, the first moving (analogous to the theme itself) from B minor to the dominant of G, the second from G to an implied dominant of D, the third providing a climactic statement in D, and the last a rapidly dissolving fugato in the tonic. Proceeding simultaneously with the strophic variations is a larger "wave" form that aptly gives shape to the whole: statement and intensification (mm. 1–26), climax and dissolution (mm. 27–32), afterwave (mm. 33–39).

Interestingly enough, the second piece in the cycle discloses striking resemblances to the first, both in melodic content and formal disposition. By measure 7, which brings a variant of the opening tenor melody in the bass, we realize that the principal idea of this second piece can be easily mapped onto that of the first (cf. Ex. 6.1, mm. 1–2, and Ex. 6.3, mm. 7–8). In addition, the shape of No. 2 — a welling up to two climaxes (at mm. 16 and 29), each answered by a dissolving afterwave — obviously recalls the wave form of No. 1. The second piece, in other words, emerges as a kind of variation (artfully disguised by a more animated texture and an increase in chromaticism) of the first.

EXAMPLE 6.3. Schumann, *Gesänge der Frühe,* No. 2, mm. 1–8

Now we may begin to understand Schumann's hesitation over the inclusion of the first piece. In that the close relationships between Nos. 1 and 2 will not extend to the other pieces in the cycle (the several attempts to interpret the opening figure of the first piece as a generative motive for the cycle as a whole are fundamentally misguided)[28] a curious but, as we will see, compelling disequilibrium results: the logic of the variation procedure that governs the initial stages of the cycle (Nos. 1 and 2) appears to give way to random succession.

Yet it is likely that Schumann's approach to large-scale coherence, as highlighted by his decision to retain all five pieces in the *Gesänge der Frühe,* tended neither toward the absolutely logical nor the merely random. Broadly speaking, there are three alternative means of organizing a multimovement entity. At one extreme, a composer may opt for the harmonious unity (for which the variation chain is paradigmatic); at the other is the loose assemblage (the collection of character pieces, determined neither by number nor order, comes to mind here). Schumann, however, most frequently takes a third course. After all, his was the "mad" world (as Barthes would say) of the continual interruption, of the fragment.[29] His cycles therefore take shape as heterogeneous totalities. Since they possess no fixed structure, the critic and performer must rather *construct* them anew with every hearing or playing.

Schumann's ultimate retention of the first piece of the *Gesänge der Frühe* thus throws into relief the dialectical play of alternate modes of coherence employed throughout the cycle. On the one hand, the apparent connections — both processive and thematic — between Nos. 1 and 2 serve as agents of logical continuity. On the other hand, the links between and among Nos. 3, 4, and 5 are of a wholly different order. Specifically, Schumann employs a number of elliptical harmonic touches as a means of imparting a kind of veiled unity to the later stages of the cycle: the plagal coloring shared by the codas of each of the last three pieces; the emergence of F♯, a subsidiary tonality in No. 3, as tonic in No. 4; the subtle reinterpretation of the closing F♯ (major tonic) of No. 4 as dominant of the submediant at the opening of No. 5; the microcosmic summation of the cycle's main tonal argument in the closing gesture of No. 5: an F♯-minor *appoggiatura* harmony to the final D-major chord.

By retaining the first piece, Schumann emphasizes the esoteric construction of the work *as a cycle.* Cycles are, in the simplest sense, circles, emblems of perfection achieved through completion. And while Schumann in part conceives the *Gesänge der Frühe* along these lines — by way of the thematic recall binding the first two pieces, or the similarities in tonal and melodic character between the first and last pieces — he projects an alternate mode of cyclicity as well. For cycles are not only emblematic of closure but also of stasis, profound calm. Schumann emphasizes these qualities, in the first place, through the persistent (almost obsessive) D-ishness of his musical cycle. D, after all, is not just the tonic of Nos. 1, 2 (which eschews decisive modulation altogether), and No. 5; the same tonality strongly colors the A major of No. 3 and the F♯ minor/major of No. 4. The pieces do not move purposively toward a goal, but rather describe a potentially

infinite alternation of extroverted and reflective characters. The
stylized "Lieder ohne Worte" of Schumann's cycle thus yield a pattern
on the order of the following: No. 1 — Chorale (group song); No. 2 —
Duo (for treble and bass); No. 3 — Heroic Chorus (replete with horn
fanfares); No. 4 — *Kunstlied* (monologue); No. 5 — *Volkslied* (yet
another group song). Static too are the singularly lyric forms of the
individual pieces, most of which elaborate some variety of strophic
design: "processive" chorale variations (No. 1); tripartite, strophic form
with "wave" elements (No. 2); modified strophic form, $A^1$, $A^2$, $A^3$
(No. 3); expanded period (No. 4); "evolving" A–B–A$^1$ (No. 5).[30]

Here too Schumann opts for the path less often taken in
nineteenth-century music. His music of motionless contrasts sharply
with the forward-driving, teleological mainstream of the period. To be
sure, there is an element of prophecy in Schumann's predilection for
atemporal structures; one thinks of the quasi spatialization of the
musical flow in Wagner's *Parsifal* or Mahler's symphonies. Although
the time-scale in these works is considerably grander than that in
Schumann's far more compact cycle, the end is fundamentally the
same in each case: an overcoming of the temporal dimension. But
Schumann's prophecy is likewise tinged with an element of "madness,"
or at least of profound irony. For it is indeed unusual that Schumann
should have inscribed his temporal experiments within the limited form
of the miniature, the fragment, the realm (to paraphrase Barthes again)
of the continual interruption.

## V

Schumann's indecision over the constitution of his cycle finds a
parallel in the checkered history of its title. As Michael Struck has
recently discovered, Schumann's first thoughts about the work date
back to sometime between 1849 and 1851, when he jotted in his
*Projektenbuch* under the heading "Composition (im Plan)": "Gesänge
der Frühe. An Diotima." The mysterious Diotima reappears in the title
as recorded in the composer's "Notizen aus der Düsseldorfer Zeit" of
1851.[31] Similarly, the original title page of the *Stichvorlage* (probably
drafted in late October 1853) reads: "An Diotima/Gesänge der
Frühe/für/Pianoforte."[32] But in the wake of Bettina von Arnim's visit
with the Schumanns on 28–29 October 1853,[33] Schumann crossed out
the reference to Diotima on the first title page and drew up a second,
this time substituting a dedication to the celebrated poetess: "Gesänge
der Frühe/Fünf [previously 'Vier'] Stücke/für das Pianoforte/der hohen
Dichterin/Bettina/zugeeignet/von/Robert  Schumann/Op. 126  [*sic*]."[34]

Who is the Diotima of the original title? What are the poetic implications of the reference? Why was it ultimately dropped? How do the two components of the original title relate to one another? The reference to Diotima was a source of mystery from the start. Joachim, to whom Schumann had sent a copy of his manuscript in late November 1853, replied with characteristic frankness: "The goddess to whom your pieces are addressed has caused me to cogitate quite a bit. Diotima! Who is she? Even Johannes [Brahms] didn't know . . ."[35] There are two possible interpretations. While assembling the materials for his *Dichtergarten* (a collection of literary references to music), Schumann wrote to Joachim that he had come upon "splendid spots" in Plato.[36] If some of these spots were drawn from the *Symposium*, then possibly the "Diotima" of Schumann's title refers to the celebrated figure from Plato's dialogue. More probably, however, Schumann's reference derives from the works of Friedrich Hölderlin. Inspired by his beloved Susette Gontard (the wife of the Frankfurt banker in whose household the poet served as tutor from 1796 to 1798), the figure of Diotima makes frequent appearances in Hölderlin's elegies, many of which are titled either "Diotima" or, foreshadowing Schumann, "An Diotima," and likewise serves as one of the principal characters in his epistolary novel, *Hyperion*. While there is no direct evidence that Schumann turned to these poetic works as a source of inspiration for his last cycle of miniatures, we know from the *Erinnerungen an Robert Schumann* of his boyhood friend Emil Flechsig that already in his youth the composer had cultivated a taste for Hölderlin's quixotic verse. And in the "Materialien zu einem Lebenslauf," Schumann's autobiographical account of his literary education up through 1827, Hölderlin appears along with Klopstock and Schiller as one of the poets who most occupied the composer in his early years.[37] Lastly, it is tempting to conjecture that Joachim's plans for a "Hyperion" Symphony in the spring of 1854 were influenced by his older colleague's musical reaction to the poetry of Hölderlin in the fall of the previous year. The circumstantial evidence, in short, would seem to support the commonly held view that Hölderlin's Diotima served as a model for Schumann's.

This intersection of music and poetry has been variously interpreted. For Irmgard Knechtges, the *Gesänge der Frühe* emerge as a reflection of the intertwined *topoi* of nature, youth, and love associated with the Diotima of Hölderlin's poetic works.[38] Gerhard Dietel finds in the Diotima of *Hyperion* a symbol of peaceful (as opposed to revolutionary) reform, a political stance shared by Schumann and the eventual dedicatee of his cycle, Bettina von Arnim.[39] According to Michael Struck, the poetic idea of the *Gesänge der Frühe* is embodied in its representation of the shift from night to day, a motif of central importance in Hölderlin's *Hyperion*.[40] Hans Köhler, who views the poetic Diotima as an emblem of the synthesis of ideal and natural qualities, interprets Schumann's original title as a veiled allusion to the figure who occupied a comparable position in the composer's world, that is, Clara.[41]

Either explicitly or implicitly, all of these views feed on the notion of Diotima as a poetic representation of ideality. In Hölderlin's works, however, the figure is somewhat more finely nuanced. Indeed, Diotima's efficacy as a poetic symbol derives precisely from a richly textured complex of related motifs: the recollection of a lost paradise and simultaneous anticipation of a future Golden Age ("Menons Klage um Diotima"),[42] the wholeness of the individual attuned to Nature ("An Diotima" ["Komm und siehe"]),[43] the enlightened calm and poise of classical Greek culture ("Diotima" ["Du schweigst"]),[44] the alienated presence of such a figure of enlightenment in the modern world ("Diotima" ["Komm und besänftige"]).[45] But in *Hyperion* and the elegy "Der Abschied," Hölderlin develops an additional poetic *topos* of greater significance for our purposes. Here Diotima appears as the figure of ideality *from whom the mature poet must part*. In *Hyperion,* the illusory quality of the ideal is thematized through Diotima's gradually emergent role as destroyer of the hero's naïve hopes, and even more emphatically, through the separation occasioned by her death.[46] The theme of separation is clearly announced in the title of the elegy on Diotima's departure, "Der Abschied" ("The Farewell"), where it is configured as the sublimation (or "bleeding away") of desire.[47] Schumann replicates Hölderlin's gesture. For if Diotima is the ideal image that the mature poet summons up only to reject, then Schumann's withdrawal of the invocation in his original title may be viewed as a decisive renunciation of the subjective impulses inherent in the *Erlebnislyrik,* the lyric of personal experience. Though the reference to Diotima was removed from the title of Schumann's cycle, it remains a vital element of the work's poetic substrate.

The portion of Schumann's original title that survived — "Gesänge der Frühe" — is no less rich in poetic implications than the suppressed inscription to Diotima. Schumann provides us, through the medium of music, with a diurnal counterpart to such lyric cycles as Novalis's *Hymnen an die Nacht,* or Hölderlin's own *Nachtgesänge.* In a letter to Friedrich Arnold of 24 February 1854, Schumann noted that his latest cycle consisted of "musical pieces depicting sensations at the approach and onset of morning, but more through the expression of feeling than tone-painting."[48] Hence the "morning" of the description is not to be construed in its literal sense. As a metaphor for renewal, it may even call to mind Schumann's turn, in the fall of 1853, to some of the concerns that had occupied him in the earlier phases of his career. After a hiatus extending for almost a decade, he appears for one last time in the role of critic (and prophet): "Neue Bahnen" holds out the promise of a new *Davidsbund* headed by Brahms, Joachim, and Schumann himself. With the renewed critical activity comes a revived interest in the literary hero of his youth, Jean Paul, whose *Siebenkäs* and *Titan* Schumann and Clara reread in September and October of 1853.[49] And of course the renewed cultivation of the poetic cycle of keyboard miniatures in the *Gesänge der Frühe* (and the *Drei Phantasiestücke,* Op. 111, as well) signals a return to the "morning" of Schumann's career — and additionally, to "childhood," for each piece in the cycle resonates unmistakably with portions of the *Kinderszenen, Op. 15.* The speech-quality of Nos. 1 and 5 hearkens to the chorale-*cum*-recitative of "Der Dichter spricht." The treble-bass duo of (the D-major) No. 2 recalls the similar disposition of "Glückes genug" (another D-major piece). The dotted-rhythm fanfares of No. 3 echo the mock pomposity of "Wichtige Begebenheit" (both pieces again share the same tonality, A major). The arabesques of No. 4 offer a textural enrichment of the similarly conceived melody-accompaniment pattern of "Fast zu ernst." But while the earlier cycle presents a portrait gallery of childhood in all its immediacy, the later work filters the same motif through the reflective medium of its disembodied textures, cryptic harmonies, and "atemporal" forms. Indeed, the hyper-reflectivity of the *Gesänge der Frühe* may help account for the fact that nearly every pianist studies the *Kinderszenen* while the later cycle languishes in relative obscurity. Hopefully my comments will convince performers interested in broadening their repertory that Schumann's final poetic cycle is just as masterful, in its way, as his better-known works of the 1830s.

These observations in turn resonate with the Hölderlinian theme of reawakening. "'Dear dreamer, why must I wake you? why can I not say, 'Come, and make them true, the beautiful days that you promised me!' But it is too late, Hyperion, it is too late.'"[50] The dream from which Diotima rouses the hero of Hölderlin's novel is a metaphor for the unreflected innocence of childhood, just as the awakening motivated by her exhortation is an emblem of maturity won through reflection. Hence, Hyperion's life describes a quadripartite trajectory: from innocence to a "first" awakening of hopefulness, and from disillusionment to a "second" awakening of heightened consciousness. In "Der Abschied," the same goal (a "second" awakening to maturity) is beautifully allegorized as the poet's reunion with Diotima at some remote point in the future: "Later perhaps one day,/Diotima, we'll meet — here, but desire by then/Will have bled away . . ."[51] To put the relationship between these poetic motifs and Schumann's last cycle in figurative terms: The *Gesänge der Frühe* is situated at the point of Hyperion's "second" awakening; it is the music heard by the poet on the occasion of his reflective "second" meeting with Diotima.

We seem to have strayed far afield from our original theme. But in fact the dialectic of madness and prophecy is not so very far removed from the themes explored in Hölderlin's poetry, for it is not difficult to detect, in the idiosyncratic harmonies, forms, and textures of the *Gesänge der Frühe* a "second" and prophetic encounter with the bizzarreries of the keyboard miniatures of the 1830s that so puzzled Schumann's earliest critics and that even led the composer himself to disavow much of this music in the ensuing decade.[52] In the *Gesänge der Frühe,* the bizzarrerie (the "madness") is still present, though now tinged with the hard-won reflectivity of the mature artist. Students of Hölderlin's equally prophetic verse have had to come to terms with the poet's removal, at the age of thirty-six, to the Autenrieth Clinic in Tübingen; although he was soon released into the care of a local family, he would live out his remaining thirty-five years writing occasional poetry of little aesthetic worth, singing, and playing the piano and flute. Before their respective collapses, both poet and composer had certainly known madness — not the madness that enshrouded Hölderlin in Tübingen and Schumann in Endenich, but rather the poetic madness of the rhapsodist thematized in *Ion,* Plato's dialogue on the dialectic between inspired frenzy and cool-headed calculation in the creative process.

# Notes

1. See, e.g., Anthony Newcomb's otherwise thoughtful "Schumann and the Marketplace: From Butterflies to *Hausmusik*," in *Nineteenth-Century Piano Music,* ed. Larry Todd (New York: Schirmer Books, 1990), 258–315.

2. Carl Dahlhaus, *Ludwig van Beethoven: Approaches to His Music,* trans. Mary Whittall (Oxford: Clarendon Press, 1991; orig. publ. *Ludwig van Beethoven und seine Zeit,* Laaber: Laaber-Verlag, 1987), 219.

3. Eduard Melkus, "Zur Revision unseres Schumann-Bildes," *Österreichische Musikzeitschrift* 15 (1960): 186–88. Clara destroyed the *Romanzen* for 'cello in 1893, just as work on the collected edition (Breitkopf & Härtel) of Schumann's compositions was coming to an end. See Martin Schoppe, "Schumann und Brahms: Begegnung in Düsseldorf," *Brahms Studien* 7 (Hamburg: Patriotische Gesellschaft von 1765, 1987), 87–88.

4. Walter Dahms, *Schumann* (Berlin: Schuster & Loeffler, 1916), 300.

5. Dieter Schnebel, "Postscriptum zu Schumanns Spätwerken," *Musik-Konzepte Sonderband: Robert Schumann II* (December 1982), 367.

6. Michael Struck, *Die umstrittenen späten Instrumentalwerke Schumanns* (Hamburg: Wagner, 1984), 711–12.

7. See Gerhard Dietel, *"Eine neue poetische Zeit": Musikanschauung und stilistische Tendenzen im Klavierwerk Robert Schumanns* (Kassel: Bärenreiter, 1989), 432–87; Helmuth Hopf, "Fehlinterpretation eines Spätstils am Beispiel Robert Schumanns," in Julius Alf and Joseph Kruse, eds. *Robert Schumann: Universalgeist der Romantik* (Düsseldorf: Droste Verlag, 1981), 238–49; Reinhard Kapp, *Studien zum Spätwerk Robert Schumanns* (Tutzing: Hans Schneider, 1984); Irmgard Knechtges, *Robert Schumann im Spiegel seiner späten Klavierwerke* (Regensburg: Bosse, 1985); and Norbert Nagler, "Gedanken zur Rehabilitierung des späten Werks," *Musik-Konzepte Sonderband: Robert Schumann I* (November 1981), 303–46.

8. Hopf, "Fehlinterpretation," 245, 247.

9. Nagler, "Gedanken zur Rehabilitierung," 333–37.

10. Kapp, *Studien zum Spätwerk,* 79–101. Harold Truscott, one of the earliest — and loneliest — of the apologists for Schumann's late style, likewise called attention to the concision born of motivic limitation that, for him, characterizes the *Concert-Allegro mit Introduction,* Op. 134, for piano and orchestra, the *Faust* Overture, and the Violin Concerto; see "The Evolution of Schumann's Last Period," *The Chesterian* 31, no. 189 (London, 1957), 105–11.

11. Although the work was in the publisher Friedrich Arnold's hands by late February 1854, and although its imminent appearance in print was announced a month later in the *Signalen für die musikalische Welt,* plans for publication did not materialize until November 1855. Struck suggests that, since publication arrangements continued after Schumann's removal (on 4 March 1854) to the asylum at Endenich, the delay may have been related to the composer's illness. See *Die umstrittenen späten Instrumentalwerke,* 472–73.

12. See Robert Schumann, *Tagebücher [TB]*, vol. 3: *Haushaltbücher*, Pts. 1 (1837–47) and 2 (1847–56), ed. Gerd Nauhaus (Leipzig: VEB Deutscher Verlag für Musik, 1982), 637–41.

13. Roland Barthes, "Loving Schumann," in *The Responsibility of Forms,* trans. Richard Howard (New York: Hill and Wang, 1985), 295–97.

14. Berthold Litzmann, *Clara Schumann: Ein Künstlerleben nach Tagebüchern und Briefen* (Leipzig: Breitkopf & Härtel, 1902–10), 2:283.

15. Dahlhaus, *Beethoven,* 219.

16. Kathleen Dale, "The Piano Music," in *Schumann: A Symposium,* ed. Gerald Abraham (London: Oxford University Press, 1952), 70. Though seldom described as such, the first-inversion B♭-major chord at the outset of Brahms' D-Minor Piano Concerto, Op. 16 is just as intractable.

17. See the letter to Joachim, 8 October 1853, in *Robert Schumanns Briefe, Neue Folge,* ed. F. Gustav Jansen (Leipzig: Breitkopf & Härtel, 1904), 379.

18. See Schumann's "Neue Bahnen," in Robert Schumann, *Gesammelte Schriften über Musik und Musiker,* 5th ed., ed. Martin Kreisig (Leipzig: Breitkopf & Härtel, 1914), 2:301.

19. Entry of 2 October 1853; *TB* 3, 637.

20. See Clara's diary entry for October 1853, in Litzmann, *Clara Schumann,* 2:80–81.

21. Entry of 4 October 1853, in *TB* 3:638.

22. See, e.g., Schoppe, "Schumann und Brahms," 86–88.

23. See *TB* 3:635–37.

24. See Hans Joachim Köhler, "Nachwort" to Robert Schumann, *Gesänge der Frühe,* Op. 133, ed. H. J. Köhler (Leipzig: Peters, 1984), 16. Cf. also Peter Ostwald, *Robert Schumann: The Inner Voices of a Musical Genius* (Boston: Northeastern University Press, 1985), 267–68.

25. Köhler, "Nachwort," 16 17.

26. Cf. Köhler, "Nachwort," 16.

27. The title page is reproduced in facsimile in Paul Kast, ed., *Schumanns rheinische Jahre* (Düsseldorf: Droste Verlag, 1981), 132. Cf. also the commentary on pages 133 and 135.

28. See Arnfried Edler, *Robert Schumann und seine Zeit* (Laaber: Laaber-Verlag, 1982), 193; Dietel, *"Eine neue poetische Zeit,"* 437–45; Knechtges, *Robert Schumann,* 153–63; and Struck, *Die umstrittenen späten Instrumentalwerke,* 477–79. Although the melodic materials of most of the pieces emphasize scale degrees 1, 5, and 6, this observation alone is hardly sufficient to support the notion of a unifying *Kernmotiv.*

29. According to a provocative, soon-to-be-published study by Markus Waldura ("Zitate vokaler Frühgesänge in Schumanns *Gesängen der Frühe* Op. 133"), the *Gesänge der Frühe* consist of a mosaic of quotations from Schumann's earlier songs. I would like to thank Professor Waldura (Saarbrücken) for sharing the results of his research with me.

30. For a discussion of the prominence of strophic forms in the *Gesänge der Frühe,* see Struck, *Die umstrittenen späten Instrumentalwerke,* 480.

31. Struck, *Die umstrittenen späten Instrumentalwerke,* 465.

32. Reproduced in facsimile in Bernhard R. Appel and Inge Hermstrüwer, eds., *Robert Schumann und die Dichter: Ein Musiker als Leser* (Düsseldorf: Droste Verlag, 1991), 190.

33. *TB* 3:640.

34. See the facsimile in Kast, *Schumanns rheinische Jahre,* 132. "Diotima" was probably dropped from the title by mid-January 1854, when Schumann referred to the cycle simply as "Gesänge der Frühe" in a letter to August Strackerjan (see *Briefe, Neue Folge,* 391). Likewise, an unpublished letter of 24 February 1854 to Friedrich Arnold (quoted in Struck, 469) concerning publication arrangements for the *Gesänge der Frühe* makes no reference to "Diotima."

35. Quoted in Struck, *Die umstrittenen späten Instrumentalwerke,* 468.

36. Letter of 6 February, 1854; in *Briefe, Neue Folge,* 392.

37. See Struck, *Die umstrittenen späten Instrumentalwerke,* 466.

38. Knechtges, *Robert Schumann,* 151–52.

39. Dietel, *"Eine neue poetische Zeit,"* 484–86.

40. Struck, *Die umstrittenen späten Instrumentalwerke,* 481. Struck also suggests that the opening gesture of the cycle was conceived as a *soggetto cavato* on the names D̲iotim̲a̲ and H̲yp̲e̲rion (483, n1).

41. Köhler, "Nachwort," 16–17.

42. Friedrich Hölderlin, *Hyperion and Selected Poems,* ed. Eric L. Santner (New York: Continuum, 1990), 168–77.

43. Friedrich Hölderlin, *Sämtliche Werke* [*HW*], ed. Friedrich Beissner (Stuttgart: Cotta/Kohlhammer, 1946–74), 1/i:210–11.

44. *HW* 2/i:28.

45. *HW* 1/i:231.

46. Hölderlin, *Hyperion and Selected Poems,* 120.

47. Hölderlin, *Hyperion and Selected Poems,* 149.

48. Quoted in Struck, *Die umstrittenen späten Instrumentalwerke,* 470. As several writers have pointed out, Schumann's qualifying phrase bears comparison with Beethoven's designation of his "Pastoral" Symphony as: "Mehr Ausdruck der Empfindung als Malerey."

49. Entries of 9 September and 5 October; *TB* 3, 635, 638.

50. Hölderlin, *Hyperion and Selected Poems,* 120.

51. Hölderlin, *Hyperion and Selected Poems,* 149.

52. According to Carl Koßmaly, author of one of the first comprehensive surveys of the early keyboard music, Schumann did not always observe the fine line between fantasy, on the one hand, and confusion or excess, on the other; see "Ueber Robert Schumann's Claviercompositionen," in *Allgemeine musikalische Zeitung* 46 (1844), col. 17. By the mid-1840s, Schumann felt that only the *Phantasiestücke,* Op. 12, *Kreisleriana,* Op. 16, *Novelletten,* Op. 21, and *Romanzen,* Op. 28, demonstrated his fully formed artistic character; see his letter of (ca.) January 1844 to Koßmaly, in Hermann Erler, *Robert Schumanns Leben aus seinen Briefen geschildert* (Berlin: Ries & Erler, 1887), 1:304.

# CHAPTER SEVEN

# Franz Schubert and Franz Liszt:
# A Posthumous Partnership

## Cristina Capparelli Gerling

*In music, one of the discoveries of Romanticism was
how to hide convention, yet have it too. Established
patterns — the cadential gestures, harmonic progressions, and formal structures of the Classical
style — could be used but were generally disguised in
some way.*

Leonard Meyer[1]

## I

IN REVIEWING the many occasions in Liszt's life when he took upon
himself the task of reworking Franz Schubert's output, one is
compelled to ask, "Why?" Why did Liszt come back again and
again to Schubert's music? Those still clinging to stereotypes of Liszt
as a showy virtuoso may be puzzled over his enthusiasm for
Schubert's often simple and reserved music. And it was a true
devotion — Schubert's songs alone account for almost sixty piano
transcriptions by Liszt, later orchestral versions not included.[2] Other
Schubert works he transcribed include a considerable array of
arrangements of waltzes, marches, and the *Wanderer Fantasy*. Liszt
even undertook the first production of Schubert's opera, *Alfonso und
Estrella,* at Weimar.

Liszt's interest in Schumann and Beethoven is easier to understand. It is not surprising that, having played Schumann's Fantasy,
Op. 17, for the composer himself and heard his "Göttlich!" as
spontaneous praise, Liszt would admire Schumann's unique piano
music. And it is not difficult to perceive Liszt as the untiring cham-
pion of Beethoven. In fact, Liszt transcribed all of the Beethoven

symphonies for both solo and duo piano in order to familiarize
Europeans with these works. His generosity explains why he paid
large sums of money from his own purse to help erect a Beethoven
monument in Bonn. There is no mention of a Schubert monument, but
Liszt certainly built a "musical monument" with his large collection of
transcriptions of Schubert songs.


# II


To understand the issues involving Liszt, Schubert, and transcriptions,
we must not jump to conclusions about the status of composers whom
we now rank as giants. During the 1830s, commercial concert life
supported popular pianism, that is to say, salon music — galops and
lighthearted dances. Circus performances of the kind provided by
Thalberg, Kalkbrenner, and others delighted audiences thirsty for
spectacle and drama. This repertoire was extremely popular and
enjoyed wide circulation among both aristocratic and middle-class
audiences. A surprisingly large number of composers that have since
fallen into oblivion supplied the market with the kind of lighthearted
music audiences wanted to hear: opera fantasies, variations, rondos,
favorite opera tunes. And why not? Piano transcriptions from other
media — popular songs, marches and other light fare — were offered
up weekly by these "Philistine" composers, as Schumann called them.
Its negligible musical content leads one to wonder if this paltry
production was tolerated among artists of the rank of Frédéric Chopin,
Clara Schumann, Robert Schumann, and Franz Liszt.

The 1830s witnessed the emergence of an avant-garde movement
exemplified by the piano music composed by Schumann and Liszt.
This refined repertoire, which today is responsible for the bulk of
concert and recording programming, was not well received by the
audiences of a century and a half ago. Composers walking in Beethoven's footsteps offered a lofty, sophisticated music that could not
reach lay audiences. Robert Schumann, for instance, did not produce a
single operatic fantasy, nor did he compose conventional variations or
rondos that would have appealed to the general public taste. It is
bewildering to us to imagine that the composer of now-recognized
masterpieces such as *Davidsbündlertänze* and *Papillons* was viewed as
a remote, alien artist. His peers had to come to grips with the fact that
their compositions did not sell; their circulation was restricted to the
initiated only.[3] Even in the case of Chopin, it was the waltzes and
lighter pieces that sold well, not the larger works.

During his lifetime, Schubert's music was seldom in the public eye. At the time of his death in 1828, he was virtually unknown outside Vienna, and little known outside his own restricted circle of close friends. His instrumental music remained unfamiliar to the great majority of concertgoers.[4] In spite of having written over six hundred songs, Schubert received scant recognition in the press. Favorable mentions such as the one made in the *Allgemeine musikalische Zeitung* (April 30, 1826) by Röchlitz were rare, isolated events.[5] His songs were published thanks to the efforts of his brother Ferdinand. Between the 1830s and 1851 Ferdinand managed to issue fifty installments under the general title "Nachgelassene musikalische Dichtungen." Schumann, as the editor of the *Neue Zeitschrift für Musik*, tried to keep Schubert's music alive.

# III

Enter Franz Liszt. Liszt saw himself as an agent, a high priest with power to preserve and promote the diffusion of the holiest kind of art. He sought to give dignity to commercial music by using the transcription as a medium to divulge worthy composers far and wide. In 1835, he published a manifesto, *"De la situation des artistes,"* to make his position clear to all. It is a work in which he exhorts his fellow musicians and "all who possess a wide and deep feeling for art" to form a fellowship, a holy band, a brotherhood whose task should be:

> 1. To call into existence, encourage, and exemplify aspiring activity and unlimited development of music, and
> 2. To raise and ennoble the position of the artist through abolition of the abuses and injustices with which they are faced, and to take the necessary steps to preserve their dignity.[6]

Although Schubert and Liszt never met, their mutual teacher Antonio Salieri in Vienna constituted a link between them. Another link was the publication of Diabelli's notable variation album of 1822. In that collection, the eleven-year-old Liszt (the youngest composer in the album) appears side by side with Czerny, Cramer, Moscheles, and Schubert. Sources also cite Chrétien d'Urhan, a violinist and concert master at the Paris Opéra, as being a decisive influence on Liszt's lifelong devotion to the music of Schubert. As documented by Alan Walker, Liszt accompanied renowned singers in 1837 and 1838 in France and Austria.[7] Mme. d'Agoult, then Liszt's mistress and traveling companion, translated the texts of Schubert's songs into French.[8] Walker treats Liszt's return to Vienna as a crucial moment when the considerable number of transcriptions "that started to pour from his pen."[9] The transcriptions were performed consistently during his European tours. The challenge of transferring the sound of the voice to the piano seems to have mesmerized Liszt.

Liszt never lost the idealism of his manifesto — during his years as a traveling virtuoso he became more acutely aware of the growing disparity between his artistic vision and public demand. An advocate and selfless promoter of the music of others, Liszt not only kept abreast of each of his contemporary's achievements, but strove to promote and give encouragement to all deserving musicians he encountered. His dazzling transcriptions, along with his Rhapsodies, outsold his more serious works, which, like the works of Schumann and Chopin, had to await future generations to touch the hearts of the audience and gain a permanent place in the concert hall.

Transcriptions sold very well, as attested by the many printed editions published during the 1830s and subsequent decades. The amateur pianist in his or her drawing room was less likely to play Chopin's Op. 10 or Schumann's Op. 17 (both of which were dedicated to Liszt) or Liszt's own Paganini transcriptions, than a transcribed song in which a memorable melody with a graspable beginning, middle, and ending could be understood and followed throughout. Amateurs desired the kind of music that, if not actually lightweight, was at least accessible, directly understood, making a strong, immediate impression.

That the transcriptions were well received is consistently documented in the press of the day. The Viennese Joseph von Seyfried expressed his contentment as follows: "One must hear Liszt's Schubert in order to fully appreciate his genius."[10] Commentaries and concert reviews were usually based on the value of the transcriptions and some mentioned the fact that these were among Liszt's strongest works. While the transcriptions were heralded as a turning point in Liszt's career, his own compositions *Apparitions* and *Harmonies* were neither well received nor understood by audiences at large. Schumann referred to the *Apparitions* (1834) as "somber fantasies which resemble Chopin, but the latter has form. . . ."[11] The reviews complained about his inability to set limits, and his sense of disgruntled poetry. Critics did not hesitate to label Liszt's own compositions as formless, esoteric and opportunistic, full of "Paganinismus," and, even worse, "beautiful but without substance."[12]

By the mid-1840s, Liszt had already written and revised some of his most extended and important piano pieces, including the Transcendental Etudes, most of the pieces in *Années de pèlerinage*, and many portentous fantasies and paraphrases from current operas. How could he remain attached to the styles of the past at a time in which his own writing was already moving forward on an original path? He created a third alternative, neither his own nor Schubert's. It is no coincidence, then, that the mid-1840s witnessed the demise of his song transcriptions.

Liszt never ceased entirely to revise, to play, and even to undertake new projects. It is noteworthy that he worked on the "Wanderer" Fantasy and his Sonata in B Minor around the same time. Extended motivic transformation provides the rules for long-term connections while disturbance, turmoil and fragmentation are the expected short-term conduct of his own works. Still he could work side by side on his own extended compositions and Schubert's transcriptions. It is remarkable that the collection of waltzes selected for the *Soirées de Vienne,* as charming and delightful as they are, exhibit the same proportion of compositional integrity and care given to any of his own works.

Schubert's music can be characterized as symmetrical and based on a clear overall harmonic scheme (a clear but by no means simple one), and abundant use of indirect third relations, altered chords, and flexible modal colorings. The tonic chord tends to be stated unequivocally at the outset and at the conclusion, and the sections tend to be clearly distinguished from one another. Emphasis is placed on tonal and modal contrasts which are employed to achieve color effects.

The songs tend to be anchored to a highly emphasized tonal center. Triadic configurations function as building blocks out of which passing-note and neighbor-note motions appear as expressive.[13] There is a clear reliance on a fundamental bass line. The dominant as a secondary tonal center tends to be dodged or at least delayed. This procedure leads to extensive tonic prolongations, bringing about a frequent modal (major/minor) mixture. One of Schubert's most original procedures is to approach the flat side of a lower third by means of a common tone.[14] His transit from parallel major and minor keys develops possibilities of arresting a prominent word, of producing a subtle turn of phrase in conveying a particular mood.[15] Schubert's melody is fluent, that is, constructed within a  unified span of an overall shape "in which each individual tone is a constituent part of the whole, as well as an end in itself."[16]

The interaction and balance between the voice and piano is one of Schubert's greatest accomplishments. The manner in which he depicts the text is reflected in the setting of a magical atmosphere. The great variety of accompanying patterns provide a masterful synthesis between words and music. Each accompaniment gives a graphic reinforcement for the inner meaning of the poem.[17] The external details of the poet's scene are revealed in the lyricism of the melodic element and in the use of unexpected chromatic modulation. What could be closer to Liszt?

As in his own mature piano music, Liszt favored replacing a theme with a variant. In the Schubert transcriptions, however, he allows the melodies to stand out clearly, regardless of the amount of added figuration. In his approach to the transcribed material, one can see an attitude of devotion and respect in relation to the melodic/harmonic structure. A close examination of the transcribed songs show that the embellishments highlight, but never hide, the melody.

The vast output of Schubert songs can be classified as (1) strophic, (2) modified-strophic, (3) through-composed, and (4) "scena" type. Most of the strophic and modified-strophic songs tend to exhibit a "bite" in the last stanza. Liszt carried this practice into his transcriptions, as seen in some exquisite cadenzas added to the end of some songs; he was not deterred by the soft *diminuendo* endings.

Dieter Presser divides song transcriptions into three periods. The first runs until 1837. The middle period witnessed the greatest number of transcriptions: a total of forty-four songs arranged in cycles. This period coincides with the height of Liszt's career as a traveling pianist. The last period of simplified elegance lasts until 1847. In other words, Liszt's settings of Schubert's songs are closely and intensely associated with his years of travel.

Once settled in Weimar, Liszt no longer transcribed songs, but there are numerous accounts of his playing a few favorite transcriptions for his own enjoyment and no doubt for that of others. His dedication to Schubert lasted through the Weimar years and beyond, as attested by the transcription of other pieces, notably the cycle *Soirées de Vienne* and the *Wanderer Fantasy*. As late as 1860, Liszt worked on a voice and orchestra arrangement of six songs, and, in 1871, a choral version of *Die Allmacht*.

Though they may never have articulated it, audiences definitely expected a degree of recognition from composers as far as accepted grammar, norms, and syntax were concerned. Conventional patterns of tonality were an ingrained condition in the comprehension of the musical language. The paying public anticipated understanding relationships established between sounds. After all, hearing music depended then, as it does now, on the recognition of patterns and familiarity with the conventions.

As the foremost traveling virtuoso of the century, Liszt was constantly confronted with the overwhelming preference for the more conventional repertoire as opposed to the disparagement, even hostility generated by his own original music. Audiences found solace and comfort in an idiom heavily dependent on tonic-dominant relationships. A minimum degree of intelligibility was a necessary prerequisite. The possibility of relating one piece to another, finding common traits, were part of common expectations.[18] Clear-cut phrase structures, well-formed cadential patterns, rhythmic play, and circumscribed tonal limits shaded by interesting harmonic coloring were ingredients that assured the success of a composition.

The superimposition of two styles, Liszt's progressive and Schubert's conservative, stands at the heart of Liszt's transcriptions. His survival as the most famous and fêted artist meant the maintenance of a strong connection with public expectation. How much innovation can an artist offer without alienating his public? The experimental composer of the *Harmonies* and *Apparitions* seems to have dispensed with clear-cut cadences and other features of regularity and punctuation. Such conventions were (and still are!) the basis of learned and culturally accepted habits displayed by audiences.[19] Liszt's own music at this time displayed much originality and individuality of a kind distrusted by the conservative but paying public. How to grasp a music in which so much innovation is possible? The audacious young composer abandoned the prevalent code of restrictions as he boldly projected his fertile imagination. He intentionally attempted to develop a new musical logic and create a new discourse. By so doing, he defined a new and idiosyncratic stylistic territory, a new harmonic language within which his resourceful and venturesome instrumental usage was written.

Given the fact that the transcriptions ensured and reinforced the characteristics of the preferred stylistic mold, Liszt's readings not only maintained but also reinforced and clarified structural levels as they related to one another. It may be paradoxical of a forward-looking artist to preserve such a devout attitude to a previous manner of composing. On the other hand, Schubert stands as a midpoint between the Classical and early Romantic traditions. Liszt's use of Schubert's material is seen as a break, an interruption towards the opposite pole of increasing freedom so tenaciously sought after by later Romantic composers.

Liszt took the most effective action toward increased recognition of Schubert's music by transforming forgotten pieces into concert hits. The quality of the transcriptions attest to the utmost seriousness of purpose and intention. Liszt elevated the category to an unheard-of status as he treated the songs with all due respect, bestowing all his care to the treatment given them, as seriously as he treated Lamartine's poems inserted as epigrams in letter and spirit into his *Harmonies poétiques et religieuses* or Petrarch's *Sonnetti* into his own three piano sonnets.

According to Dezső Legány, "as far as the borderline between the original work and the transcription is concerned, it may by no means be drawn so rigidly. . . ." Whatever the source from which Liszt drew his theme, if he wrote a work in his own style it became original. But when he transcribed a work for piano without any change, as he did the symphonies of Beethoven, this was an arrangement.[20] As stated previously, Liszt established a posthumous partnership with Schubert, and as difficult as it is to give a proper classification to the process of transforming works originally composed for voice and piano into piano works, the transcriptions became *autonomous* piano pieces.

Most of Liszt's transcriptions of Schubert were published in Vienna between 1838 and 1840.[21] Other pianists were influenced by his success. Clara Schumann and Anton Rubinstein also presented Schubert's songs in concerts. The novelty eventually wore off — Walker comments that, already in 1839, Liszt complained "for the moment I am rather tired of this work."[22] As early as 1841 there were unfavorable reviews concerning the fact that the delicate melodies were overburdened by the pianist's might. Concerning the demise of the song trnascription, Norbert Miller commented that, by the fall of 1847, "[Liszt] had championed the romantic ideal of unity between interpreter and creator to an unbelievable degree. He produced so much that in the end he had to refute himself."[23]

Liszt published two cycles in 1846. The first one with six songs (R. 248, S. 563) was probably arranged in 1844.[24] The words are meticulously printed along with the melody (an exception being the first version of *Ungeduld,* in which the poem appears above the music), and the metric and harmonic construction is carefully retained. There are changes in length and in the number of stanzas used. These songs display in full the compromise between authenticity and the rich and opulent piano effects audiences demanded. However, they seem to be simply a collection of six transcriptions, with no overall harmonic or psychological unity.

By contrast, the second set, appearing in 1846 under the title *Six mélodies favorites de la belle meunière de François Schubert* (R. 249, S. 565), differs from any of Liszt's other transcriptions. He clearly intended these as a unified cycle, with structural links and connecting scaffolding. The songs and their harmonic plan relate to each other, not unlike Beethoven's *An die ferne Geliebte,* which Liszt later transcribed in 1849. For his new set of Schubert transcriptions, Liszt used songs Nos. 1, 19, 14, 17, 2 and 7 (in that order!) from *Die schöne Müllerin* (D. 795).[25] Schubert had based this cycle, as well as the later cycle, *Die Winterreise,* on the poetry of Wilhelm Müller (1794–1827). Liszt seized an opportunity to write an original piano cycle, creating his own vision of unity and coherence apart from that of Müller and Schubert. It is on this uniquely cohesive set of song transcriptions that the rest of this chapter will focus.

## IV

The six songs that Liszt chose — *Das Wandern, Der Müller und der Bach, Der Jäger, Die böse Farbe, Wohin?,* and *Ungeduld* (third version) — are arranged, transposed, and combined in such manner as to reveal a common thread. The songs exhibit a symmetrical key scheme: B♭ major, G minor, C minor, C major/C minor, G major, B♭ major. The second song in G minor has its middle section in the major parallel key; the penultimate song is written in G major. The two songs, *Der Jäger* and *Die böse Farbe*, are combined as a large ternary form. In order to secure this arrangement, the latter was transposed to C major. Modal change and modal mixture occur frequently in both middle songs. The last song, *Ungeduld*, was transposed to B♭ major, the key of the first song. Songs 1, 2, and 5 are also externally related by allusions in their texts to a brook — nature is vividly conjured in all of them. It is also significant that the musical material is treated with a freedom not previously encountered in the transcription. These songs signal some strategic departures from the original in terms of phrase disposition, inclusions of initial and final measures, suppressions and additions. Each poem appears printed before each song and no longer engraved over the melody.

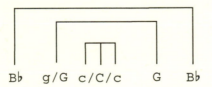

B♭   g/G   c/C/c   G   B♭

EXAMPLE 7.1. Key scheme of Liszt's *Six mélodies favorites de la belle meunière de François Schubert*

*Das Wandern.* First, a look at Schubert's setting. *Wanderschaft* is the original title Müller gave to the first poem. Schubert changed it to *Das Wandern* for the first song of *Die schöne Müllerin*. There it is set as a strophic song; that is, all verses (five in this case) are set to the same music. Schubert indicates *Mässig geschwind (Allegro Moderato)* and the accompaniment figure suggests a lively walking pace, but with a suggestion of the heaviness of a mill wheel. The sung phrases are surrounded by recurrent and identical introductions and postludes (mm. 1–4). Each unit consists of four-measure phrases arranged in pairs. The first pair is made up of two identical four-measure segments in tonic harmony (mm. 5–8, 9–12). The following two segments establish a limited degree of contrast and consist of a sequence moving from the submediant (vi, minor) to the dominant (mm. 13–16). The final segment (mm. 17–20) reiterates twice the authentic cadence and leads to the postlude. The structure of the song is shown in Ex. 7.2:

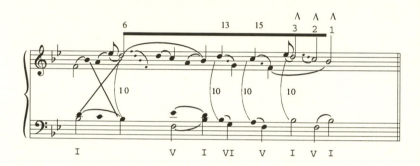

EXAMPLE 7.2.  Structure of *Das Wandern*

*Das Wandern* is based on a triadic scaffold that features D as the main melodic tone. As the principal tone, the pitch D is maintained throughout measures 5 through 12. D is also present and supported by the submediant harmony as a form of contrast (m. 13), followed by C, a lower neighbor-note configuration (m. 15). The reinstating of D signals the descent D–C–B♭ (mm. 17–20) and rounds off the melodic contour.

The fifth degree, F, like the tonic B♭, is given a high profile. Its presence is also preserved by its offbeat placement in the opening accompaniment figure (mm. 1–12). The song is built on tenths, readily allowing exchange of voices, as can be seen in Example 7.2 in measures 6, 13, 15, and 17. The pleasant tune in which D is the main tone is concealed somewhat by the accompaniment melodious counter subject in the contrasting pair of phrases (mm. 13–16). The interval of a rising sixth, F–D, enhanced by the upper neighbor-note E♭ as the main melodic feature, creates a memorable melody with which the song concludes (mm. 17–20).

The text describes a yearning for wandering about the world. This idea finds an echo in the walking pace of the accompaniment, but the harmony seems to contradict this desire: it is so basic that it hardly leaves familiar territory, shown in this instance by the use of the submediant as the only tonal contrast. The appearance of G minor (mm. 13–14) is the sole moment in which F is not present as a sustaining tone. The absence of F coincides with the temporary abandonment of the quasi-ostinato figure in the right hand of the piano. At the same time, the descending bass figure acquires a more distinct profile, which is combined with a new and insistent right-hand pattern. The change in figuration coupled with the use of vi is followed by V at the crucial point of each stanza. The idea of taking off to see the world is constantly contradicted by the return to the tonic, punctuated by authentic cadences. Schubert's setting affirms that wandering is an all-but-impossible pursuit. The figures invoked in the poem, such as the mill's owner, the mill wheels, and stones, are firmly bound to the place where they stand. The water, like the poet's thoughts, can roam freely in wayfaring dreams.

Liszt transforms Schubert's five strophes into a theme-and-variations of the tenderest sort. His composition is seventy-six measures long instead of Schubert's hundred twenty measures; the tempo marking remains the same. The introductory measures (mm. 1-4) show the compression of the B♭ figuration into a tighter hand position than Schubert's, the avoidance of the low register of the instrument, and the maintenance of the B♭-major arpeggio in the right hand. The *leggiero* vocal theme is set in a straightforward manner: that is, the pattern is remarkably simple and unencumbered. There is, however, an irresistible instance of rounding off the end of the melody with an ornamental figure (D–C–B♭, second beat of mm. 20) and a *ritardando*. This subtle addition strengthens the main melodic contour.

As the second stanza deals with lessons learned from restless waters, Liszt creates literal rivulets by adding arpeggio figures (mm. 25-26, 29-30), resulting in a very fluid setting of the second verse that cascades into higher regions of the instrument. (The melody is set in varying registers according to the hand movement so that the employment of octaves is considerably widened in the higher register.)

The third verse addresses the mill wheels. The piano writing portrays incessant movement by means of upward/downward arpeggios encompassing four octaves in four measures. This figuration creates an impression of continuous movement and reinforces the quadrature [*Vierhebigkeit* — four-squareness *Ed.*] of the phrases. The melody itself is entrusted to the left hand, which creates a remarkable depiction of wheels turning, yet another testimony of Liszt's predilection for setting melodies in the mellow medium-to-low register of the instrument. This procedure is employed in some of his most beloved transcriptions, including Schubert's *Ständchen* and Liszt's *Rigoletto* paraphrase.

Instead of writing new variations for the remaining stanzas, Liszt sums up the fourth and fifth stanzas in a *dolce armonioso* ritornello. This passage conveys the image that wandering remains but an unfulfilled desire as the B♭ bass remains fixed and unmovable. The poet's aspiration to wander is frustrated by the insistence on familiar harmonies. From measure 71 to the end, the indication of *perdendo* does not necessarily mean slackening of tempo, only of volume. Liszt's version concludes on the high D (final measure), whereas Schubert's translation of the Poet's aspirations lingered much after actual sounds could be heard.

*Der Müller und der Bach.* The last pitch, D, in Liszt's transcription of *Das Wandern* sets the stage for *Der Müller und der Bach*. The brook offers a solution to the Poet's unrequited love — that is, "down there," at the bottom of the water. This is a song of sorrow in which death is announced as a peaceful solution. In the Schubert collection it appears second to last; the Poet's decision to die is a definitive solution.

The key scheme developed by Liszt in these songs can explain at least partially the choice of this somber song as the second in his cycle. The first song is hopeful, but the poet later decides to give up life.

*Der Müller und der Bach* is written in a tripartite scheme articulated by modal changes. The protagonist announces his resolve to seek ultimate peace in part A (mm. 1–28), his voice supported by simple, grave chords. This bittersweet melody evokes a gypsy cimbalom in its use of oscillating tones shown in the example below.

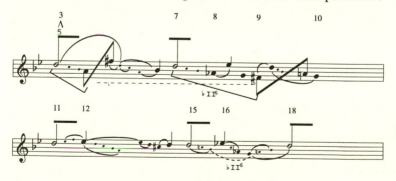

EXAMPLE 7.3. Structure of *Der Müller und der Bach,* mm. 3-18

The tonic-minor harmony, which sets the mood, is contrasted with its dominant, but G is firmly grounded as a pedal sonority. The sorrowful mood is enhanced by the use of a chromatically altered sonority. The words "Lilien," "Thränen," and "singen" ("lilies," "tears," and "[angels] sing") are accompanied by the Neapolitan chords (mm. 8, 16, 25). The word Thränen in particular receives poignant treatment as the music moves chromatically towards the cadence, C–C♯–D–G (mm. 16–20).

The brook "speaking" (section B, mm. 29–60) manifests itself in the tonic-major key and is sustained by an accompaniment figure which displays a delicate embroidery of contrary movement around tonic, dominant, and tonic (mm. 29–39, 40–48, 49–59).

EXAMPLE 7.4. Prolonged dominant in *Der Müller und der Bach,* mm. 33–40

The accompaniment in the third and final part (mm. 60–89) tells us the story is about to end. The poet's tragic yodeling in part A and the accompaniment pattern of the brook in part B are fused together. Schubert works a sensitive and deft change to G major (m. 75) which leaves no doubt as to the boy's tragic fate.

Liszt sets part A (mm. 1–28) with little or no modification. The melody is written one octave lower to better reproduce in the piano the actual sound of the male tenor voice. The indication *malinconico espressivo* faithfully indicates the mood. In Liszt's version, it is necessary to decide which version, the primary one written in tenths, or the *ossia* written in thirds, is most satisfactory. Pianist Vladimir Sofronitsky is absolutely masterful in bringing out this exchange between the lines of accompaniment while playing the upper melody.[26]

Schubert makes a quick return to part A (see mm. 59–61) as he chooses to linger one measure longer both in G major and minor. This enlargement signals a departure from the original song (see Liszt's transcription, mm. 60–64). At measure 64, Liszt offers an *ossia* version written with nine notes per measure, producing cross rhythms and undulating waves.

After measure 90, Schubert's original ends with two measures of pure, calm G major. But Liszt, with chilling effect, goes on to make explicit what has already been implied — the Poet has "taken the plunge" and has accepted the brook's offer of peace. We hear the Miller's song, filtered through a tremolo in both hands, bubbling up to the surface. [The pianist is well advised, as Liszt specifies, to use plenty of pedal. *Ed.*] This third and modified appearance of the Miller's G-minor melody, by the way, is set in a style reminiscent of Paganini's sixth Caprice, also written in the key of G minor. This Caprice was reworked as the first of Liszt's "Paganini" Etudes is the model of violin tremolo figuration extensively transferred to the piano. The final three measures of Schubert's song appear in the left hand of Liszt's version. No matter how far his imagination took him, Liszt always acknowledged Schubert's version as his fundamental source.

*Der Jäger* and *Die böse Farbe.* The most ingenious aspect of the cycle of six transcriptions, R. 249, S. 565 is the way Liszt combined two songs, numbers 14 and 17 of the original cycle into an instrumental scherzo-and-trio form. Liszt finds motivic unity in these apparently disparate songs and strives to make it clear.

Müller's text tells us that the Miller's daughter is blonde and blue-eyed, the morning stars are blue, the flowers along the brook are blue, but the girl's favorite color is green (*"Ich hab das Grün so gern!"* [song No. 13]). She admires the pretty green ribbon tied to the Poet's lute, and he quickly gives it to her as a gift. Then the Hunter appears. As the Poet realizes the extent of his beloved's attraction to green, and to insolent hunters wearing that color, he sings two increasingly bitter songs: *Die liebe Farbe* and *Die böse Farbe* (The Good Color and The Evil Color). *Die liebe Farbe* has more than a hint of sarcasm, but Liszt chooses *Die böse Farbe,* another case of making explicit what Schubert had only implied; "hunter" and "green" are now forever linked. *Die liebe Farbe* does not lend itself to the kind of development envisioned by Liszt. Thus Liszt's *Der Jäger* becomes a composite of both melodies.

Both songs are linked motivically. The descending fifths (*Der Jäger*) and ascending fourths (*Die böse Farbe*) tend to be filled in by triadic figuration followed by motion by step. Both melodies display rapid changes of tonal focus. *Der Jäger* presents constant shifts between the tonic minor and its relative major, and *Die böse Farbe* dotes on modal mixtures of tonic major and minor. A prominently placed descending arpeggio constitutes the ending pair of phrases of *Der Jäger* (mm. 23–24, 27–28). The descending arpeggio reverses direction at the very end and becomes an ascending fourth. The beginning of *Die böse Farbe* exhibits a tonic-major arpeggio (mm. 5) after the fourth has been sounded.

EXAMPLE 7.5. Motivic similarities between Schubert's *Der Jäger* and *Die böse Farbe*

Both songs rely on the fifth degree of the scale and its upper neighbor, G–A♭. As stated by Walter Everett, "the decoration of the fifth scale degree with its semitone upper neighbor note, is Schubert's principal means of portraying the wanderer's grief . . ."[27]

Although Everett was referring to the *Winterreise* songs, the observation applies to these specific songs as well. The recurrent theme in both cycles is the fate of a wandering Poet. One of the more salient melodic contour in both songs is the articulation of G–A♭ at strategic points. The G–A♭ articulation defines the profile of the first phrase of *Der Jäger* and provides an ending to *Die böse Farbe*.

Schubert's *Der Jäger* is offset by a four-measure introduction and postlude in which the left-hand figure (m. 1) is imitated canonically at the octave in the right hand (m. 2). As the song proper begins (m. 5) the voice and the piano are in unison. As the Poet extols the Hunter to

leave undisturbed the tender creature (a deer) and again to put his
hunting gear away, contrary motion underlines the situation (Ex. 7.6).

EXAMPLE 7.6. Strong contrary motion that mimics the contrasting sentiments of the text in *Der Jäger*

In *Der Jäger,* Liszt "outdoes" Schubert by taking the imitation
one step further. First there is a discarding of the introduction. The
transcribed version begins at the point where the voice makes its
entrance. Second, Schubert carries the imitative procedure for a pair
of measures. Liszt, on the other hand [literally the left one! *Ed.*],
extends this passage (See Liszt's mm. 6–7). A comparison of
Schubert's measures 13–20 with its transcribed equivalent shows the
discarding of the vocal line in favor of accentuating the contrary
movement between the parts. This pianistic design brings to mind
Liszt's own *Au bord d'une source.* This passage (mm. 10–17) is
marked *spiritoso,* almost redundant if one knows the text. Third,
Schubert writes a deceptive chord progression. The dominant of C
moves to an Ab-major chord (m. 21) and the next chord, the dominant
of Eb, moves to a C-minor chord (m. 22):

EXAMPLE 7.7. Comparison of Schubert's and Liszt's right-hand figuration in *Der Jäger*

Liszt's version creates the illusion of a three-voice invention garbed with filigree. He prolongs the discrepancy between bass and soprano by filling in the passage with a kind of chromatic writing that allows the exploration of conflicting harmonies in greater detail and creates the illusion of a prolonged time span. The "scherzo" in Liszt's version ends in a portentous cadence leading to the "trio" — *Die böse Farbe*.

Schubert's *Der Jäger* is thirty-two measures long, and the obligatory repetition extends it to sixty-four. Liszt's transcription is exactly sixty-four measures long. It has no repeat signs, and the phrases are at once related and contrasted to each other. The text has an impassioned and agitated character masterfully mirrored in Schubert's music, although the psychological time of this song is longer. Schubert mingles regular and irregular phrases and abrupt changes of mode to convey the Poet's affliction. The contrast between sections is conveyed mostly by the disquiet shown in the piano accompaniment. The main melodic characteristic is the upward melodic thrust of the fourth, the sixth, and the octave, followed by a descent at the cadence. Schubert represents the Poet's conflicted states of mind by alternating major and minor phrases. This process is further maximized by changing from one mode to the other within a single phrase:

| Intro. | Antecedent–a<br>Consequent–a¹ | b + a² | Interlude | c + a³ | Postlude |
|---|---|---|---|---|---|
| mm. 1–4 | 5–22 | 22–41 | 41–42 | 43–61 | 61–64 |
| I–i | I–i–I | iv–III V–(I–i–I) | I | I–i–I | I–i |
| | ♭II (m. 20) | ♭II (m. 39) | | ♭II (m. 59) | |

EXAMPLE 7.8. Form of *Die böse Farbe*, highlighting frequent modal shifts and three appearances of Neapolitan chord (♭II)

The first section of Liszt's transcription is based on an antecedent–consequent phrase structure (mm. 5–12 and 13–22) characterized by a great deal of modal instability. Both antecedent and consequent phrases begin by announcing the major mode in a fanfare-like figure, although the consequent phrase (a¹) is shaded by minor coloring until the resolution at the cadence (m. 22) where a return to major occurs. Similar modal mixtures occur throughout the entire song. A passage (c) in major is later changed to minor (mm. 46–51), only to change back to major where there is a phrase overlap (m. 52). The diverse accompaniment patterns chosen by Schubert depict agitation and the feeling of loss.

Liszt saw the possibility of establishing a clear and solid motivic connection between the two songs. This is achieved by placing the interval of G–C (a descending fifth in *Der Jäger* and its inversion, an ascending fourth, in *Die böse Farbe*) in an undisputed position of prominence. He accordingly transposes the latter to the key of C in order to create a strong and logical bonding with *Der Jäger*. The writing in the middle section of this newly conceived three-part structure is grandiose, and the pianistic demands are similar to some of Liszt's most taxing transcriptions in which sustained melody is decorated with varying chordal patterns of shorter duration.

Liszt departs from Schubert's song in many ways. Both the introduction and the postlude (mm. 1–4, 61–64) are discarded completely, so that the middle part is 58 measures long, six measures shorter than the original. Schubert's poignancy expressed by the use of the Neapolitan (mm. 20, 39, 59) is replaced by the minor subdominant.

Liszt displays a formidable command and mastery of harmonic schemes. It may seem a bit surprising, therefore, to note that he altered a few of Schubert's Neapolitan chords in favor of the minor subdominant. The reliance on the common key of C might account for the choice of reinforcing the link between the two middle songs of the cycle. The melodic contour of *Der Jäger* delineates a $\hat{5}$–$\hat{6}$–$\hat{5}$ melodic profile in which the $\hat{6}$ is supported by harmony associated with the minor subdominant. Likewise in *Die böse Farbe*, the $\hat{5}$–$\hat{6}$ articulates words like *todtenbleich* (pallor of death, m. 20), *Ade* (goodbye, m. 39), and *[zum Abschied deine] Hand* (saying "goodbye" to your hand, m. 59). These passages end on rapid conclusive cadences. Liszt earnestly invokes the use of the minor to produce the desired mood, matched by the descending scale pattern. Schubert's descending scale mirrors the ascending melodic minor (Schubert, m. 17), but Liszt flattens the A, producing a harmonic-minor scale (Liszt, m. 13).

The use of the minor subdominant assures a tighter connection between the two pieces in terms of character and mood; Liszt also gives measures 29–31 considerably greater weight. He expands the passage to five measures and aggrandizes the pianistic effects. As if to compensate for the missing Neapolitan sonority, Liszt turns to chromatic writing to prepare the return of the main melodic idea (m. 30).

What follows contains a profusion of octaves, arpeggios, and repeated chordal patterns. The volume of sound consequently grows. At each return of the initial section (see mm. 30–38 and 50–58) Liszt provides varying alternatives (*ossia*) of greater technical demands and challenges. The emphatic cadences merit some consideration. Some of

Schubert's cadences in *Die böse Farbe* are prepared with a tonic-minor chord preceding the dominant and resolve to a tonic-major chord which in turn overlaps with the following phrase. At the first occurrence Liszt does not adopt this harmonic scheme (compare Schubert's mm. 21–22 and Liszt's mm. 17–18). However, he does comply with the proposed blueprint at the second occurrence (see Liszt's mm. 38–39). At the third occurrence (Liszt, m. 58) the resolution is theatrically presented. The dominant chord is not immediately resolved, the next strong beat is filled with rests, and finally we arrive at . . . *Der Jäger!*

*Wohin?* The fifth song of Liszt's transcription appears also in Sauer's edition[28] in a collection entitled *Sieben Lieder von Franz Schubert;* however, both versions are identical. In Liszt's 1846 collection, *Wohin?* is the second to the last song. It is set in G major (Schubert's key).

Like the preceding song *Das Wandern, Wohin?* is about flowing water. Both songs share the fifth degree of the major scale as the main melodic tone:

EXAMPLE 7.9. Opening theme of *Wohin?*, showing emphasis of fifth degree of the scale

The six stanzas of *Wohin?* each consist of four lines of alternating rhyme. The title question, *Wohin?* (where to?), appears in line fourteen. Schubert's irregular seven-measure phrase which asks this question, supported by a chromatically altered sonority, an augmented Italian-sixth chord leading to the dominant of E (vi of G), divides the song in two halves. The song is eighty-one measures long and the question is repeated exactly at midpoint (mm. 39–41), resulting in a phrase extension. Schubert emphasizes the word "Wohin" through irregular phrase construction. The four-measure phrase is extended to six measures, not simply doubled to the more predictable eight, producing a feeling of compression. The Poet asks his question three times, but the ubiquitous brook goes on without furnishing an answer.

Schubert sets the poem as a ternary structure. The final restatement is tinted by elements of the contrasting middle part (mm. 62–65). The final descent from D to G occurs in measures 71–72, followed by

a reiterated cadence in the final tonic. The vocal line sustains a long
D, because the poem implies that the wanderer will follow the stream.

At this early stage in the original cycle the questions addressed to
the brook are still hopeful. The right-hand figuration represents the
murmuring of the brook against the walking-bass figure, which
sometimes shadows the voice (mm. 23–26, 42–45). At the return of
part A (m. 53), Schubert combines elements used both in the initial
and middle section, thus creating a synthesis followed by a coda.

Liszt, who otherwise transcribes the song as faithfully as his
wonderful pianistic and musical imagination permitted, expands the
middle six-measure phrase to ten measures and sets the question
*wohin?* to an augmented French sonority. This sonority is made of two
tritones, which urges an impending resolution. Liszt adds *crescendo,
poco rallentando,* and *espressivo,* in order to heighten the dramatic
coloring of the passage (Schubert's mm. 42–49 and Liszt's mm. 45–
56). The added measures are the result of a direct transposition of the
D-major phrase (mm. 27–34) to E minor (mm. 45–46). Liszt sets the
return section an octave higher and the piano carries the melody in
broken chords as it does in the second song of this cycle. Beginning at
measure 75, the writing changes to what Suttoni describes as presenting "the melody played by alternate hands in the midst of sweeping
arpeggios."[29] This device was originally "invented" by Liszt's rival,
Thalberg, but the latter used it so much that his audiences grew tired
of it. Liszt made frequent use of this splitting of the melody among the
hands as shown in the first and second versions of *Die Forelle,
Morgenständchen,* and his own *Un Sospiro!* In fact, its employment
became assimilated into the core of Liszt's piano technique and
musical imagination. At the final measures of *Wohin?,* Liszt explains
how to end the piece, writing *in tempo più tosto animato* and also *ppp
murmurando* (m. 89). He later adds *smorzando* (m. 94) and *mancando*
(m. 95). This last expression mark has been discussed and demonstrated by pianist Gerald Moore in his recording, *The Unashamed
Accompanist.*[30]

*Ungeduld.* For Liszt, this transcription of *Ungeduld* is his third. Liszt
transposes it to B♭, the key of *Das Wandern,* returning to the deceptive
mood in which the cycle began. To understand Schubert's and Liszt's
musical procedures, it is important to be aware of the song's title.
*Ungeduld* means "impatience." The Poet is *impatient* to declare his
love, breathlessly enlisting everything in nature to assist him. This
pervading feeling of *impatience* is transferred into music by Schubert.

The introduction poses some perplexing problems of harmonic
and rhythmic structure. A mediocre composer, insensitive to the

theme of *impatience*, for example, might have written two pairs of four-measure phrases, as illustrated in Ex. 7.10.

EXAMPLE 7.10. Hypothetical version of *Ungeduld's* introduction

In Schubert's version, however, *impatience* takes over, the balancing fourth measure of each hypothetical four-measure phrase is dispensed with — you can almost hear the "splice"! (Ex. 7.11.) The strong dominant cadence proves unstable, V becomes v, which in turn becomes ii and proceeds as ii--V--I in the subdominant. The bass line leads the way from IV to ♯IV to V, just in time to welcome the singer.

The question of irregular phrase construction in Schubert's music merits consideration. He created some very beguiling problems of phrase rhythm by the use of extensions and overlaps in the opening phrases of his most memorable pieces. The opening measures in the first movement of the last two piano sonatas, D. 959 and D. 960 (1828), are worth mentioning as examples of irregular phrasing. The song *Täuschung* (Deception) from *Die Winterreise* is a virtual catalog of musical deceptions, sideslippings, and devious three-measure phrases.

EXAMPLE 7.11. Schubert's actual version of *Ungeduld's* introduction

EXAMPLE 7.12. Simplified sketch of *Ungeduld,* mm. 1-9

In *Ungeduld,* Schubert needs to accommodate five lines of poetry in each part to depict the intense, *impatient* pursuit of a goal. Propulsive iambic figures create the illusion of constant progress toward each sixth line of verse, in which impassioned declarations of eternal love are expounded (mm. 19–26). Each declaration, complete with word repetition, is given a luxurious eight measures all its own.

The text, ironically, is written in the imperfect subjunctive and expresses what the Poet ardently wishes for. Schachter observes that "this is typical of Schubert's method, which sustains a remarkable equilibrium between sensibility to text and compositional integrity."[31] As Ex. 7.11 shows, the verses are accommodated in duple hypermeter.

The song itself (without the piano introduction) discloses a melodic ascent D–Eb–F, already present in the introduction, and confirmed at length in the song proper. The harmony moves by tenths and there is constant voice exchange. The song can be understood as the unfolding of the tonic harmony (mm. 9–18) followed by a vigorous display of dominant harmony (mm. 19–24), and a brief conclusion in the tonic (mm. 25–26):

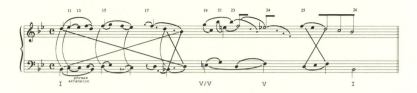

EXAMPLE 7.13. Graph of *Ungeduld* without the piano introduction

The ascent to F is articulated by supporting passing harmonies (mm. 9–18), but the overall motion displays B♭ major as the main guarantor of the harmonic scheme, as seen in the slow-moving exchange of voices:

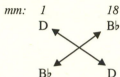

After the built-in haste of the introduction, the song proper is constructed in a sequence of five phrases (mm. 9–18) arranged in pairs corresponding to the five verses that precede verse six, the declaration of love (Ex. 7.14).

The interval of a rising sixth (m. 9, F–D; m. 11, G–E♭) provides the necessary impulse for the forward-moving melody. The initial phrase segments show that the melody receives support from the bass so that both voices move sequentially at the interval of a tenth (mm. 9–10, 11–12). This movement comes to a temporary halt at measure 13, as the soprano F (first eighth note) is soon resolved to E♭. The bass note C lingers, thus delaying the appearance of D and F until the next measure (m. 14). When the apparent goal F is reached in the next pair of measures (m. 15), the harmonic context changes to that of a diminished chord resolving back to C minor. Rhythmic displacement between the main melodic tones in their relationship to the bass dislocates the interval of a tenth. As a result there is dissonance between the parts (see mm. 13–18). The ensuing harmonic delay provides the two extra measures in which to carry the fifth line of verse. As the voices exchange places, a few subsidiary but nevertheless colorful sonorities emerge (see the diminished sonority in m. 15) and the illusion of movement is created. The declaration of love unfolds over the next eight measures, featuring a series of elaborate dominant-preparation chords.

EXAMPLE 7.14. *Ungeduld* graph, illustrating slower harmonic motion of the phrase beginning at m. 20, the "declaration of love"

The constant urge to move forward is supported by the diminished-chord sonority (mm. 21–22). This conveys a sorrowful tone, matching the insistent utterance. The diminished sonority leads on to an inverted tonic; there is no firm ground on which to stand until measure 24. The psychological time of the eight-measure refrain is at least equivalent (if not longer!) to the preceding ten-measure phrase. Schubert supports the text with unstable sounds which expresses unfulfilled longing.

Liszt was obviously intrigued by *Ungeduld* — S. 565 represents his third transcription of it. There is ample evidence in his own works that he was attracted to irregular phrase constructions and unusual uses of *Vierhebigkeit*. His *Mephisto Waltz* breaks the molds of regularity and sets an unusual *Vierhebigkeit* simply by beginning with a clearly indicated measure of silence. The expected strong points then fall out of their expected places, posing an intriguing problem for the performer.

We have shown how Schubert musically highlighted *impatience* within Müller's poem; there are subtle indications that Liszt added his own contributions of *impatience* to Schubert's song. Liszt transcribed three verses, omitting the anxiety-ridden fourth. Was he *impatient* to end it? Furthermore, the introductory piano measures feature jumps and hand-crossings, an odd and challenging choreography for the performer. The ornaments briefly pose as melody. It is quite difficult not to look hectic and *impatient* while executing those first six measures! When they return between verses 2 and 3, Liszt adds *incalzando,* which means "chasing or pursuing" — *impatiently,* of course.

The first stanza displays piano writing not very far of Schubert's original. The texture is made thicker as a result of doubling chord tones. The transition between the first and second stanzas incorporates denser texture and modified placement of hands (mm. 26–33).

The second stanza exhibits what can be defined as orchestral writing adapted for the piano. Contemporaries like Bellini were fond of passages in which the singer's voice is echoed by orchestral instruments a fraction of a beat later. Schumann absorbed this manner of writing in the first episode of his *Humoresque,* Op. 20. Chopin occasionally uses this kind of writing but he is much more subtle. Examples can be seen in the Preludes, Op. 28 (specifically Numbers 1 and 8), and the Etudes (Op. 10, No. 1, and Op. 25, No. 12). Liszt's operatic fantasies incorporate this device with mind-boggling variety and subtlety. The transcriptions of the second stanza of *Ungeduld,* like its counterpart in *Das Wandern,* expands the scope of Schubert's figuration while maintaining his basic harmonic and melodic structure.

Liszt's transcription of the third stanza pays the clearest homage to Schubert's own style of piano writing.[32] Liszt sets this stanza in the same piano texture as Schubert's Impromptu in B♭ (first variation). Liszt adds his own touch of *impatience* by contributing a nervous four-against-three rhythm between the hands. Finally, Liszt adds the finishing touches by echoing the last melodic fragment in the left hand while the right hand ascends to F. By transposing *Ungeduld* to B♭, Liszt has brought the cycle full circle, and presented a more life-affirming view of the world than has Schubert.


# V


*Six songs of Franz Schubert in simple style* is a deceptive title. The songs are scarcely "light" piano music for bored ladies. The pianistic requirements are equal to the ones found in some of his own piano pieces, especially the ones with descriptive titles: *Au lac de Wallenstadt, Eglogue,* and the *Etude paysage.* These are Liszt's own "songs without words." His transcription of Schubert's cycles transformed the songs into character pieces. In the process, Liszt drifts between

absolute and program music. The pianist acts out the melody, the
poem provides the backdrop for the action.

Schubert was not known as a gifted or virtuoso pianist, but his
melodic imagination left Liszt spellbound. Liszt combined Schubert's
unambiguous melodies with the instrumental demands of a later
period. The result, however, is not merely the addition of virtuosity to
attractive and well-formed melodies — it is musically cogent.

There is a degree of permanent alteration involved in the process
of transcribing — as Leonard Meyer said, "interpretation always
involves some deformation of prior meaning."[33] Liszt's transcriptions
are not merely a substitute medium for presenting Schubert *Lieder*
when no singer is present; rather, they represent Liszt's own vision
and understanding of Schubert's music.

# Notes

1. Leonard Meyer, *Style and Music: Theory, History and Ideology* (Philadelphia: University of Pennsylvania Press, 1989), 222.

2. Alan Walker, "Liszt and Schubert Song Transcriptions," *Musical Quarterly* 75 (winter 1991): 248.

3. Anthony Newcomb, "Schumann and the Marketplace: From Butterflies to *Hausmusik*," in *Nineteenth-Century Piano Music,* ed. Larry Todd (New York: Schirmer Books, 1990), 265–75.

4. [Schubert's friends hounded him to present himself and his works in concert. One night he finally relented, and programmed, among other works, the première of the Bb-Major Piano Trio. Sadly, he received almost no mention in the press — Paganini had come to town. *Ed.*]

5. Maurice Brown, "Franz Schubert," *The New Grove Dictionary of Music and Musicians,* ed. Stanley Sadie (London: Macmillan Publishers Limited, 1980), 18:773.

6. Alfred Einstein, *Music in the Romantic Era* (New York: W. W. Norton, 1947), 31.

7. Walker, "Liszt and Schubert."

8. Paula Rehberg, *Liszt: Eine Biographie* (Mainz: Schott, 1978).

9. Rehberg, *Liszt,* 50.

10. Thomas Kabisch, *Liszts Transkriptionen Schubertscher Lieder,* vol. 23 of *Berliner musikwissenschaftliche Arbeiten* (Munich: Musikverlag E. Katzbischler, 1984), 69.

11. Kabisch, *Liszts Transkriptionen,* 71.

12. Kabisch, *Liszts Transkriptionen,* 70.

13. Robert Cogan, *Sonic Design* (Englewood Cliffs, NJ: Prentice-Hall, 1976).

14. James Webster, "Schubert's Sonata Form and Brahms' First Maturity (II)," *19-Century Music* 3 (July 1979): 61.

15. Brown, "Schubert," 18:773.

16. Heinrich Schenker, *Counterpoint,* trans. Rothgeb and Thym (New York: Schirmer Books, 1987), 20.

17. Brown, "Schubert," 18:775.

18. Leonard Meyer, *Explaining Music* (Chicago: University of Chicago Press, 1973), 16.

19. Meyer, *Style and Music,* 208.

20. Dezső Legány, "New Directions in Liszt Research," *Journal of the American Liszt Society* 20 (December 1986): 126.

21. David Owen Norris, "Liszt's *Winterreise,*" *The Musical Times* 126 (September 1985): 521–25.

22. Alan Walker, *Franz Liszt: The Virtuoso Years, 1811–1847* (New York: Alfred A. Knopf, 1983), 257.

23. "Das romantische Ideal der Einheit von Schöpfer und Interpret zum Siege und ad absurdum. Er schöpft alle Möglichkeiten aus, um sich am Ende

selbst zu wiederlegen." Norbert Miller, "Musik als Sprache zur Vorgeschichte von Liszts symphonischen Dichtungen," in *Beiträge zur musikalischen Hermeneutik,* ed. Carl Dahlhaus. Studien zur Musikgeschichte des 19. Jahrhunderts, vol. 43 (Regensburg: G. Bosse, 1975), 223–87.

24. Imre Sulyok and Imre Mező, preface to *Liszt Klavierwerke, Freie Bearbeitungen,* vol. 7 (Budapest: Editio Musica, 1988), xi.

25. Sulyok and Mező, preface to *Liszt Kavierwerke,* xii.

26. Vladimir Sofronitsky, *Schubert/Liszt Transcriptions,* vol. 2, ARL2.

27. Walter Everett, "Grief in *Winterreise*: A Schenkerian Perspective," *Music Analysis* 9 (July 1990): 157–75.

28. Franz Liszt, *Lieder Bearbeitungen,* vol. 9 of *Liszt Klavierwerke,* ed. Emil von Sauer (Frankfurt: Peters Edition), 66–71.

29. Charles Suttoni, introduction to *Piano Transcriptions from French and Italian Operas* (New York: Dover Publications, 1982).

30. Gerald Moore, *The Unashamed Accompanist,* Seraphim 60017.

31. Carl Schachter, "Motive and Text in Four Schubert Songs," in *Aspects of Schenkerian Analysis,* ed. D. Beach (New Haven: Yale University Press, 1983), 64.

32. Once before, Liszt had taken a Chopin's style and, as a "template," applied it to a song; specifically, Liszt used Chopin's Nocturne style, and applied it to his otherwise light-hearted song, *Meine Freuden,* to produce in effect, a "new" Chopin Nocturne! See Liszt's *Lieder Bearbeitungen,* ed. Sauer, 177–80.

33. Meyer, *Style and Music,* 144, n. 23.

# CHAPTER EIGHT

# Brahms: Where Less is More

## Antony Hopkins

## I

WHEN his first piano teacher Otto Cossel unselfishly passed on the ten-year-old Brahms to Eduard Marxsen, with whom he himself had studied, he did so in the belief that his gifted pupil deserved the best tuition available in Hamburg. Marxsen was renowned as both pianist and composer and had initially been unwilling to accept Brahms at such a tender age; however, fears that the child might be exploited as a prodigy caused him to relent, and though at first he insisted that lessons with Cossel should continue, it was not long before he became the boy's sole musical mentor.

Little Brahms had created something of a sensation when he had played chamber works by Mozart and Beethoven as well as some solos at a public concert, so Marxsen was aware that he had been entrusted with the development and nurturing of an exceptional talent. Fortunately for the child, Marxsen proved to be an exceptional teacher, for although the original intention was to develop the boy's pianistic talents it soon became clear that something far more than keyboard studies was desirable. Refusing to accept payment from the impoverished parents, Marxsen proceeded to give young Brahms a thorough grounding in harmony and theory in addition to conventional piano lessons.

In many respects Brahms' adolescence was far from ideal, making his contribution to the family's expenses by playing popular music in the notorious dockside taverns (Lokale). There, during his most impressionable years, he would be surrounded by foul-mouthed drunken sailors and shrill-voiced whores who were not above flirting outrageously with the good-looking youth as he played. The experience produced a psychological inhibition with regard to any emotional relationship with women that was to remain for the rest of his days. He was shocked, indeed revolted, by much that he saw going on

around him, and would keep a volume of German literature open on
the music stand; reading as he continued to play was a way of shutting
himself off from the distractions of blatant lewdness and, if nothing
else, it certainly taught him the art of concentration. For anyone less
strong-willed, these formative years might have proved morally
destructive, leading almost inevitably to alcoholism and a pile of
unfinished works. Fortunately for us, he was able to emerge with his
integrity intact, and with a determination to storm the heights as
pianist and composer.

Even the most gifted student needs time to practice, time to
develop the purely physical dexterity that concert performances
demand. With Marxsen's help and encouragement, Brahms was
anxious to improve his skills in both capacities, but the need to earn
his keep meant that he was too often deprived of time; endless late
nights thumping the piano in smoke-filled taverns so exhausted him
that he would stagger home in the small hours reeling from tree to tree
like a drunkard. Keenly self-critical as he was, he must have realized
how detrimental such a life-style was to the development of his gifts,
and it seems that a profound insecurity began to affect him so that
even in his maturity he was often plagued by doubts about whatever
composition he was engaged on. (A classic instance is the D-Minor
Piano Concerto, Op. 15, which began as a sketch for a symphony,
developed as a two-piano sonata, and finally materialized as a
concerto.)

Those who are insecure often speak loudest, and Brahms' first
serious compositions show a determination to impress. The Scherzo in
E♭ Minor, Op. 4 (1851), written when he was only eighteen, treads
unashamedly into Beethoven's territory both in its terse rhythms and in
the way they are developed. The three piano sonatas, Opp. 1, 2, and
5, completed when he was still only twenty, seem to set out to conquer
the world by force of arms.

Already the keyboard appears to be an inadequate medium; indeed
many passages in the Third Sonata, Op. 5, sound and feel more like
the transcription of an orchestral score than a work conceived for solo
piano. This is especially true of the fourth movement, where Brahms
uses the title "Intermezzo" for the first time, coupled with *Rückblick*
[Reminiscence].

The opening phrase provides a deeply saddened remembrance of
the untroubled lyrical theme that began the second movement (*Andante
espressivo*), but who can play these notes without imagining the sound
of two clarinets, or climb to the anguished climax (mm. 38–43) and
not long for trombones and timpani? Here, the very same composer
who was so unsure of his ability to write for the orchestra that time

and time again he held back from committing himself seems to be thinking in purely orchestral terms.

Since the piano sonatas had earned considerable praise from Schumann, Liszt, Berlioz, and Joachim, Brahms had every right to feel proud of them, yet doubts about his ability to handle these large forms must have assailed him. It is interesting to note that, superb pianist though he was, he never attempted to write another solo sonata for his favorite instrument.[1]

The three violin sonatas, the two for cello, and the two for clarinet, are works of high quality, but none has the heroic aspirations so evident in the much earlier piano sonatas.

Aware that his compositional technique was still not adequate to cope with major forms, Brahms embarked on a period of self-tuition that is probably without parallel. As a boy he had been well taught by Marxsen — that cannot be doubted; but the lessons had not provided him with the technical resources he needed to realize his ambitions as a composer. Although he was already in his twenties with some substantial compositions behind him, he entered into an agreement with Joachim that they should regularly exchange exercises in counterpoint and fugue. Punctilious about completing his own contributions on time, he would reprimand Joachim when he failed to deliver, even establishing a system of fines, the penalty to be paid in books rather than money. The fruits of this self-imposed drudgery are lost, but we need not be concerned with them save as an indication of his character. More to the point, he became almost obsessed with variations as a form, realizing that there was no better way of developing his technique as a composer.

A string of such compositions ensued over the next few years — Thirteen Variations on a Hungarian Song (1853), Sixteen Variations on a Theme by Robert Schumann (1854), Eleven Variations on an Original Theme (1857), Twenty-five Variations and Fugue on a Theme by Handel (1861), Ten Variations on a Theme by Robert Schumann for piano duet (1861), and Twenty-eight Variations on a Theme by Paganini in two books (1862–63). Understandably, these works are variable in quality as for that matter are the variations written by Mozart and Beethoven, but all show considerable inventiveness, while those on the themes of Handel (Op. 24) and Paganini (Op. 35) are outstanding. Moreover, while their prime purpose was clearly to develop his skills as a composer, they also served to extend his technique as a player, even though a career as a virtuoso held little appeal for him. All those who heard him play admired his musicianship and interpretive insight but, at a time when Liszt's virtuosity had set an unprecedented standard, Brahms' command of the keyboard appears to have been less than absolute. Even Eugenie Schumann, who must have thought of Brahms almost as an uncle, wrote that his performance of his own music was highly interesting "if not always satisfying." If this seems to damn him with faint praise, she made up for it when she described his playing of the more passionate passages "as though a tempest were tossing clouds, scattering them in magnificent fury."[2]

The cultivation of piano technique clearly held a considerable fascination for him. When he was only twelve, he told Marxsen that he was practicing Weber's testing *Moto Perpetuo* by transferring the continuous rapid passages from the right hand to the left, an exercise in pianistic masochism that was later published in 1869. Other transcriptions exist, such as the arrangement of Bach's famous violin Chaconne which Brahms gave to the left hand only, or the fiendishly difficult version of Chopin's Etude in F Minor, Op. 25, No. 2, in which the swiftly murmuring notes of the original are turned into sixths and thirds. But perhaps the most striking evidence of his preoccupation with technique — even more than the Paganini Variations, which he called "Studies for the Pianoforte" — is to be found in the book of Fifty-one Exercises (1893); designed to search out every possible weakness in the control of fingers, hand, and wrist, they also cultivate a feeling for tonality since they should be transposed into every key. (Their publication date is totally misleading, since they were developed over the period when he was still forced to give lessons to earn some welcome cash.)

After the strain, both physical and intellectual, of so many sets of variations, it is hardly surprising that the next work for piano was by way of light relief. Originally conceived in 1865 as a set of sixteen waltzes, Op. 69, for piano duet, they were rewritten in the same year as piano solos. Compared with the elaborate waltzes of Chopin they are true miniatures; few extend beyond a single page, yet each establishes its own character in a matter of seconds. It is as though the composition of so many variations had established a particular time-scale in Brahms' mind so that he was hesitant about stretching his material to more conventional lengths. Yet although the waltzes may be lacking in development, they positively luxuriate in melody; few composers can challenge Brahms, let alone surpass him, in sheer melodic beauty when he is in this amiable mood. It was a mood he was to return to a few years later in the enchanting *Liebeslieder* waltzes for vocal quartet and piano duet (Op. 52, 1868–69; Op. 65, 1874). One feels that such deliciously tuneful music could only have been written in Vienna where, for much of the latter part of the nineteenth century, the Strauss family had provided a seemingly inexhaustible flow of waltzes. Was it not Brahms who autographed a fan belonging to Frau Adèle Strauss with the opening notes of the "Blue Danube" Waltz and the words "Unfortunately not by Brahms . . ."

After the waltzes Op. 39 of 1865, Brahms seems to have lost interest in writing for piano solo. Certainly the piano still features in a number of works and in various roles — as collaborator in chamber works, as the accompaniment in songs, and in providing the original two-piano version of the so-called Variations on a Theme of Haydn.[3] It was not until 1878 that Brahms returned to the piano with the eight short pieces of Op. 76, the point towards which this essay has been aiming. If so far there seems, in this chapter, to have been a suggestion more of a catalog than a study, it is because one cannot fully appreciate the achievement of the many short pieces which thereafter appeared without being aware of the long and often arduous progress which ultimately led to them.

To summarize briefly: at first we find Brahms as hero-figure, setting out to conquer the world with the classically respectable "weapon" of the Sonata; secondly we find the long period of self-tuition when, through the extensive use of variations, he develops a technique more suited to his aims; third comes a period (not discussed here) when he responds to the lure of the human voice with a great number of songs, choral compositions, as well as substantial chamber works, and, after much heart-searching over some twenty years, the first two symphonies. What prompted him to return to the piano as a solo instrument after a period of thirteen years we cannot say. Preoccupied as he had been with the Second Symphony and the Violin Concerto, he may have felt the need for a less demanding form of composition. It was a form that had been anticipated as early as 1854 in the Four Ballades, Op. 10.[4] Here the word "Ballade" does not imply any similarity to Chopin's far more extensive compositions sharing the same name. Schumann, of whom Brahms was a devoted disciple, much preferred descriptive or literary titles for his compositions, and it seems likely that Brahms in his Op. 10 was simply trying to follow Schumann's example. Brahms was often at a loss for titles and even, when submitting the Op. 76 pieces to his publisher Simrock, wrote "Can you think of a title?" He finally opted for "Capriccio" and "Intermezzo," the latter term being allocated to the gentler, slower pieces. What is certain is that it was in these more economical and concentrated forms that he found the ideal mould for the presentation of his mature inspirations; if there is any truth in the saying "Less is more," it is to be found here, for while the piano sonatas and some of the sets of variations are seldom performed, these short works will undoubtedly continue to give joy and satisfaction to performers and listeners alike for as long as piano music survives. If the essence of genius can be distilled, we will find it here.


# II
# Piano Pieces, Op. 76

The first of the set was composed in 1871, but it was not until 1878 that Brahms seems to have decided to devise a group of contrasting pieces; five were written in that year as his enthusiasm for the project increased and the full collection of eight was duly published in 1879.

CAPRICCIO IN F♯ MINOR, OP. 76, NO. 1, *Un poco agitato 6/8.* The influence of Schumann is very evident in this, both in the figuration and in the mood. It is an autumnal piece with gusting winds and scurrying leaves and was a favorite of one of Brahms' dearest friends, Elizabeth von Herzogenberg, who was a talented enough pianist to be able to master its considerable difficulties. (Clara Schumann thought it "horribly difficult.") The swirling sixteenths are looped around a sequence of basic harmonies, one to a measure. After a descending cascade of the dominant C♯ major, played by both hands two octaves apart, the main theme appears:

EXAMPLE 8.1. Op. 76, No. 1, mm. 14–17

Change the second note D♮ to a D♯ and we find a curious reminder of Mozart's favorite "motto" theme, so brilliantly exploited in the finale of the "Jupiter" Symphony.[5] Although this is surely no more than coincidence, Brahms treats the first four notes in quite a symphonic manner, modulating through various keys (A minor, G minor), extending them through a wider arc and even producing an ingenious variant involving augmentation and a sort of retrograde inversion.

EXAMPLE 8.2. Op. 76, No. 1, mm. 38–41 — reversal of pairs of measures reveals strong resemblance to Ex. 8.1

This leads to a more exact inversion of Ex. 8.2 in a middle register before a return to the opening material, its coils now thrown even wider. A long descent in broken octaves (which surely supplied the formula for the comparable descent in the Second Concerto, first movement, measures 338–419, sketched in the same year) leads to an altogether calmer treatment of the four-note motif which shows an increasing longing to be allowed a resolution into F♯ major. Brahms had a particular gift for bringing compositions to a close with an expressive coda and this is one example of many. Although the ultimate destination of the tonic major has been implied for eleven measures it is only in the last three that the music finally comes to rest, free of any suggestion of dissonance.

CAPRICCIO IN B MINOR, OP. 76, NO. 2, *Allegretto non troppo 2/4.* In this piece, perhaps more aptly named "Capriccio" than its predecessor, the bass notes provide an important feature. The first four measures show a chromatic descent from B to E; next we find a circling around the dominant (F♯) which is then established as a new tonic with a genuine cadence into F♯ major. After a repeat (which must be observed) the music turns surprisingly towards D major with playful thirds dancing above a reiterated D which stays constant for four measures regardless of harmonic considerations. The expected resolution onto A major (the dominant of D) is neatly by-passed with an unexpected E-major chord before some measure of harmonic propriety is restored with a dominant seventh on A leading us back to D major. This can truly be described as "capricious," as can the couple of joking modulations ("If at first you don't succeed, try, try again.") which lead us back to a reprise of sorts in the original B minor; this time the phrase ends in B major instead of modulating to the dominant.

A contrasting middle section follows in the unforseen key of C major, although occasional B♭s cast doubts on the new tonality. These enable Brahms to play an ingenious trick, a musical pun which exploits the enharmonic change B♭–A♯. Just when the B♭ seems to be taking charge it is called to order by several A♯s which duly take the proper turning that leads back to B major.

EXAMPLE 8.3. Op. 76, No. 2, mm. 56–62

An ingenious reprise reassembles the original material in a different order, with some intriguing new arrangements of the opening theme, none more so than this, where what is written on the page effectively disguises what the ear detects with ease.

EXAMPLE 8.4. Op. 76, No. 2

A brief flirtation with the alien territory of F major during the last few measures makes the final resolution onto B major all the more satisfying.

INTERMEZZO IN A♭ MAJOR, OP. 76, NO. 3, *Grazioso 4/4.* The avoidance of first beats in the main theme gives it an almost disembodied quality that conveys an especial tenderness. Although only the piano can convey the sounds Brahms had in mind, there is a suggestion of a harp in the delicate accompaniment, while the triplet figure that takes over in measures 11–13 has a distinctly oboe-like quality, topped briefly by imagined violins in measures 14–15. However, strings would bring too great a richness of sound in a movement where restraint must ever be the watchword. Nowhere is there a dynamic above *piano* and even the one measure that looks like a real climax (m. 14) has a precautionary *pianissimo* in the left-hand part. It is the first of a number of what I call "Dear Diary" pieces, surely designed for the player to perform in the intimacy of a room in the home rather than in a public concert hall.

INTERMEZZO IN Bb MAJOR, OP. 76, NO. 4, *Allegretto grazioso 2/4.* Here too there is an avoidance of technical display with not a single *forte* to be found. The opening melody is poised delicately above a dominant pedal point and a gently rocking rhythm. In the fifth full measure, the left hand discreetly prompts the right, suggesting the next phrase which, after a brief excursion into Ab major, settles rather poignantly into G minor. There is a subtle chromatic counterpoint in the "alto" part whose essential resolution onto a Bb is not always conveyed in performance (mm. 11–13).

EXAMPLE 8.5. Op. 76, No. 4, mm. 11–13

There follows a little flurry of thirds and sixths in the shadows that can scarcely be regarded as a concession to virtuosity, though it demands playing that is both supple and subtle. The repeat that Brahms then requests seems perhaps to be more an observance of a convention than a musical necessity, but it may be that its purpose is to draw greater attention to the lovely excursion into Gb major that now follows. This is the lyrical heart of the piece, though there is a suggestion of anguish in the strange dissonances that appear (albeit by logical progressions) in measures 28–30. A classical reprise brings back the material of the first page, this time with an ending that seems to disappear into thin air.

CAPRICCIO IN C♯ MINOR, OP. 76, NO. 5, *Agitato, ma non troppo presto 6/8 (3/4).* The warning against too reckless a tempo is just as well, since stormy waters lie ahead. This is not merely the most substantial of the set but also the most demanding technically. In it Brahms exploits one of his most characteristic rhythmic patterns — the combination of 3 x 2 and 2 x 3, the accompaniment a surging and chromatic 6/8, the melody a boldly striding 3/4. From time to time, progress is briefly halted *(sostenuto)* as though a hunter stands to scan the horizon before plunging onward; a dramatic climax is reached when, for three measures, the right hand has three G♯ octaves in different registers over snarling chromatic octaves in the bass (mm. 33–35).[6]

A reprise of the opening material leads to a brief respite *(poco tranquillo)* which may or may not be intended to suggest an inversion of the initial theme but which at any rate bears a family resemblance.

Three times more we find the curious momentary halts (*sostenuto*), at first *pp*, then *fp* and lastly *f sempre più*. There follows a stormy passage with energetically leaping octaves in the bass and agitated syncopations in the right hand; it concludes with an ingenious new version of the clanging G♯s of measures 33–35. Equally striking is the way in which the opening material is now given even greater urgency by an accompaniment in sixteenths. Gradually, the music seems to become more expansive and even appears to be heading for a quiet ending, but Brahms has a further surprise for us in a brilliant coda which like a sudden tidal wave threatens to swamp us. The effect is produced not just by a tumult of notes but also by the way in which the bass notes are grouped in fives.

EXAMPLE 8.6.  Op. 76, No. 5, mm. 111–114

INTERMEZZO IN A MAJOR, OP. 76, NO. 6, *Andante con moto 2/4*. This gently flowing but not sentimental piece is full of rhythmic subtleties, not just the three against two which is so characteristic of Brahms, but a modification in which the first note of an implied two is replaced by a rest.

EXAMPLE 8.7.  Op. 76, No. 6, mm. 1–5

This imparts a curious unease to what might otherwise have been altogether too bland. The importance of the left-hand syncopations can best be appreciated by bringing them forward by an eighth and playing them *with* instead of *after* the melody notes in the right hand. The melody itself raises questions; does it consist primarily of rising sevenths (E–D, B–A) so that the triplets are simply an enfolding accompaniment, or are the second and third notes of the initial group (E–E–A–D) integral to the melody? Such questions must be answered by the performer; analysis can only pose them.

The central section in the related key of F♯ minor is notable for the greater length of the phrases, here four measures long in contrast to the two-beat units that have predominated in the first part. Gradually the phrase length is contracted as the music heads towards a clearly defined cadence. After a moment's silence there is a reprise of the opening material. Flattened sevenths (G♮s) bring a special poignancy to the coda and the undemonstrative ending; on no account should the final chord be held longer than the indicated duration.

INTERMEZZO IN A MINOR, OP. 76, NO. 7, *Moderato semplice 4/4.* Here we find Brahms in the strangely bleak mood that first appeared in the Intermezzo *(Rückblick)* of the Op. 5 Sonata and in the *Edward* Ballade from Op. 10.[7] Some commentators have drawn attention to a similarity between the opening phrase and that of Chopin's Nocturne in F Minor, Op. 55, No. 1, but as Brahms scathingly said in another context when accused of plagiarism, "Any fool can see that." After the warmth of the previous piece there is an impression of profound loneliness in these two pages. Of particular interest is a comparison of his treatment of the recurring pattern E–D♯–E–C with a similar shape in possibly the greatest of all the late piano works, Op. 118, No. 6. In this Intermezzo it is simply used as a springboard to move the music onward out of the doldrums; in Op. 118 it becomes eloquent of the deepest sorrow.

Op. 76/6

Op. 118/6

EXAMPLE 8.8. Op. 76, No. 7, mm. 8–9 and Op. 118, No. 6, mm. 1–4

The final return to the opening measures brings a feeling of desolation, emphasized by Brahms' refusal to linger on the last note.

CAPRICCIO IN C MAJOR, OP. 76, NO. 8, *Grazioso ed un poco vivace 6/4.* Whereas in the previous piece the melody is given to us in unmistakable tones here there is an enigmatic quality, as though Brahms is playing a game with us — "Now you see it, now you don't . . ." In a nonstop flow of eighth notes, there are certain ones which catch the ear as being more significant, so that we begin to sense that amidst all the movement there is a more serene element.

EXAMPLE 8.9. Op. 76, No. 8, mm. 1–4

How conventional and plodding this could sound if it were to be presented in quarter-note chords with a rum-tum-tum waltz accompaniment; how subtle and elusive is the version we find here. After a repeated first section, gently sustained offbeat chords (*dolce, sotto voce*) have a calming influence despite the continuing activity in the left hand. A more openly lyrical phrase comes to flower out of a rising five-note scale, at first in the related key of F major, but later in the more remote tonality of B major (initially shown as Cb major!). A flashing descending arpeggio in triplets leads the way into a reprise that soon moves in new directions with, for the first time, a sustained melody in the left hand. Gradually the music seems to lose impetus until, after a considerable ritenuto, Brahms produces one last surprise, a substantially slower version of the rising five-note phrase (*più adagio*). However, it is not allowed to create too great a change of mood and after only two measures vitality is restored with a brilliant ascending passage confirming the proper tonality of C major.

# III
# Two Rhapsodies, Op. 79

These two substantial works were composed in 1879 and dedicated to one of Brahms' dearest friends and a one-time pupil, Elizabeth von Herzogenberg. The man whom she eventually married was a composer of considerable gifts whose admiration for Brahms is revealed in many of his compositions but she, in addition to being an accomplished pianist, had an exceptional ear allied to a remarkable memory; it was reliably reported that she could write down a new orchestral work by Brahms in its entirety after a single hearing. Not surprisingly, he had been much attracted to her when, as an outstandingly lovely blonde, she had come to see him for lessons. Fearful of any emotional entanglement with the opposite sex, he passed her on to a pianist-colleague named Julius Epstein. Once she was safely married, Brahms was able to feel much more at ease with her, and an enduring friendship was formed, which involved much correspondence. Although Clara Schumann remained his greatest confidante, he would often turn to Elizabeth for her approval or advice. For instance he had been characteristically undecided about what to call the two pieces of Op. 79, originally thinking that Caprice might be suitable. He then thought of Rhapsody, but in a letter to Elizabeth asked if she could think of a better title, stressing that he would not dream of altering the dedication, "that is, if you will allow me to put your dear and honored name on this trash."[8] He often employed this half-joking denigration of his work in his letters as if hoping to be reassured of its excellence.

RHAPSODY IN B MINOR, OP. 79, NO. 1, *Agitato 2/2*. Without preamble, Brahms launches the first theme, its dotted-quarter to eighth-note rhythm driven forward by restless broken chords in the bass. The little triplet in sixteenths seems at this stage to be nothing more than decoration, but it later proves to be capable of considerable development. The thematic interest is divided between the hands though it is the left hand that increasingly takes charge. A curiously choppy episode centers around the dominant F♯ before sustained D-major chords exert a calming influence. References to the opening theme are given a darker tone as a brief chromatic ascent in quarter notes climbs out of the depths. (As sometimes happens, Brahms' classical instincts led him to ask for a repeat here, but it seems both unnecessary and unconvincing.)

The spirit of *Edward* (Op. 10) reappears with a strangely bleak theme in the unexpected key of D minor. In a sonata-form movement it would be designated the second subject, but whether Caprice or Rhapsody, this is no sonata and it is soon swept aside by explosive B♭-major chords that reintroduce the initial theme. A masterly development ensues, making much use of that same brief chromatic ascent which previously had done little more than cast a dark shadow over snatches of the opening. During the next twenty measures, Brahms visits a number of keys in dramatic fashion, spanning most of the keyboard and constantly revealing the relevance of the passage by use of the triplet in sixteenths which had first appeared in the very opening measure. Two scales, one in F one in G♭, sweep across the keyboard like gusts of wind leaving an isolated F♯ stranded in their wake. "What will it lead to?" we ask ourselves, as it hangs suspenseful in the air. Logically, it might be expected to open the way to a gentler contrasting section; instead, Brahms returns to the opening material, now more agitated than before. Athletic leaps lead to a huge climax which finally subsides onto the lowest possible octave B♮. The five measures that follow, briefly reminding us of the bleak D-minor

theme, were an afterthought. In the original version Brahms had
introduced a triplet figuration which was subsequently transferred
most effectively to the coda. Much to Elizabeth's approval, he
substituted a more concentrated, simplified allusion which made a
more satisfying link to the lyrical episode which now follows.

This is an expansive tune, which brings the D-minor theme into
the sunshine of B major. More relaxed though it may be, it is not
allowed to fly as free as some of Brahms' melodies; it stays anchored
to a repeated tonic bass that only changes as modulations demand.
Gradually the sunlight fades as D♮s cast a chill; finally all movement
ceases as a quiet B-minor chord is sustained for two measures.

An unusually exact recapitulation ensues, so much so that it
suggests, perhaps unworthily, that Brahms had become overeager to
finish his largest-scale piano composition for many a year. Inspiration
is rekindled in the coda, which transfers the bleak D-minor theme
(now in the tonic B minor) to the left hand against a flowing triplet
accompaniment that contains subtle suggestions of an inversion of the
tune, though it is far from exact in its outline. The final measures,
even though in the major, bear more a weight of sorrow than a feeling
of release.

RHAPSODY IN G MINOR, OP. 79, NO. 2, *Molto passionato, ma non
troppo allegro 4/4.* There is such a suggestion of narrative in this
piece that it is surprising that Brahms did not choose to call it
"Ballade." Many listeners must have found themselves imagining
events in some heroic tale as its various episodes unfold. The opening
phrase is instantly memorable with its soaring melody given extra
panache by the crossing of hands and the leaping octaves in the bass.
It is played twice, the second time a third higher and finally coming to
a dramatic pause on a B-major chord. This conveniently proves to be
the dominant of E minor, which even more conveniently provides easy
access to G major, in which key Episode Two makes its explosive
entry (mm. 9–13). Here the triplet rhythm is ingeniously distributed
between the hands, giving a rough-hewn effect that adds enormous
vigor to what might otherwise have been a rather conventional and
uninteresting passage. In the music of a minor eighteenth-century
composer we would hardly be roused by anything so limp as this:

EXAMPLE 8.10. Hypothetical version of Op. 79, No. 2, mm. 9–10

Yet Brahms' version, with brusque chords in the right hand and athletic octaves in the left is electrifying.

EXAMPLE 8.11. Brahms' actual version of Op. 79, No. 2, mm. 9–10

A sudden shift to the minor catches us unawares, as does the unexpected pause on the A-major chord — the dominant of D.

Episode Three follows, a total contrast to what has gone before, its wailing chromaticism suggesting an impassioned lament. Is it coincidental or subtly contrived that the semitone A–Bb with which it begins seems related to the D–Eb interval which launched the opening phrase? Certainly its importance can hardly be overestimated for it soon becomes a dominating feature in the recurring A–Bb–A ostinato triplet that is heard throughout Episode Four.

This proves to be a strange march, full of menace, with the main interest given to the left-hand octaves. Starting quietly, it builds relentlessly towards a considerable climax, culminating in a descending D-minor arpeggio which swoops down through three octaves. (Once more Brahms asks for a repeat which does not seem really justified; with a tale as gripping as this, one does not want to go back and read the first chapter again.)

There follows an extensive development of the opening theme, now in more restrained a mood and visiting many different tonalities in its progress. An F# pedal point finally provides an anchor for the wayward harmonies, reeling them in to the dominant of B minor.

Episode Four now reappears driven by the ostinato triplet, but scarcely has the march got on its way than its stride is elongated:

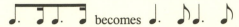

For the very first time, we find the dynamic *ff*, drawing forcible attention to the most strident dissonance in the whole piece (E♭ octave against Gm$_4^6$). Like a massive wave beating against a cliff face, the phrase recedes, then re-forms and strikes again. Almost without our being aware of it an episode that began in B minor has arrived at G minor, the constantly shifting tonalities being a notable feature of the work.

Episode Five creates a strange and ghostly atmosphere with the unusual dynamic *ppp* and *sotto voce*. The essential melody is played with both hands in unison an octave apart; the harmony is bare and stark (the ghost of *Edward* stalks again) while the triplet ostinato continues almost hypnotically. Above, faintly bell-like, paired quarter notes try vainly to recall the very opening theme but the mood is too dark to allow its return. The whole section could be taken for a transcription of a Schubert *Lied* as though the *Erlkönig* were once more abroad, seeking some innocent prey. The episode disintegrates with a magical descending figure that is like an owl gliding down to earth from the top of a ruined tower.

A classic but condensed recapitulation follows, the first alteration simply being the necessary change of direction that allows Episode Three to appear in the tonic key of G minor instead of the original D minor. A similar transposition affects Episode Four, whose left-hand octaves extend their leaps over a wider span before the gradual unwinding that brings the piece to a close — or nearly so, since just when it seems to have come to a complete halt, two crashing chords provide a dramatic cadence.

# IV
# Fantasias, Op. 116

It is further evidence of Brahms' confusion about titles that he calls this set of seven pieces Fantasias and yet names them individually either Capriccio or Intermezzo. The fourth (in E major) was originally intended to be called Nocturne but it is possible that he was reluctant to be thought of as following in Chopin's footsteps. They were composed in 1891–92, and it is clear that Brahms was feeling unusually satisfied with this relatively new medium; he composed no fewer than twenty pieces in a little over a year (Opp. 116, 117, 118, 119).

CAPRICCIO IN D MINOR, OP. 116, NO. 1, *Presto energico 3/8.* Brahms may have been fifty-nine when he wrote this, but in spirit it belongs to the period of his early twenties when he set out to conquer the world by force of arms. It could well be taken for the scherzo of an early sonata, save that it lacks the obligatory contrasting Trio section, for here nothing is allowed to check the forward impetus of the music.[9] As in the opening dozen measures of the B-Minor Rhapsody, Op. 79, No. 1, he passes the thematic interest from one hand to the other until, in measures 17–20, there is a fleeting moment when the heady rhythm of a waltz brings a glorious release from the asperities of the opening. Suddenly the triple pulse of the music is changed so that although the 3/8 barring stays unchanged we now hear the music as 2/8. Further variety is provided by a change from four-measure phrases to ones of only two measures suggesting a 3/4 signature.

EXAMPLE 8.12. Op. 116, No. 1, mm. 59–67 and mm. 21–28

Rising chromatic basses such as those shown here are much favored by Brahms and there have already been examples in the B-Minor Rhapsody and in the Capriccio, Op. 76, No. 5. Its ascent is closely matched in the inner part of the right-hand chords before the sequence rises irresistibly to the top revealing its full melodic potential.

The pianist's left-hand technique is now put to the test as Brahms asks for four descending diminished seventh arpeggios in *legato* octaves with the added hazard of a considerable leap to a low C to finish. Four detached chords offer a moment's respite before a brief reprise of the opening measures.

A new section begins with chords or octaves tossed between the hands to create a curious hopping effect, suitable music for a kangaroo ballet. It continues for thirty-six measures, modulating through several keys but refusing to settle in any one, until at last a low-Bb octave appears as an anchor note, establishing Bb minor. Four times more we find the descending diminished sevenths in octaves followed by an extended and considerably easier descent shared by both hands. A comparable passage to the one indicated in Ex. 8.13 ensues as part of a résumé of all the material of the piece. In the brief coda we find the octaves spread in both hands to give the sort of snap to the rhythm that a side-drum might impart. Was Brahms perhaps unconsciously echoing a passage from the tenth variation in Op. 24 (mm. 6–8) as the two examples below suggest? (Ex. 8.13). Certainly the spread octaves in the Capriccio produce an effect markedly similar to the *gruppetti* in the variation, while the *forte* indication four times in a single measure suggests the 3/8 time signature of the later work.

(a)  Op. 116, No. 1, mm. 193–96

(b)  Op. 24, Var. 10, mm. 6–8

EXAMPLE 8.13.  Rhythmic  similarities  between  (a) Op. 116,  No. 1, mm. 193–96, and (b) Op. 24, Var. 10, mm. 6–8

INTERMEZZO IN A MINOR, OP. 116, NO. 2, *Andante 3/4*. After the intense virility of the previous piece, there is a danger that this very different composition might be dismissed as wan and colorless. On the other hand, it could be argued that the Capriccio is a display of bravado — "Look, I am still as young in spirit, I can still storm the heights" — while this piece is a truer picture of a man whom love has passed by and who now feels his loneliness more acutely. Loneliness is certainly the emotion that seems to be conveyed here; time and again movement freezes for the second and third beats of the measure as though the composer waits for a response that does not come. Once more we are reminded of the bleak harmonies of the *Edward* Ballade (Op. 10); indeed, this could well be the desolate song his mother sings after his departure into exile.[10] The repeated cadences in measures 8– 9 are reminiscent of the falling fifths E–A of the *Edward* Ballade, Op. 10, and while I am not suggesting any conscious allusion on Brahms' part, he has unquestionably tapped a very similar vein of ore.

The first nine measures are repeated in a slightly elaborated version before a complete change of figuration and of time signature — 3/8 in place of 3/4. The directions to the performer are explicit: *Non troppo presto; molto piano e legato.* The right-hand part consists entirely of broken octaves, alternately in upward or downward motion; the left hand has a repetitive gently rocking figure which may well be related to the very first measure of the piece since it too tends to linger on the second and third beats. The almost disembodied feeling of this passage may partly be attributed to the strangely unpredictable length of the phrases — five measures, ten measures, seventeen measures, during the last of which the rhythm changes from three-pulse to two-pulse, the same variation that, in a very different context, had appeared in the previous Capriccio.

With the return to 3/4, a glimmer of sunshine seems to lift the mist, for during the next ten measures the music is in A major. Again we find the strange halting of forward movement, but whether by accident or design there is now a characteristic Scottish rhythm, the so-called "snap"

which bears out my suggestion that *Edward* might indeed be in the composer's mind. The only *forte* in the piece signals the emotional climax and a cadenza-like passage leads by a tortuous chromatic route to an almost exact reprise of the opening music. The final cadence, which ends with a single unsupported low A, brings confirmation of the essential loneliness of this intimate and intensely personal piece.

CAPRICCIO, OP. 116, NO. 3, *Allegro passionato 2/2.* There is an ambiguity of rhythm here that raises an intriguing question for the performer since the barline appears to be in the wrong place. It is almost inevitable that the first half note sounds like an upbeat:

EXAMPLE 8.14. Hypothetical perception of the meter at the beginning of Op. 116, No. 3

The *sf* that is indicated in the second half of measures 1, 3, 5, 7, and the like, suggests that Brahms felt the rhythmic stress to fall in the way shown above; indeed, the augmented version of the opening figure that appears in measure 13 seems to make the necessary adjustment that places the melodic accent where it belongs — on the first beat. There is no confusion when we reach the chromatic development of the initial four-note group in measures 9–12, nor when the same figure is extended through eight measures in a dramatic ascent to the dominant seventh. However, in the splendid augmentation of the initial group that brings this first section to an end it is quite possible to put the stress onto the second note of the phrase, that is to say, the written first beat.

EXAMPLE 8.15. Op. 116, No. 3, mm. 29–33

Would Brahms have preferred that we perceive the following (Ex. 8.16) instead of what we usually hear?

EXAMPLE 8.16. Hypothetical perception of the meter of Op. 116, No. 3, mm. 29–33

Such problems need not concern us in the triumphal march which constitutes the central section of this piece. Set in E♭ major and marked *Un poco meno Allegro,* it offers not just a change of mood but also a change of texture. The many unison passages that occur in the first part are replaced by dense harmonies, often widely spaced for maximum richness. Any suggestion of stodginess is countered by the swinging triplets which sustain a forward impulse without any sacrifice of dignity. A sudden transition into G major might be considered as woodwind after brass, the whole section sounding like a piano transcription of a stately march for military band. The triplet in the bass of the very first measure of this central part provides the pattern with which Brahms cunningly slows the music, bringing it to a complete halt before launching a thunderbolt of a reprise. Apart from rather more athletic versions of what originally were straightforward unison passages there are no significant alterations. However the final five measures offer a greatly expanded version of the material shown in Ex. 8.15.

INTERMEZZO IN E MAJOR, OP. 116, NO. 4, *Adagio 3/4.* After the turbulence of No. 3 this is indeed a journey into a different land where all is peace and tranquillity. The original intended title Nocturne conveys the mood more clearly than Intermezzo which, as we have seen, bears many interpretations. Brahms' disposition of the notes, asking that the right hand should cross over to play the E in the bass, gives the note a special bell-like significance (See Ex. 8.19). The falling intervals of a fifth and then a sixth that constitute the first elements of the melody are like sighs of contentment; one has the impression of a reluctance to move, a delicious idleness that pervades the whole piece despite the increased movement in the accompanying bass that occurs later. Brahms even amuses himself by taking the energetic opening notes of the previous Capriccio and turning them into a phrase so lazy that it might be taken for a yawn.

EXAMPLE 8.17. Op. 116, No. 3, m. 1, compared with Op. 116, No. 4, mm. 15–17

Since the upper part in the example above retains the falling intervals of the original melody (mm. 2–4), it produces a neat fusion of elements from two completely different compositions.

In measures 22–25, we find some elegant two-part counterpoint in the right hand, a dialog between imagined soprano and alto parts that reminds us of Brahms' fondness for choral composition.

EXAMPLE 8.18. Op. 116, No. 4, mm. 22–25

Vaguely wandering phrases in triplets drift aimlessly round a tonal center of G♯, uncertain whether or not to treat it as the dominant of C♯ minor. Even the rhythm becomes disoriented, finding duplets in a forest of triplets so that for a time all relation to the original pulse seems lost. This first section is brought to a close by a proper cadence in G♯ minor, preceded by a beautiful new harmonization of the very opening phrase.

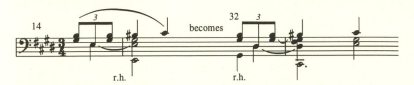

EXAMPLE 8.19. Op. 116, No. 4, mm. 14–15 compared with mm. 32–33

The central section, so essential a part of the structure of nearly all of these late piano works, appears to be more active when we see the arpeggio figures that rise in sixteenths in so many of its measures. But these are but the gentlest of breezes when compared to the gusting winds of the previous Capriccio, and Brahms writes a restraining *dolce, una corda* to discourage any displays of athleticism in the left hand. There is a hint of a dreamy waltz here, and it is quite instructive to make a comparison with Op. 39, No. 5 (mm. 9–12), where we can find a much more concentrated version of a rather similar idea.

For several measures, Brahms lingers tantalizingly on the doorstep of E major before creating a diversion with yet another harmonization of the opening phrase.

EXAMPLE 8.20. Op. 116, No. 4, mm. 49–52

But the remaining measures can scarcely be called a reprise; rather, they are a nostalgic glance back at the previous material from which Brahms takes the tenderest farewell.

INTERMEZZO IN E MINOR, OP. 116, NO. 5, *Andante con grazia ed intimissimo sentimento 6/8*. The unusually long instruction from Brahms and the unique request for "the most intimate feeling" tell us that he was anxious that the piece should not be misunderstood. In clumsy hands it could sound jerky or lumpish, yet played with sensitivity it has a strange, almost ethereal, beauty. A composer with a liking for descriptive titles might have called it "Footsteps in the Snow," for there is a soft "crunch" on each of the chords that begin each pair of eighths. For those who like their tunes out in the open with nice supportive accompaniments, the piece does have problems; indeed there are moments when the player has a choice of several options — is the melody here or there, when either is possible? Without attempting to provide a definitive answer, I would propose this solution:

EXAMPLE 8.21. Extraction of the melody of Op. 116, No. 5, mm. 1–12

The silences are as important as the notes, for it is they that give a special fragility to this unique composition.[11] Occasional dissonances occur when the two thumbs find themselves uncomfortably close to each other, but they should be gently brushed aside rather than accented.

After the repeats (both of which should be observed) the gaps are filled, the more sustained legato bringing welcome warmth. Soon a problem for the interpreter does appear. From the second ending, Brahms establishes a melodic pattern of rising thirds in this rhythm:

EXAMPLE 8.22. Op. 116, No. 5, mm. 11–13

But after a mere four measures, an additional note an octave lower modifies the pattern somewhat (Ex. 8.23).

EXAMPLE 8.23. Op. 116, No. 5, mm. 14–18

Interwoven with this is a similar octave-plus-a-third pattern in the left hand.

EXAMPLE 8.24. Op. 116, No. 5, mm. 15–17

The duet nature of this exchange is really hard to convey without creating a muddled texture from which neither part benefits. In performance, one tends to hear only the top two notes in the right hand as being of significance, but needless to say this fails to convey the subtlety of the dialog, something that could be more clearly shown by a string quartet. The little sighing phrases from the first section duly return, leading ultimately to a lingering cadence in which even the last expressive melodic line is enfolded in rich harmony rather than being allowed to rise above supporting chords.

INTERMEZZO IN E MAJOR, OP. 116, NO. 6, *Andantino teneramente 3/4*. The word *Andantino* warns the player not to take this lovely piece too slowly. Each individual harmony is so beautifully spaced that it is only too tempting to become overindulgent, enjoying the sheer sensuality of the sound and thereby losing the shape of the melody. There is such richness here that one is hard put to know which part to bring out, "soprano" or "alto," but as in the central section of the previous Intermezzo, Brahms is clearly thinking in terms of a duet, and it is up to the performer to convey this. Although a feeling of forward movement is essential, there are occasional pauses which allow us to savor for a moment the beauty of the latest modulation — for example, how to extricate oneself from C sharp major and return to E. In passing, we find possibly the most exotic notation ever devised for a chord of C major (B#–E♮–F×–B#), which may make academic sense but seems to have no relation to what the hand feels on the keys.

After the second pause, we find a reprise of measures 3–6 followed by an unexpected diversion into B♭ major, which could well extend into more remote keys were it not for the fact that Brahms decides to turn it gently back to the "home" key of E major. And there we could stop; quietly and questioningly he proposes a chord of G♯ minor, poised on its dominant, and mysteriously opening the door to the contrasting central section.

Against a harplike accompaniment of descending triplets, this new melody, tinged with melancholy, is based on a segment of a falling scale. Even though only one melodic line appears at a time, there is still the suggestion of a duet when the tune is transferred from "soprano" to "baritone," a point which is emphasized when towards the end of the section they exchange "sweet nothings" in the tenderest way. No attempt is made to link this to the reprise that now follows; there is a definite pause complete with double bar line, as though Brahms was really reluctant to move back to the original phrases. For a time all is as it was before, but the shift into B♭ major now leads to an extended cadenza-like "duet," perhaps the most openly expressive passage of the whole piece. Just as we think that the final chord is imminent, Brahms produces a characteristically beautiful coda that takes a last nostalgic look back to the falling-scale theme of the central section, now more richly harmonized. Did Shakespeare dream of such a phrase when he wrote "That strain again, it had a dying fall . . ."? (*Twelfth Night,* Act 1, Scene i)

CAPRICCIO IN D MINOR, OP. 116, NO. 7, *Allegro agitato 2/4.* Although any one of the pieces in Op. 116 may be played on its own, the obvious resemblance between this Capriccio and the third suggests that Brahms was intending to impose some sort of thematic unity on the whole set. Remembering his devotion to Schumann, from whom he might have derived a delight in cyclic form, it makes an attractive hypothesis. We have already seen a tenuous link between the third and fourth pieces (see Ex. 8.17). Yet surely if he had really wanted to unify the whole set, he would have pursued the idea more consistently and planted a rhythm or a melodic fragment in such a way that we would have become increasingly aware of a relationship between movements. (There can be no more brilliant example of this than Schumann's *Carnaval,* which Brahms would certainly have known intimately.) It seems more sensible to assume that he took a fancy to the idea of devising a completely different working-out of a similar pattern; after all, a diminished-seventh arpeggio is almost as basic as one based on the "common" major or minor chords.

From the start, the two hands are in violent opposition to each other, batting the little group of five notes from side to side with the ferocity of two tennis players in a match-point rally at Wimbledon. The eleventh measure sees the introduction of a modified version of the pattern with the first note of each group omitted so that the music seems positively breathless. With the arrival of the inevitable central section, there is a complete change of texture; we now find a long seamless melody in A minor, which weaves its way between ascending and descending arpeggios. There is an intriguing twist to the rhythm, for the tune seems perpetually out of step, an eighth note later than it might be expected to be. The first eight measures are repeated before Brahms extends the theme further, now reinforced with chords or octaves but still as offbeat as ever. This section, sixteen measures in all, is also repeated before coming quietly to rest on a chord of A major.

There follows a brief toccata-like passage, a gesture of homage to Bach, perhaps; it springs from the diminished-seventh figure which began the piece but flies free thereafter. A seemingly exact reprise ensues, but it is rudely cut off by forceful chords which condense the four-note groups into massive chords in 3/8, which, using a technique we have now seen several times, Brahms duly compresses into an implied 2/8. The last four chords triumphantly affirm D major, a tonality he has managed to totally avoid up to this climactic moment.

# V
# Three Intermezzi, Op. 117

INTERMEZZO IN Eb MAJOR, OP. 117, NO. 1, *Andante moderato 6/8.* Not since the slow movement of the Sonata in F Minor, Op. 5, had Brahms declared the content of the music by putting a quotation from a poem at the top of the page. There it was: three intensely romantic lines from Sternau, describing a moonlit evening and two lovers, their hearts united in happiness. Here we find two lines from an old Scottish ballad, "Lady Anne Bothwell's Lament," in Johann Gottfried von Herder's translation of a collection of folk poetry of which Brahms seems to have been unusually fond:

> Schlaf sanft mein Kind, schlaf sanft und schön!
> Mich dauert's sehr, dich weinen sehn.

To judge from this example alone, Herder seems to have been a faithful and honest translator, for in the original ballad we find these lines:

> Balow, my babe, lie still and sleep!
> It grieves me sore to see thee weep.
> (spelling modernized.)

Lady Anne's sad tale is told in seven verses. Briefly, she had been deserted by a faithless lover who, unwilling to face up to the responsibilities of fatherhood, left her with their baby. In the two outer sections of the piece we find the tender cradlesong she sings to her child, while in the central portion, in the dark tonality of E♭ minor, she broods unhappily on her miserable plight.

This piece with its hauntingly beautiful tune instantly became popular, so much so that Brahms actually attempted to orchestrate it; but its essentially pianistic quality did not easily transfer to the orchestra, so he abandoned the idea. He once referred to this piece as "the lullaby of my griefs,"[12] confirming that it had a special and personal significance for him. Did he feel that he shared Lady Anne's loneliness, or was it a wish that he might have had a child?

The simple melody, initially based on no more than a descending scale of an octave, is clearly designed to be a setting of the German text shown above. In measures 6–7 its span widens by a third before the memorable moment when the tune is taken over by the bass whose last few notes are echoed touchingly in the right hand. It is notable that the melody in this piece is nearly always enfolded by harmonies rather than just supported by them, a symbol perhaps of the mother's arms wrapped protectively round the child. In measures 13–14 there is a beautiful extension of the opening phrase in which Brahms hints at a canon that is due to be developed more fully in the reprise. Spread chords in the left hand disturb the easy flow of 6/8 by proposing 3/4 as an alternative, so that for three measures the hands fail to agree. A potent A♮ in the bass adds a more expressive twist to the harmonization of the opening phrase. Suddenly there is a real chill as the tune is taken into the remote tonality of A♭ minor, first with both hands in stark octaves, then in the bass with doom-laden chords above. Twice more we hear this minor version, at first more impassioned and then sinking down in despair, as though the distraught mother is asking "What have I done to deserve this?"

There follows one of the strangest passages to be found anywhere in these late piano works. Marked *più adagio,* each measure is like a huge sigh, with mysterious suggestions of a melody that never really materializes. Occasionally what small movement there is freezes, with the two hands in unison playing abortive fragments of the original theme two octaves apart and embedded in dark harmonies. The last two measures of this section remind us a little more positively of the first notes of the opening tune.

Gently, as though warmed by the sun's rays, the song appears once more, now divided ingeniously between the hands so that it seems to pass through the accompanying chords. A decorative frill of sixteenths provides a new sound, its repetitive pattern possibly reflecting the "winsome smiles" of the babe referred to in the sixth verse of the poem. Serene as before, the tune returns in its original guise, only to be momentarily diverted by an unforseen modulation into G minor. Starting on a high E♭ the canon that had been suggested earlier (mm. 13–14) now blossoms as a charming variation, apparently destined to bring the tune to a final cadence. Just as we imagine that we have arrived there, Brahms inserts a sudden subdominant chord, marked both *rf (rinforzando)* and *espressivo*, a last stab of pain as the anguished mother clasps her babe more tightly.

INTERMEZZO IN B♭ MINOR, OP. 117, NO. 2, *Andante non troppo e con molto espressione 3/8.* Simply to look at this music gives a misleading impression for one might take it to be a study in rapid arpeggios made the harder by the need to play quietly; it might even have been given such a title as "Will o' the wisp" or "Fireflies." However, a more thorough exploration reveals one of the subtlest pieces that Brahms ever wrote in which, for the most part, tunes are implied but seldom revealed and in which the pianist must combine scrupulous articulation with veiled impressionistic tones. It is helpful to imagine the sound of an unaccompanied violin (admittedly with an abnormally wide compass!) as it might be heard in a Bach Partita. The performer needs to pay the closest attention to the details of notation. During the many little groups of four (or three) thirty-second notes, Brahms has been meticulous about indicating which notes should be sustained and for how long; for example, he clearly intends there to be a difference between no notes sustained:

*one* note sustained:

and *two* notes sustained:

The temptation for the pianist is to treat the top (first) note of every group as melodic, which nullifies the effectiveness of those occasional measures where eighth notes are actually required. The brief ascending phrases in the left hand are not just accompanying figures but integral parts of a continuous ribbon of melody, of which only a few notes draw attention by being briefly sustained. If we in the audience imagine that the very first notes spell out this melody, then we are being misled:

EXAMPLE 8.25. Oversimplification of melody of Op. 117, No. 2, mm. 1–3

Every note counts, and the extra length shown on the first note of the Bb or F groups might be compared to a touch more *vibrato* from a violinist playing the same passage. (Manifestly this is not violin music and it would be most awkward to play, but I suggest thinking in violin terms to avoid the overlaps that the pianist's hand will be tempted to allow.)

Just why these details are so significant is revealed when, in Db major, a sustained tune at last appears. The previous wisps of sound, delicate and translucent as they were, coalesce to form solid harmony. Here the contrasting central section almost invariably used in these pieces is no separate entity but a natural growth emerging in a deeply satisfying way. At times the texture has a special richness as both hands duplicate a chromatic inner part, as though violas and cellos in unison were to intensify the emotional content of a phrase.[13] This profoundly expressive passage lasts no more than sixteen measures. Austere octaves lead into an increasingly passionate development of the opening material, the two hands now disputing their importance until they form a continuous chain of notes extending over four octaves. The music seems on the point of disintegration as a few poignant harmonies float down from the heights followed by a marvellous wash of sound based on a diminished seventh. Tentatively we are reminded of the initial patterns and a reprise of sorts begins. After a mere ten measures it begins to stretch its arcs, building in volume to the first *forte* in the whole piece and a substantial climax in the alien key of E major. This is instantly contradicted by a similar phrase in Bb major, albeit tinged with minor tones during its descent. A ritenuto leads into a *più adagio* in which memories of the central (Db major) tune are overlaid with deep sorrow, made the more painful by the grinding E♮–F in the bass that occurs no less than seven times. The chromatic movement in these last harmonies is skillfully contrived to go in opposite directions as though searching for some solace but not knowing where to find it. The final cadence brings no release.

EXAMPLE 8.26. Op. 117, No. 2, mm. 76–85

INTERMEZZO IN C♯ MINOR, OP. 117, No. 3, *Andante con moto 2/4.*
There is a unique austerity in this Intermezzo; in no other piece does
Brahms so extensively use unison octaves unsupported by harmony.
With the instruction *molto piano e sotto voce sempre,* the opening
phrases seem to grope their way forward, reaching step by gradual
step from C♯ to the B a seventh above, only to sink back into the
shadows. A modified repetition, now supported by the simplest
indications of harmony, makes the same journey but by a slightly
different route with A-sharps bringing a brief modulation into B
major, a destination no sooner reached than quitted with a descent into
the even darker region of G♯ minor. The same technique is employed
with the new theme that now appears; it is presented in bare octaves
and then repeated with simple harmonies and a change of modulation
— a return to the tonic C♯ minor instead of the dominant G♯. Notice
the subtle interchange between imagined viola and cello in measures
16–18. (More than in most of these late works, one can easily imagine
much of the music being transferred to a string quartet.)

EXAMPLE 8.27. Op. 117, No. 3, mm. 16–18

The first theme returns, still *sempre sotto voce,* but with an
unexpected harmonization based on the subdominant and with soft,

bell-like chords above. Increased movement in the left hand helps to lift the music out of the shadows, but there is no sunlight here and the second element reappears, as gaunt as before. *Poco più lento,* the first section ends in despair, the opening theme now harmonized more densely but anchored firmly to a low C♯ regardless of dissonance.

The central section in A major, *più moto ed espressivo,* brings some relief from the gloom, but the new theme, such as it is, is presented in such an elusive manner that at first it seems little more than a series of floating harmonies such as we found in the previous Intermezzo. It helps to clarify the melody if at first we confine it to the same octave and simplify the rhythm:

EXAMPLE 8.28. Simplified version of melody in Op. 117, No. 3, mm. 47–56

How infinitely more subtle is Brahms' version with its gentle syncopations and constant shifts of pitch. After a double bar and repeat, we find a development in F♯ minor with occasional moments of stability as a tune materializes on the beat. A reprise of the A-major section has some small modifications of harmony but brings no change of mood.

The return to the original theme is like autumn leaves drifting down from the tree, the one passage in the whole piece that allows some warmth and sensuality in the harmony. Almost unnoticed, Brahms plants a little three-note motif in an inner part so that it seems quite a revelation when it proves to be the start of the opening theme, now harmonized over an unexpected D♯ (as the dominant of G♯ minor). The second part of the phrase is treated as though in F♯ minor; indeed every harmonization of the initial unisons sheds new light on them. Even in the very last line of the piece, Brahms finds yet another harmonization, bringing a greater emotional intensity than has been allowed at any previous moment. Restraint is put aside, the inner sorrow exposed. The deadening hand of the musical anatomist can never explain the profound effect of such a phrase as this (Ex. 8.29).

EXAMPLE 8.29. Op. 117, No. 3, mm. 103–108

# VI
## Piano Pieces, Op. 118

We cannot be certain of the precise order in which these six pieces were written but we do know that in May, 1893, Brahms sent the sixth (in E♭ minor) to Clara Schumann as a birthday present. Only later in the summer did the remainder of the set follow, usually one at a time. Now it is possible that the sixth was indeed the first to be composed, but it may be that several had been sketched and that Brahms, realizing that it was indeed the finest, put the finishing touches to it first, making fair copies of the others later. As a birthday offering it would appear to be excessively gloomy but as a composition it must surely establish a claim to be the greatest and most profound of all the thirty short piano works discussed here.

INTERMEZZO IN A MINOR, OP. 118, NO. 1, *Allegro non assai, ma molto appassionato 4/4.* "Impassioned" is indeed the word to describe this splendid piece whose opening phrase bestrides the keyboard in heroic style. The wide-ranging arpeggios which surround it, covering no less than four octaves in two measures, add to the air of flamboyance. The first two phrases are brief, only two measures, the second reproducing the first a third lower. Unusually, they are followed by an extension spread over eight measures in all, so that the opening section (repeated) is ten measures in length. After the double bar line Brahms produces an inversion of the opening phrase so that it rises to a high C instead of falling to a low E, but before its answering phrase is allowed to appear he inserts one of his favorite descending diminished sevenths, plunging downwards across nearly four octaves as though rivalling the *rising* figures that appeared at the beginning. This has the effect of lengthening the initial phrase from two to four measures, setting a new pattern which we assume the answering phrase will follow. Here Brahms has a nicely plotted surprise for us, for the response is interrupted just as it seems set to copy this extended version. Over a bass that rises chromatically from A to E, increasingly urgent figures whip up the excitement until, after hinting at the opening theme in a diminished rhythm, the initial two measures reappear as the climax. A further surprise follows immediately as the answering phrase rises even higher before breaking off into an angular descent. From this point we find six measures corresponding to the original plan (mm. 5–10 = mm. 25–30) though so modified that they bring a return to the tonic key of A minor instead of the previous modulation to C major. After the obligatory repeat, there is a coda in which, after a huge diminished-seventh arpeggio extends in a lazy arc over four octaves, the music seems to sink exhausted, the opening heroic gesture now reduced to half speed, the final major chord quenching the fire.

INTERMEZZO IN A MAJOR, OP. 118, NO. 2, *Andante teneramente 3/4.* This tender and lyrical piece would seem to be more like the traditional birthday gift that Clara Schumann might have expected. It suggests warmth and affection in almost every phrase. Easily taken for granted as undemanding to both performer and listener, it repays detailed examination. Many phrases or segments of phrases are repeated, but usually with subtle variations of harmony. For instance, compare the three differing treatments of similar passages in Ex. 8.30.

EXAMPLE 8.30. Three varied treatments of a thematic idea in Op. 118, No. 2

As is so often the case in Brahms' music, a pair of short phrases is followed by an extended phrase, not only in the main thematic material (mm. 1–16) but in the contrasting melody that ensues with its slightly disturbing hints of C major or F major, quickly denied. A slow chromatic ascent leads to a top A, harmonized on the subdominant, after which subtle reminders of the very opening notes appear in the bass as though to prevent the music from being carried too far away from the matter in hand. A brief diversion into A minor (*calando*) is followed by a ravishing inversion of the initial theme complete with wide-spread harmonies and a new counterpoint centered on A.[14] The ensuing *codetta* (*crescendo un poco animato*) refers back to the contrasting phrases originally found in measures 17–24 before offering a last reminder of the very opening melody, now darkened by being placed an octave lower.

The central section brings a new, more freely ranging melody in F♯ minor with suggestions of canonic imitation in a "tenor" part that are not followed through. However, in the F♯-major section, which next appears almost like a chorale, the left-hand chords do follow the right hand in nearly perfect canon. A pause on the dominant seventh of F♯ minor leads to a new and somewhat more elaborate working-out of the central section before a genuine if slightly modified reprise brings this charming work to a close.

BALLADE IN G MINOR, OP. 118, NO. 3, *Allegro energico 4/4.* Sometimes referred to as "the schoolgirl's war-horse," this dramatic and stormy piece shows a very different aspect of Brahms' musical *persona,* while its chunky chords and leaping octaves give us insight into his seemingly preferred style of playing. Forthright though it appears to be, it contains plenty of surprises, as for instance in measure 10 where instead of the expected cadence in G minor we find G major, which in turn is instantly contradicted by a flattened seventh (F♮) on the third beat. A transitional passage follows in slightly more restrained mood; it is basically in E♭ major, but flirts briefly with F minor and even D♭ major before returning, reinvigorated, to the opening theme. Here too, as in the previous piece though in a very different mood, Brahms provides a *codetta.* Indeterminate in tonality, it manages to retain a strong feeling of G minor despite the contradictory B♮s which keep appearing. After three measures in a gently rocking rhythm, these same B♮s (apparently heading for C minor) prove to be the tonic of the new tonality of B major in which a beguiling new theme now makes its entrance. Marked *pp una corda,* it ambles easily on its way in an extended phrase of no less than eight measures, indeed a contrast to the brusque abruptness of all that has gone before. Its progress is interrupted by a memory of the opening music, now in D sharp minor and considerably tamed by the context in which it now finds itself. Consequently, when it is due to return it takes several measures to gather strength before launching with renewed vigor into an unusually exact reprise. One last surprise awaits us: the coda, now resolutely in G minor, seems to disintegrate, and a last faint memory of the middle section brings the piece to an unexpectedly quiet ending.

INTERMEZZO IN F MINOR, OP. 118, NO. 4, *Allegretto un poco agitato 2/4.* If one regards the previous piece as a boldly executed oil painting, this next Intermezzo is like a delicate pencil drawing, full of exquisite detail but avoiding any obvious statement. The phrases could scarcely be shorter; only in Op. 116, No. 5 do we find even greater economy of utterance. There is an intimate exchange of thoughts between right and left hands which is only occasionally allowed to rise above a whisper. At one point a touch of shading is added to the sparse lines by the addition of thirds, an extravagance that is soon countered by a reduction to single notes, unsupported.

The central section (in the related key of Ab major) is almost as reluctant to reveal a melodic line. The rests indicated in every measure give a curious impression of breathlessness, while the left-hand chords, doggedly following every move of the right, have more substance than a shadow, serving as a brake that prevents the tune from taking wing. Only with the reprise on the final page is some passion allowed but even that is suppressed in a last diminuendo.

ROMANCE IN F MAJOR, OP. 118, NO. 5, *Andante 6/4.* Despite its romantic title, this is the most classically designed of all the late pieces, combining a ground bass in the outer sections with the baroque technique of "doubles" (variations in which the number of notes to each beat is proportionately increased) in the center. The extended melody, four measures of 6/4 in length, is presented in sonorous chords, sometimes duplicated in the two hands, providing an exceptionally rich texture. With only small variants it is unfolded four times over a recurring bass that would not seem surprising in a *chaconne* by Handel or Purcell.

There follows a change of tempo, tonality, and mood. With the instruction *Allegretto grazioso* and in the contradictory key of D major, Brahms embarks on a surprisingly strict set of miniature variations. Each is four measures long, the first three rooted in tonic harmony, the fourth still based on the tonic but with a sharpened fourth to add spice. The movement in the right hand progresses through stages of increasing complexity:

Variations 1 and 2: smooth eighths.
Variation 3: smooth triplets.
Variation 4: more athletic, angular triplets.
Variation 5: sixteenths.
Variation 6: widely spread chords, four to a measure.
Variation 7: trills and runs.

It seems more than likely that Brahms was using Chopin's Berceuse, Op. 57, as a model here since the compositional technique he uses is markedly similar.

Three measures with murmuring trills in the bass return us to the initial theme in its original form. It is immediately followed by a modified version even richer in texture which brings us smoothly and effortlessly to the final peaceful cadence.

INTERMEZZO IN E♭ MINOR, OP. 118, NO. 6, *Andante, largo e mesto 3/8*. In this magnificent piece, Brahms returns to the quasi-orchestral writing that is to be found in the F-Minor Sonata, Op. 5. Even the waves of diminished-seventh arpeggios that appear to be entirely pianistic actually have an authentic orchestral equivalent in the first movement of the Fourth Symphony (mm. 107–9, 114–16, *et sim* ). The opening phrase, an unsupported cry of sorrow, suggests a clarinet as surely as its response an octave lower does a bassoon. The many phrases in thirds equally suggest a pair of oboes, a pair of bassoons and so forth, while the darkly brooding unison separated by two octaves would sound well on violas and contrabasses with sombre horns or trombones providing the sustained dominants.

The despairing, sorrowful character of the first two pages is suddenly dispelled by the sound of a distant march whose taut staccato rhythms offer a complete contrast to the vague wanderings of a lost soul that preceded them. Again the orchestral implications are clear, the left hand providing the beat of a drum with subdued trumpets and horns above. Unison strings make a characteristic entry from a top B♭ while a densely harmonized version of the very opening phrase brings in the full orchestra. The second time this occurs the tune is diverted into D♭ major, an extraordinarily effective moment of relief. However, a "moment" it indeed is, followed instantly by a return to the bleakness of the opening. The subsequent paired notes now tend to be sixths rather than thirds, but in essence the music duplicates the mood if not the notes of the first page. Four measures from the end, Brahms asks for the biggest sound of all, a massive chord with the unusual indication *sff*. It is like a last convulsive shudder before the spirit leaves the body, bringing a welcome release from despair.

# VII
# Four Pieces, Op. 119

INTERMEZZO IN B MINOR, OP. 119, NO. 1, *Adagio 3/8*. Here we find an exceptionally interesting study in harmonies formed from chains of thirds, chords of the ninth or the eleventh which look forward to the idiom of Mahler or even Britten. Again it is helpful to think in other than purely pianistic terms, imagining an oboe with soft harp accompaniment in the opening measures and full strings, possibly muted, after the first double bar line. Although the texture seems at first to be conceived almost entirely in harmonic terms, counterpoint is not forgotten in a series of delicate exchanges between the hands, often using no more than three notes (mm. 12–16).

The shift into D major brings a flood of warmth and one of Brahms' most expressive passages. It climbs step by gradual step over a widely striding bass until a splendid climax is reached on a high E, followed by a long decline through two octaves. The D-major tune returns, now enhanced by a chromatic descent in the "alto" part. The dense, closepacked harmonies are soon opened out by two brief phrases which are like outstretched arms pleading. This is the most impassioned section, easily recognized by the first and only appearance of triplet sixteenths in the bass. Again the "pleading" figure recurs, now stretched even wider but gradually sinking into the shadows. Falling thirds reappear, briefly grouped as two times three (hemiola) instead of the previous three times two. The actual reprise is signalled by additional notes in the "harp" accompanying figure, now falling triplets with added chromaticisms. A touchingly expressive coda is notable for the little silences which separate one three-note phrase from the next, while the penultimate harmony consists of the most extended chain of descending thirds, which coalesce into a chord of a minor thirteenth, a moment unique in Brahms' output.

INTERMEZZO IN E MINOR, OP. 119, NO. 2, *Andantino un poco agitato 3/4*. The instruction *piano, sotto voce e dolce* should ensure that the fluttering sixteenths which provide the pervading rhythm are not played percussively. This elusive piece demands a suppressed urgency that is particularly hard to convey for there is also a wistful, almost forlorn character that seems at odds with the constant patter-patter of the rhythm. Indeed the break into somewhat less agitated triplets (m. 13) comes as a release from tension. A sudden deviation into F minor over a dominant pedal point (C♮) introduces a new rhythmic figure which, whatever its appearance, must not suggest the onset of a toccata. Tonalities change swiftly here with E minor leading to a climax on the dominant of B major. The promise of change that a major key might be expected to bring fails to materialize, and the urgent pattering of the accompanying sixteenths in support of a more openly expressive melodic line continues. A brief codetta introduces a new texture, legato two-part writing in the right hand over still somewhat agitated broken chords in the left. As the music slows there is a broad hint that we are approaching E major.

With the new and welcome indication *Andantino grazioso,* Brahms introduces a dreamy waltz that harks back to the felicities of the *Liebeslieder* waltzes of Op. 52. It takes a moment to realize that it begins with an ingenious transformation of the opening music, now with all its *angst* removed.

EXAMPLE 8.31. Comparison of melodic contour within contrasting sections of Op. 119, No. 2 (mm. 1–2 and 36–39)

This is developed at some length until, after some excursions into other tonalities, E major is confirmed with a gradual loss of impetus.

Tentatively the inevitable reprise begins, not significantly different save for the elimination of the triplet figuration originally found in measures 13–16; this time a rather more flowing version of the sixteenths gives some rhythmic continuity. At the last Brahms rekindles a memory of the central waltz, offering needed comfort at the end of a piece whose prevailing mood has been tinged with melancholy.

INTERMEZZO IN C MAJOR, OP. 119, NO. 3, *Grazioso e giocoso 6/8.* We have already seen in Op.117, No. 3 (mm. 20–30) Brahms' fondness for putting the melody line into the middle or "alto" part. In this delightful Intermezzo we find him using a similar technique though to a very different purpose, for here, instead of introspection and sadness, we find humor and high spirits. Few pieces by Brahms

are as genuinely lighthearted as this; it shows no signs of the blustering or lack of refinement that is sometimes evident when Beethoven or
even Brahms himself aims to be humorous in music. For the most part
it should be played quietly, with a light touch (*leggiero*). The tune in
the inner part chatters happily on its way from C major towards the
dominant of A minor — or is it A major? Brahms toys with the two
possibilities in a delightfully teasing way before rejecting both and
returning to the initial C major and the opening tune. This time round,
A major seems to be preferred — the two hands join in unison to quote
the opening measure, but with the slight modification that causes it to
begin on the (new) tonic, A, instead of the third of the scale. In a
flash, we are whisked off into F♯ minor, bounced along in C♯ minor
and eased into D♭ major. These rapid changes of key are like a game
in which Brahms constantly catches us wrong-footed; A♭ major is no
sooner achieved than it becomes F minor, and just as we think "Home
again" in C major it turns out to be merely the dominant of F minor
again.

The tune makes an abortive attempt to come back (A♭ major) but
is frozen on its third note. Next, and most beguilingly, it reappears in
the proper key of C major but in notes of twice the length, a trick that
brings the musical equivalent of a delighted laugh from Brahms. Yet
again the tune tries to make a comeback but it is swiftly diverted into
D minor. "Where to now?" says the composer, and introduces a
change of character by smoothing everything out into a flowing legato.
Over the well-tried device of a chromatically ascending bass (F–B) the
music climbs in sequences before settling happily on a dominant pedal
point as Brahms unwinds a new pattern derived from just three notes
of the original tune. A quicksilver ripple of sixteenths whisks this
away, before dancing chords provide a brief coda. Catching us
unawares, two loud chords slam the lid down on one of Brahms'
happiest inventions.

RHAPSODY IN E♭ MAJOR, OP. 119, NO. 4, *Allegro risoluto 2/4*.
*Risoluto* — and there is resolve in every measure, resolve that the
inspirational flame could still burn as brightly, resolve that at the age
of 59 he could still write with the power and virility of a twenty-year-
old. Not even in the early sonatas do we find a bolder, more forceful
theme than the one which opens this splendid work, made the more
unusual by its Hungarian-style five-measure phrases. Once the
opening theme has run its course (mm. 1–21) there begins a contrasting episode in which strong chords in fourths alternate with descending arpeggios in sixteenths. Was Brahms influenced here by memories
of Chopin's Scherzo in C♯ Minor, Op. 39, whose central chorale

alternates with glittering cascades of notes? Was it his intention to
devise a condensed, more classical conception of the same idea?

The first theme returns but is halted dramatically by two bell-like
chords. Quietly and mysteriously a march begins in C minor, its
triplet rhythm suggesting the beat of a drum. As it grows in volume it
is gloriously transformed into C major, a celebration (one feels) of a
great victory. The triumph is short-lived as its progress too is halted
by similar arresting chords.[15] These set a three-note pattern (C–D–
Eb), which provides the seed for the graceful new theme that now
appears. The sounds of a harp were not far from Brahms' imaginings
here, and there is an unusual effect of harmonies spread upwards in
the left hand and downwards in the right. After this has been developed for some length, the "march" returns more brightly scored.
Unexpectedly it is replaced by a quiet staccato variation on the
opening theme, now in C major. For no less than twenty measures the
music remains poised on a dominant pedal point (G) with fragments of
the first theme alternating with reminders of the "fourths" episode.
Gradually, *pp ma sempre ben marcato,* this takes command until, long
postponed, the initial theme returns in splendour. A coda of formidable difficulty concludes this, Brahms' farewell to the piano as a solo
instrument. In rhythm and figuration it echoes passages in the finale of
the Concerto in Bb Major, Op. 83, written eleven years previously,
but too much significance need not be attached to this. It only proves
that for all the twilight character of many of these late pieces, the
"heroic" element still survived when it was wanted.

## Notes

1. [Brahms did produce a sonata for *two* pianos about ten years later (1864). To be more precise, it was a work that began its life as a string quintet, was rearranged as a two-piano sonata, and finally emerged as the well-known Piano Quintet in F Minor. *Ed.*]

2. William Murdoch, *Brahms* (London: Rich and Cowan, 1933), 178–79.

3. Doubts have been expressed about Haydn as composer of the original theme and it seems more likely that it was by his pupil Pleyel; however, old habits die hard and it seems unlikely that the title will ever be changed.

4. The title "Ballade" is only significant in the first of the set which is based on an old Scottish poem called *Edward*. Brahms came across it in a German translation by Johann Gottfried von Herder, although one wonders in what dictionary Herder managed to find such archaic words as "Quhy" (why), "Zour" (your), "Haukis" (Hawk's), "Erst" (once), and others — or should I say "ithers" — of like obscurity. The poem recounts a grisly conversation between mother and son in which she asks why his sword drips with blood; he palms her off with lies, saying that he has killed first his hawk and then his horse, neither of which she believes. At last he admits that he has killed his father and that in penance he must sail away, leaving his castle to become a ruin, his family to beg for their living, and his mother to be cursed to hell "such counsels she gave to me." Brahms reproduces the scansion of the poem exactly in the opening phrases.

> Dein Schwert, wie ists von Blut so roth?
> Edward, Edward?
> (Herder's translation, used by Brahms)

[Compare with the following two versions:

> Why dois your brand sae drap wi' bluid,
> Edward, Edward?

> O why does your sword so drip with blood,
> Edward, Edward!

Not only the German, but also the old English and the modern English versions scan very well with Brahms' melody! *Ed.*]

The mother's heartbroken cries of "Edward, Edward" as he leaves can be heard over and over again as paired eighth notes in the closing measures.

5. It appears in no fewer than thirteen of his compositions extending over a period of twenty-five years.

6. An intriguing comparison may be made with Op.79, No. 1, measures 53–60, where we find a similar idea developed in a more complex way.

7. See also measures 131–40 from the Piano Concerto in D Minor, Op.15, first movement, a texture which has no parallel in concertos of the period.

8. Murdoch, *Brahms*, 256.

9. The strong accents on the supposedly weakest point of each measure recall Beethoven in his most blustering mood, but Brahms had already enjoyed this exhilarating game in the fourth of the Handel Variations, Op. 24. Context and rhythm may be different but the principle is the same.

10. It seems that Brahms was still reading Herder's translations of old Scottish ballads as the inscription above Op. 117, No. 1 shows.

11. Brahms had produced a more classically conceived version of a rather similar idea in Variation 3 of the Handel Variations, Op. 24, but while that was impersonal pattern-making, this is personal and expressive.

12. Karl Geiringer, *Brahms: His Life and Work* (London: George Allen and Unwin, 1936), 221.

13. It is a texture used more extensively in the slow movement of the Piano Concerto No. 1 in D Minor, Op. 15.

14. Compare the "winsome smiles" counterpoint in Op. 117, No. 1, measures 43–44.

15. Are the three rising notes C–D–E♭ a subconscious memory of the C♯–D♯–E♯ in measures 238 and 244 in Op. 83, No. 1, which serve a rather similar function?

# CHAPTER NINE

# A Masterpiece from an Inhibition: Quashing the "Inquisitive Savage"

Joel Sheveloff

## I

PITY Musorgskii! He had to exist in a nineteenth century lacking in hot and cold showers, in a Russia lacking an aesthetically voracious middle class, amidst friends and colleagues who regarded his every stroke of genius as an error in musical grammar, and told him so in cruel terms. Worst of all, perhaps: our century has continued to enshrine nearly all the poorest judgments of his day as our own axioms. His reward for executing sixty-five of the very best *Lieder* anywhere in Romantic Europe, as well as the most wondrously telling settings of Russian words, was to have them altered, recast, even recomposed, and still most often performed in some poetaster's notion of acceptability. The greatest horrors, however, rained down on the operas *Boris Godunov, Khovanshchina,* and *The Fair at Sorochinsk;* to this day, one reads obscenities in reputable publications about the legendary Musorgskii clumsiness, lack of melodic sensitivity, misunderstanding of the requirements of the theater, ignorance of orchestration, and other incompetencies aggravated by alcoholism.[1] I wish some mechanism existed for an individual or a family, or even for admirers, to sue for posthumous slander, libel, and/or persecution; then Musorgskii's disciples would be eligible for untold fortunes.

Major work for solo piano rarely enticed the efforts of nineteenth-century Russian composers until the generation of Medtner, Rakhmaninov, and Skriabin. But the sudden early demise of Musorgskii's close acquaintance, the rather pedestrian painter-designer-architect Viktor Aleksandrovich Hartmann, induced our hero to concoct and execute a suite of piano pieces evoking his own experience touring a posthumous exhibit of Hartmann's work. This suite, *Kartinki s vistavskii* (*Pictures from* [or] *at an Exhibition*), has become so celebrated that it has maintained interest in the painter's work far beyond the intrinsic merits of any of it. I consider *Pictures,* from a purely musical standpoint, the finest epic-scale solo piano work to come from the second half of the unwieldy Romantic century; many musicians agree with this assessment, though they would not assert it in so unqualified a way. Too much detritus has clung to this work for people to praise it so. Up to this moment, Musorgskii's reward for this achievement has been a long series of editions of the pianistic text,[2] most of which alter the composer's ideas, both in large and small particulars, as well as an unending series of transcriptions of the piece for other media,[3] as though the original were merely a sketch for organ or orchestra — and finally, an incessant series of essays and monographs that evaluated all this musical parricide as great art, attempting to resurrect a noble but technically flawed work.[4]

We may forgive the early avatars of Russian music: Stasov, Taneev, Rimskii-Korsakov, Glazunov, Swan, Calvocoressi, and von Riesemann, for they lacked perspective, being so close to the creator and his creations. We must also forgive those Soviet writers, better left nameless, whose true feelings and ideas had to be sacrificed to the needs of a tyrannical regime that controlled aesthetic and critical writing as carefully as it did political opinion. We may never know how some of the very talented Soviet writers really felt, and among them may have been a few with great insight. I find it difficult, however, to forgive recent writers who have listened to and absorbed this piece, in all its versions, for the best part of a century. How can they prefer the Ravel or Tushmalov scorings to the original? How can they assert that the subject depicted counts as much, if not more, than the technical means employed to depict it? How can they continue to see *Pictures* as unsympathetic for the piano, as a torso requiring orchestral clothes? Why do they continue to attack the form of the whole and of the individual members of the suite as contorted, unrealized, and unsatisfactory? Audiences love the work, and for most of the right reasons, but most experts remain unconvinced.[5]

The curse hovering over *Pictures* recalls Apollo's curse of Cassandra for refusing his love; the god decreed that she would accurately see into the future, particularly its most unpleasant aspects, and predict it in time to warn those subject to its direst consequences — only to be believed by nobody, and thus to live to see the most horrific of her predictions come true, harming those for whom she most cared. Perhaps one of Musorgskii's many enemies cursed him similarly, allowing him to compose the very deepest and most wondrously expressive music, only to have its message misunderstood by those who needed most to comprehend it — virtuoso pianists,

critics, aestheticians, and musicologists. How else can one account for
the mass of insensitive judgment within the Musorgskii bibliography?[6]

Modest Petrovich possessed a breathtakingly beautiful handwrit-
ing, clear and filled with character, in Russian script, in Latin letters,
and in musical notes and signs. Those studying *Pictures* can examine a
thorough, excellent facsimile edition of the suite that appeared in
1975.[7] Many markings here appear to be late corrections by the
composer, indicating the extremity of care he lavished upon this
autograph. While this does not mean that the text has been freed from
all error, we can surmise that the essence of the composer's conception has been successfully transmitted to us here. I would advise any
pianist serious about performing the suite, no matter how "authentic"
the edition he owns claims to be, to repair to the nearest library
holding the facsimile to compare texts. If the comparison gets down to
the tiniest nuances of notes, dynamic markings, hand disposition, and
all the other parameters that make up a sophisticated notation like this
one, the sensitive investigating pianist cannot help but discover aspects
of the work that probe to its very nature, to the inner core of the role
of the piano in music. At the end of the process, every measure of the
work will stand above admiration, displaying the highest degree of
pianism, albeit of a maverick order, and thus its curse will ultimately
be exorcised.

## II

Who remembers the name of the critic who recognized that, while the
piano literature might be the best of all instrumental repertoires, it was
wasted on pianists? Such snap cynical judgment serves no purpose.
We all know at least one practitioner of the keyboard art, however,
who tends to regard every work as a vehicle for his or her own
magnification, and thus accepts only those factors within it that show
off his own technique to best advantage. People like this either avoid
performing, or perform in a distorted way, or go out of their way to
disparage music of great worth that fails to gratify their egos. In the
pianists' repertory, many major achievements fall into this category,
including such pieces as the following:

Beethoven — Piano Sonata No. 22 in F Major, Op. 54
Schubert — Adagio in E, D. 612
Schumann — *Novelleten,* Op. 21
Chopin — Piano Sonata No. 1 in C Minor, Op. 4
Liszt — *Scherzo und Marsch,* D Minor/Major, R. 20 (S. 177)
Brahms — Variations on a Hungarian Song in D, Op. 21, No. 2
Stravinskii — *Serenade en La* (1924)

All of the composers listed here knew the piano, composed well for it, and meant the works on the list to be positive contributions. All these pieces display seminal motives, tonal manipulations, metric surprises, formal coups, and pianistic effects of the highest caliber, but also contain elements that pianists fear and avoid as difficult to project while maintaining their own supposed mastery. Mature pianists warn their students that these pieces are "miscalculated, awkward, beneath the composer's usual efforts,"[8] or in some other way ungrateful to perform. Keyboard journals, manuals of the literature, and musicological evaluations of the music transmit these notions until they become truisms. Of all such works, *Pictures at an Exhibition* may be the most often sinned against. Most recorded performances ruin at least three movements, and render another three dully; nearly every edition makes some errors, and the evaluations, right up to the 1992 Cambridge Handbook by Michael Russ,[9] transmit short-sighted aesthetic judgments that contribute to the unending denigration of Musorgskii's achievement. What can be done to repair this complex, long-standing damage?

## III

All that one can do is attempt a thorough revaluation; unfortunately, this must begin as an extended review of Russ's work, for within its pages all the accomplishments, omissions, and errors of past writers, performers, and arrangers converge into an aesthetic Bermuda Triangle. Like all the other valuable tomes that have appeared under Julian Rushton's general editorship, this one sorts out everything you ever wanted to know into a package nearly anyone can control and use. Russ deals with just about every question you or I might ask, but most often superficially; this piece demands a far deeper probe than he essays. His review of the editions appears in a five-page section entitled "The manuscript," which just begins to discuss their differences. At its end, he prefers Manfred Schandert's rendering of the piano original for the *Wiener Urtext* series in 1984.[10] This edition, however, includes the metronome markings for each section first added in 1903 by Stasov and Rimskii-Korsakov, when they tried to resurrect interest in this all-but-dead piano suite.[11] Any attempt to specify speed with mathematical precision in a Russian Romantic solo piano work prone to *rubato,* as they have long been known to be, seems counterproductive. Even if taken merely as general guidelines, the Rimskii/Stasov numbers seem seriously faulty to me.

Take the case of the opening *Promenade,* its tempo marked by the composer: *Allegro giusto, nel modo russico, senza allegrezza, ma poco sostenuto,* to which the composer's "friends" added the metronomic indication of [ ♩ = 104]. This number seems to have influenced most performers who tend to play it somewhere between 96 and 112; some performers go even faster, but I have never heard anybody try to obey Harold Bauer's insane 152, mandated in his Schirmer publication of 1922. I offer a facsimile of the final measures of the *Great Gate of Kiev* in this edition for purposes of comparison of the most profligate recomposition in the nefarious history of Musorgskii alteration with any other rendering (Ex. 9.1).[12]

EXAMPLE 9.1. Final lines of the *Great Gate of Kiev* in the 1922 Schirmer edition, drastically altered by editor Harold Bauer. Copyright ©1922 (Renewed) by G. Schirmer, Inc. (ASCAP) International Copyright Secured. All Rights Reserved. Reprinted by Permission.

Musorgskii's words seem to me to negate these fast tempi; does anybody read past the opening *Allegro*? I take *Allegro giusto* to mean "with all deliberate speed," that is, at a measured tempo, perhaps a bit on the fast side. Add *nel modo russico (in a Russian manner),* a somewhat cryptic qualifier, which may mean something like "ponderously, thoughtful to an extreme." Then comes *senza alle-grezza,* which all but nullifies the opening *Allegro,* and finally, *ma poco sostenuto,* the clearest clause of all, and the overall meaning of these words seems to be "measured, slightly sustained — err if you must on the slow side." The governing image of this movement, that of the chunky, paunchy composer padding about from one exhibit to another, as he himself says in a letter to Stasov, "He does not hurry, but observes attentively." I do not see how anyone can project the image above at a pace that exceeds 88 to the quarter, and I would choose a range of speed somewhere between 72 and 88, with a median around 80. The inner sense of the tempo, as well as so many other parameters of the piece as we have grown accustomed to hearing it, has been ingrained in us by Ravel's orchestration which we all know so much better than the original. It is not that Ravel quotes these metronome markings — he uses none. We just hear a solo trumpeter answered by other strident brass boldly heralding the exhibition, rather than the intended vision of the composer prowling the gallery. Unconsciously, most pianists feel themselves performing a kind of transcription of the orchestral version — an intimidating situation.

As for the other metronome markings, most seem to me too fast, most often far too fast. That every so-called *Promenade,* though not so entitled in the autograph, receives the same 104 quarter note, shows the carelessness of Stasov and Rimskii; with these movements being so different from each other in every way other than motivically, the idea that "one size fits all" cannot be taken seriously. Rimskii/Stasov chose to employ the quarter note as the *integer valor* for every movement, including even *Il vecchio castello,* where its 6/8 meter makes only the eighth or dotted quarter notes the sensible standards of measurement. If they simply overlooked the dot and meant the dotted quarter rather than the quarter to equal their 56 beats per minute, I find the resultant tempo too fast to control the nuances of its message; at [ ♩ = 56], the speed seems almost correct, perhaps erring on the fast side; Rimskii/Stasov can hardly ever be said to err on the slow side. My general guidelines for these movements differ from those of Musorgskii's friends, as shown in Table 9.1.

I refuse to keep the quarter as the unit of measure in a movement in which another note value serves as motoric unit, and I add other metronome markings inside a movement in which a radical tempo

change occurs. Rimskii/Stasov only did that in *Baba Yaga.* You can
see how many of my suggestions run significantly slower than those of
Rimskii/Stasov.

| Movements | Rimskii/Stasov ♩ = | Sheveloff ♩ = |
|---|---|---|
| *Promenade* | 104 | 80 |
| *Gnomus* | 120 | 132 |
| [Interlude] | 104 | 72 |
| *Il vecchio castello* | 56 | ♩. = 48 |
| [Interlude] | 104 | 66 |
| *Tuileries* | 144 | 116 |
| *Bydlo* | 88 | ♪ = 96 |
| [Interlude] | 104 | 66 |
| *Ballet . . .* | 88 | 92 |
| *Goldenberg* | 48 | 42 |
| *Promenade* | 104 | 88 |
| *Limoges* | 120 | 100 |
| *Catacombae* | 57 | 50 |
| [Interlude] | ---- | 58 |
| *Baba Yaga* | 120 | 128 |
| *Andante mosso* | 72 | ♪ = 126 |
| *Kievan Gate* | 84 | ♩ = 40 |

Table 9.1. Rimskii-Korsakov's and Stasov's metronome markings, compared with Sheveloff's corrected markings

Performers complain that, when they try to get an audience used
to a tempo slower than the traditional one, they risk sounding dull,
listless, or lacking in the technique needed to carry off the "proper"
speed. What they must do to make up for the lack of speed, of course,
is to project details, nuances, things missed at the fast tempo. In this
opening *Promenade,* what would such details be? After all, once past
its opening *forte* marking, not a single dynamic marking appears; after
his verbose opening tempo marking, Musorgskii offers no further
advice. In fact, all markings disappear after measure 11, even the
horizontal lines indicating some form of unaccented *tenuto* that
appears above most single and chordal quarter notes. Slightly inconsistent slur markings appear above eighth notes in these opening
measures, most often linking them to subsequent quarters, but not
always — the notes then proceed without further interpretational
notation. In such a situation, one tends to assume that the composer
feels that he has given all the advice he needs to give, while the

remainder should be taken *simile,* as what had preceded it. Most players follow this path.

At a tempo of [ ♩ = 80], however, another reading of this information suggests itself. The player must keep the picture of the overweight composer in his or her mind, plodding now this way, now that. In dynamics, *forte* ought to prevail, but it should allow itself to fall to *mezzo forte* at times, and grow to *più forte* at others; the tempo should similarly allow itself a range of rubato, both on the fast and slow side, probably no greater than 72 and 88; the attacks ought to vary similarly, with an occasional small decrease or increase of weight. Musorgskii leaves it to the sensitive player, following the rise and fall of the melody, the twists and turns of the harmony, and the ebbs and flows of the tension between the relatively regular rhythm and the tricky meter, to decide when and where to make these small adjustments.

## IV

The literature about the 5/4 6/4 opening has been fairly large, but it has been hampered by unwarranted assumptions. In our century, meter signs tend to mean what they say, but in the nineteenth century, odd meters like 5, 7, 10, 11, or 13 gained no respect from contemporary theorists. Only duple and triple meters or their many multiples could serve as true bases for rhythmic organization. And yet, composers did employ odd meters, especially five. Chopin, Alkan, Reicha, and Glinka wrote some of the best-known early examples. For the first sixty years of the century, however, such examples remained very rare and thus very special; frequency did increase through this period, but very slowly. Then, in the 1870s, an explosion of odd meter took place, mostly as a measure or two here and there, but by the end of the century, pieces entirely in odd meter became commonplace. *Pictures* of 1874 comes along early enough so its use of odd meter must be defended through the sort of explanation theorists of that period were not prepared to make.

The best pedagogical model for making this point occurs in the music of, of all people, Richard Wagner. He almost never employed odd meter, but in the two notable places where he did write a bit of quintuple meter, each illustrates the two different principles underlying its use. For anyone espousing five as a mixture of two and three, such an explanation solves nothing: if one must be either in one or another, the regular alternation between them denies both as much as it affirms them. The only explanation must be arithmetic rather than geometric, that is, one based upon subtraction and/or addition rather than division and/or multiplication. The two Wagner examples demonstrate this convincingly.

In *Meistersinger,* two rare adjacent measures of 5/4 appear within an environmental meter of 4/4.[13] Wagner finds he must add an extra quarter value to these measures to take account of two extra syllables in explanatory lines sung by Fritz Kothner as he reads the rules of the Singer's Guild; the odd meter helps to convey the pedantic age-old rules, written in a style far older than that normally spoken by the people of the time of the tale. These two measures are thus not true 5/4 units, but rather a pair of 4/4 units with an extra quarter in each, thus playing a role we may fairly abbreviate as 4+1=5!

In *Tristan,* Wagner uses 5/8 in Tristan's mad scene in Act III, when the hero thinks back to the *Liebesnacht* in Act II.[14] The composer nearly quotes the love duet section in the previous act, a duet in triple meter — taking two measures of this music, subtracting one beat from the middle of the phrase, he gains the disturbed effect in a 6–1=5 way. Thus, one may add a beat to four or subtract one from six to obtain five; similarly, one may add a beat to six or subtract one from eight to gain a meter of seven. Chaikovskii's famous "limping waltz" in 5/4, which makes up the entirety of the second movement of his "Pathétique" Symphony, seems to me a six-minus-one, in which the downbeat of every odd measure of the waltz's natural 3/4 has been elided, allowing us to feel the dancers gliding an inch above the floor, so much are they in love. The sort of performance that goes 1–2–1–2–3 rather than 2–3–4–5–6 turns Chaikovskii's love magic into a ponderous plodding of barely pubescent pygmy pachyderms.

To return to the opening *Promenade:* the true meter of the movement must be understood as 6/4; of its twenty-four measures, Musorgskii only writes measures 1, 3, 5, 7, and 11 as 5/4; the remaining nineteen measures are set in the true meter. The sextuple division clearly dominates the metric environment, so the 5/4 measure would seem to be a subtractive construction. The most revealing clue to the metric puzzle comes from the motives, which seem to occur as two-quarter temporal units. For the sake of argument, I label them as they appear in the 6/4 second measure, rather than the first one of 5/4, as in Ex. 9.2.

When we compare measure 2 to measure 1, we see that the very same motives appear in both, though in retrograde order. The notes do not get reversed, but the motives do (Ex. 9.3).

EXAMPLE 9.2. Clarification of the two-quarter-note temporal units of the Promenade theme

EXAMPLE 9.3. Retrograde order of the x, y, and z motives in the *Promenade* theme

The overlap of the y and x motives on the fourth quarter of the 5/4 measure points up the "missing" beat, which I insert below to demonstrate the putative parallelism (Ex. 9.4).

EXAMPLE 9.4. *Promenade* theme with "missing" beat restored

A similar adjustment might be made in measure 3, the harmonized reiteration of measure 1 (Ex. 9. 5).

EXAMPLE 9.5. *Promenade* theme with "missing" beat restored in m. 3

The total effect of the analytically motivated adjustments, when one plays the first four measures so manipulated, may best be termed boring, thinned out, weakened. The tied melodic notes destroy the momentum of the phrase, and the C-minor (ii) chord seems timid and lame. But the altered phrase serves its purpose, revealing the back-and-forth rocking motivic action, somewhat obscured by the quintuple measures. Once one realizes the power of this motivic interaction, its effect can never again be hidden by the imbalancing effect of the odd measures.

The two-quarter-note motives project themselves unmistakably. Yet the meter signs with a denominator of 4 tend to divide the 6/4 measures in half rather than in thirds. Musorgskii knew 3/2 meter, of course, and if he wanted to bring the two-quarter-note motives into high relief, he should have used that meter. The 6/4 creates a cross-accent between the motivic division and the notated meter that enriches the unfolding sonority of the *Promenade,* keeping it thick, multilayered, and contrarily consistent. When combined with the unusually rapid tonal motion of the movement [tonic of B♭, mm. 1–4; dominant of B♭, mm. 5–6; dominant of D♭, mm. 7–11; dominant of F, mm. 12–13; uncertain and modal, mm. 14–16; returning to the dominant of B♭, mm. 17–21; and return to tonic of B♭, mm. 22–24], the picture of the ever-changing nomadic behavior of Musorgskii in the gallery attains three real dimensions. This tends to confirm the aforementioned performance flexibilities. Within a couple of minutes, the entire complex scene completes its effects, setting up the musical rendition of the first item in the exhibition. The player has to project a great many shifts of mood, position, and receptivity in a very short time — what instrument allows its performer to do this with more pinpoint control than the piano? What could be more soloistic, more pianistic, than this kind of musical portraiture? And none of this gets addressed by anyone, from Stasov through Russ.

V

Several previous writers have attempted to deal with the temporal, material form and the tonal plan of *Pictures* as a whole, with a pronounced lack of success on both fronts: the outer plan of the progressions, and the interaction of neighboring members. Nor do these pictures convey any of the drama or passion of the music; each one tends to be tabular, mechanical, and stenographic at exactly those points at which it should be explanatory, subjective, and thorough.[15] For instance, nobody brings up the anomaly of the key of the opening

*Promenade* — B♭ major is ultimately the dominant rather than the tonic of the whole. When we first hear this very impressive movement, so powerfully prolonging and weaving its structure in and around B♭, we get the strong sense that this ought to be the tonic of the whole, only to be surprised as the later movements pull us away — but something within us keeps hoping that the very end will somehow find its way back to B♭. All listeners gifted with a sense of tonality spread over time must be disconcerted by this turning away from reasonable expectations.

I recall the first piece that ever surprised me in this way: Chopin's Second Ballade, Op. 38, which prolongs F major stubbornly for forty-five measures, before suddenly shifting to A minor. It circles back to F in measure 82, but that merely teases. By the time the Ballade's 203 measures have passed by, we know the piece's real key to be A minor, and that the opening F functioned as submediant of an incomplete progression; the "key" of the beginning turns out to be illusory, but we do not know that until the very end.

Schumann's *Kreisleriana,* Op. 16, begins with a brilliant D-minor movement that ends up being the dominant of the entire collection. Many other European pieces follow similar unpredictable routes. Of Musorgskii's other piano works, only the late (circa 1880) *Derevne* (In the country) ends in a key different from that at the outset, but many of his sixty-five songs end of a tonic that makes one revaluate the opening, including every one in the *Songs and Dances of Death.* This sort of incomplete progression plays an important role in the expression of the program of a piece, and *Pictures* is nothing if not a kind of subcutaneous program music. As the pictures and promenades fly by, tonal and motivic information pile up, and the plan clarifies itself, but thus far not to professional analysts.

The long-range tonality does not become clear in the first four pieces, which proceed from B♭ major through E♭ minor to A♭ major and its enharmonic brother, G♯ minor. This falling through the circle of fifths seems aimless and acentric at first. But as the keys proceed, and the tonal directions change, even doubling back, we discover the true center to be E♭, and its ultimate pattern may be symbolized as shown in Ex. 9.6.

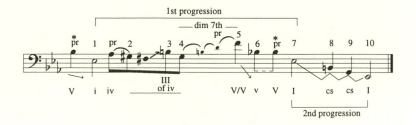

EXAMPLE 9.6. Overview of the tonal scheme of *Pictures,* revealing E♭ as the central key

Most pieces fall into one large tonal progression, but this one contains two of them, still another surprise. The first extends from *The Gnome* to *Limoges,* and the second from *Limoges* to the Finale, the *Kievan gate.* The tonal world of the first progression follows a fairly familiar sort of progression, while the second divides the octave into major thirds in the sort of symmetrical structure then rare, save for the most exploratory works of Liszt, Brahms, or Reger. The tonal language does not grow ever more radical with each new picture, but the second progression's music leans further to the left than the first.

On the matter of material organization, Russ's argumentative *ostinato* concerns Musorgskii's avoidance of German sonata-allegro form. First of all, German Romantic piano music explored many other designs apart from sonata, especially the Schumann program piano collections from Op. 2 to Op. 21. Russ does mention this, but fails to follow up on the similarities between *Pictures* and many elements within the Schumann cycles, a link that would work against the picture Russ paints of Musorgskii as a narrow, nationalistic, independent agent. The heart of his image reads: "Schumann and Musorgskii are highly divergent. In Musorgskii, structure is subordinate to content and Russianness in a way that Schumann's respect for a pure musical language would never allow."[16] The musical evidence of motivic and tonal links in both composers belies this assertion. Russ, like Ashkenazii and so many others, harps on *Pictures'* Russianness! For them, being Russian meant being irrational, unpredictable, thoughtful, but chaotic, and especially lacking in balance — totally unlike a classic sonata movement.

Once and for all, Borodin could be just as "Russian" in a sonata structure as Musorgskii in a through-composed form; and Schumann could be as pictorial, as startling in his harmony, rhythm, and other parameters of musical syntax as Musorgskii, and all that nearly a half century before *Pictures.* This may not be the place to explore all the

similarities between Musorgskii and his putative model, but any
informed student of both composers, once aware of the possibility,
cannot help but notice parallels and similarities. Recent scholarship
has drawn close attention to Rossini, Bellini, and Meyerbeer as
models for certain elements in Glinka; to Mozart, Beethoven, and
Schubert as models for Chaikovskii; to Reger as a model for Pro-
kofiev; and Mahler inspiring Shostakovich. These Russians, all as
"Russian" as Musorgskii, sought kindred spirits in the West. Why
then should we be resistant to the idea of a mainstream model for
some factors in Musorgskii? Every Russian composer essaying into the
world of serious concert music needed a guide from Western culture,
one congenial to his own aesthetic. The pictorial Schumann seemed a
perfect parent for Musorgskii, both in content and in form; even Russ
finds none of the forms within *Pictures* to be defective.

The following list summarizes the musical form of each
"picture":

*Gnomus* — a three-element rondo, beginning with the subor-
    dinate linking passage between the main ideas;
*Il vecchio castello* — a short rondo over an ostinato, with a
    sensitive variation process making each reiteration fresh;
*Tuileries* — an almost Mendelssohnian rounded binary grop-
    ing towards incipient ternary;
*Bydlo* — another ternary over an ostinato, but contrasting with
    *Castello* in mood and in placement of the climax;
*Unhatched chicks* — an old-fashioned minuet and trio, regular
    and perfectly satisfying;
*Samuel Goldenberg und Schmuyle* — a Russian combination
    form — that is, section A, section B, and then a section
    combining A and B, followed by a brief coda;
*Limoges* — a ternary with an almost sonata-like rewiring of
    parts of the return;
*Catacombae* — a unitary form, unfolding like a Baroque pre-
    lude reduced to its very essence;
*Baba Yaga* — a complex ternary, approaching rondo form;
*Gate at Kiev* — a sort of sonata rondo.

Each movement achieves its own kind of formal balance; Schumann's
*Humoreske,* Op. 20, and his *Novelletten,* Op. 21, seem more open to
criticism on this account than *Pictures.* Even the many interludes

based on the *Promenade* music seem to fill their roles satisfactorily. A few details in these interludes defy compositional norms, but only mildly, and these can be justified by anyone with a sympathetic ear. Forms within *Pictures* seem varied and balanced according to the same criteria we apply to the Romantic masters in Western Europe — so why do so many critics continue to carp about form in Musorgskii? Will the Iron Curtain between his technical brilliance and the faulty perceptions of audiences fed huge doses of disinformation ever fall?

# VI

Russ says of *Catacombae* that "with its dissonant, unbalanced chords and uncertain tonality, [it] is certainly not conceived in terms of piano sonority."[17] This climaxes his constant attack on Musorgskii's lack of real piano figures, particularly of arpeggios. While Schumann's pianism has rarely been criticized, many of the movements in his cycles employ unusual pianistic dispositions, that his contemporaries thought poor to project in performance; a very few musicians still do. It seems quite clear to me that Musorgskii, like Schumann, in trying to express the essence of a poetic or pictorial manifestation in music, strove to avoid the usual sort of pianistic effect. I believe further that, if played with understanding and sympathy, these effects would be seen and heard to work wonderfully well.

Take the case of *Catacombae,* which so many writers feel to be a mere sketch for orchestration. It probes the lower half of the keyboard deeper and more unequivocally than any other movement. It strips itself bare of figuration to depict the subterranean scene of Roman tragedy. It employs far more dynamic contrasts, one right after another, than any other movement. Russ finds these chords "Stravinskian" and "unbalanced."[18] These chords, perhaps more than any other feature of this movement, must be labelled "Musorgskiian." Sounds just like them fill the left hand of *Bydlo,* may be heard in several songs, and rattle through *Boris Godunov,* especially the music associated with the policeman in the Prologue's first act, and with the rogue monk Varlaam. Stravinskii is only one of several twentieth-century composers to ape this detail. If it seems unbalanced on pianos of our time, it may be explainable as a function of our high-pressure, thickly wrapped stringing, far beyond nineteenth-century norms.

Perhaps no other movement in *Pictures* arises so purely from the possibilities of piano sonority! What other instrument can sound out chords like these with one sound quality, with such a sense of unity? In all the orchestral versions, colors clash in profusion among the low brass, woodwinds, and strings. Strident brass proclaim the *fortissimo* chords and mellow brass answer in the *piano* chords, and any voice-leading connections between them become squashed in the color shifts. The piano, on the other hand, follows the lines with a clarity born of a single sounding board. The pianist should render *Catacombae* secure in the glory of a piano sonority that cannot be duplicated by anything else.

Strike the opening *fortissimo* triple-octave B, and revel in its fermata, as the great cavity of the full grand resounds with the aftermath of hammer on strings. Pedal the B late to keep the sound from dying away fully without being gross at its attack, and release it just as the fingers strike the *piano* triple-octave G, and the starkness of the dynamic contrast will outdo Ravel's trombone-horn dichotomy. The pianist has to breathe, but this does not affect his volume, phrasing, or ability to control a difficult passage. The orchestral winds cannot manage the lines in measures 4 through 11 [mm. 490–97 of *Pictures* as a whole) of *Catacombae* on one breath, nor can they make the dynamic contrasts without intonation problems.

Only the piano can make each dissonance ring out in proper balance, and then make each resolution identify itself by voice and direction. Only the piano can make the pedal tones sustain gently, without overpowering the remainder of the texture. Only the piano can render the deep thirds in measures 12–14 [mm. 499–500] without producing a thunder of low overtones obscuring the musicality of the combination. Only the piano can bring out the bass A pedal in measures 19–22 [505–8] in just the right way, so that its poignant sound againt the G minor chord in measure 22 [508] reveals that the G on the last quarter of that measure finally resolves this most stubborn element of the preceding progression. Only the piano can cleanly project the contrary motion in measures 25–28 [511–14] and thus make the point of the polychord in measures 29–30 [515–16].

For the pianist who loves and understands piano sonority, this movement should be the glory of *Pictures,* not its horror. Once known, however, this does not reduce the pianist's problems, for the tending of every nuance here requires enormous care. Few in an audience will imagine how much pianistic skill it takes to bring these slow-motion effects to the fore, but that should not lessen the pianist's sense of duty. The opening of Brahms' Op. 119, No. 1, in which a pedal F♯ is to be heard as melody, going to A on the final semiquaver, rather than as the first of a series of descending thirds that merely arpeggiates, rarely gets performed correctly . . . and the skill needed to solve that problem parallels that needed to make *Catacombae* the rich celebration of piano sonority Musorgskii crafted with such care.

The *attacca* problem may not seem very important, but much of the drama of *Pictures* hinges on the connections among its fifteen sections. Musorgskii marks eight of these fourteen connections *attacca*. Most of the published versions lack the vital *attacca* indication at the close of the opening *Promenade*, which causes many pianists to slow down at its end and come to a complete stop. The final chord of the *Promenade* serves as the dominant of *Gnomus*, its Bb being the common-tone link between the movements. The flow of one movement into another, if one avoids any slowing down or hesitancy, attains great dramatic power and presence, veritably pulling the viewer into the picture. This effect seems to be exactly what the composer strives for — once one has heard it this way, no other will ever seem correct. And once one has gained this insight, all the other ties, from the Interlude to *Il vecchio castello,* to *Tuileries,* and so forth, seem to gain by *attacca* treatment in the same way, for the same reason. The other connections, between the end of a picture and the resumption of the composer's lumbering walk, could take a bit of time, as he (and we, hearing through his ears) recovers his sense of reverting to his position in the gallery, and with it, his composure. Musorgskii does not mark these other connections *attacca,* confirming the unmarked promenades' primary scenic role as preludial rather than intertudial or postludial. Of all the connections, the most difficult to execute properly may be that between the *Ballet of the Unhatched Chicks* and *Samuel Goldenberg und Schmuyle,* for while the former shows an *attacca,* the *fermata* that superscribes its final measure's concluding quarter rest seems to contradict the connection's momentum, at least somewhat. The other connections present no anomalies. In about four out of five performances I have heard, both live and recorded, at least two of the *attacca* markings caused the pianist or orchestra enough difficulty to make them stumble, often nearly fatally.

# VII

In his not-quite-competent videocassette of *Pictures,* in which he both plays the piano version and conducts the Leo Funtek orchestration,[19] Vladimir Ashkenazii attacks the Ravel orchestration as entertainment music, too lovely, too well groomed, too French; he claims that the roughness and depth of feeling in *Pictures* exhibits a Russian suspiciousness, a paranoia, an unspecified sense of unease that needs to be communicated by any scoring. My views about all scorings have already been made absolutely limpid; I thus cannot agree that such alleged unease inspires this work, and would now like to suggest what does!

Musorgskii walked through the memorial exhibition and saw what all subsequent commentators on the surviving exhibits have evaluated as promising but unfulfilled work. Signs of talent in Hartmann appear everywhere, but signs of genius, of real accomplishment, hardly anywhere. The young man died just as he seemed to be about to realize his promise. Again and again, annotators of notes on programs or recordings assert that the musical rendition of the pictures glorifies them far beyond their worth. They never think that the music may be using the sketches and architectural plans as a springboard for a deep program, a spiritual revelation the exhibition may have imparted to Musorgskii, a program so transparently straightforward, when one examines the order of the pictures, that it should have appeared in print generations ago. . . .

The tragedy of Hartmann's early death cannot help but suggest many instances of similar artistic lives cut short prematurely, as well as the notion that even those who live a full life may have done still better work had they only been granted some time beyond their allotment. All we truly own is the time God lets us stay here, and we must find a way to accomplish all we can in that time. But first we must go through childhood, learning the inner workings of the world of our time, after which, and only after which, we can assert ourselves, expressing in our adult work the ways in which we strive to improve this world.

I hear the first progression from *Gnomus* to *Goldenberg,* as a depiction of vital parameters of childhood, and the remainder as the adulthood that all too often gets halted abruptly. Each picture suggests a particular aspect of the processes that contribute to our personal development, but that also takes its toll, perhaps far more of a toll than we know. Every lesson brings pain, sometimes long-lasting pain, and limits our horizons and potential for accomplishment.

We all know *Gnomus;* some of us call him the bogeyman, or the big bad wolf, or the evil spirit that lurks in every dark corner. One of the first things any child (except Wagner's Siegfried, as you recall) learns is fear. The huge and dark world is filled with danger, and the more parents dote over us and try to keep us safe, the more we worry. "He" will get us unless we behave properly, and learn to say our prayers properly, and intone them every night faithfully as well as properly. *Gnomus* teaches us fear, caution, religion, and respect for things greater than ourselves, a necessary set of lessons, as every culture knows and maintains: in every country someone like the

Brothers Grimm exists, just in case our parents insufficiently inculcate society's requisite fears and totems.

The other side of the fairy tale, in which one plays the role of knight-errant, sounds forth in *Il vecchio castello.* As one reaches that phase of childhood at which every adult comments upon how big one has grown, and how one must behave like the little man or woman one is becoming, the adventures of Gallahad and Roland and Sigurd inspire one to deeds of unparalleled courage and daring, not right away of course, but as soon as one knows his or her time has come. The element of danger remains, particularly in the constantly throbbing bass line, and one remains afraid; but no longer will one let fear win. The end of the musical picture does not tell us how the adventure finishes, for like our dreams, we awaken before the tale's *dénouement.*

The world of play, as represented by *Tuileries,* turns out not to be an unalloyed pleasure. Children can be startlingly cruel to one another, committing hurtful acts with the vigor that comes from the ignorance of just how much it hurts. As we grow and learn pain, we hesitate to inflict the sort of unthinking damage we did as children. The fast motion of events in the park covers a multitude of misdeeds, and each dissonance portrays one, only some of which are resolved. When involved in play, we all participate joyously, fully, with abandon; afterwards it all seems so mean-spirited and wasteful — still we come back the next day. The Tuileries may be a park in Paris, but the sounds of that play would not have sounded much different in St. Petersburg, Buenos Aires, or the Bronx. We all recall playing our children's games, no matter how old we get.

With the rumbling of *Bydlo,* the Polish ox-cart, we move from the world of play to that of hard work. The child watches the cart go by, perhaps thinking about his father's line of business, or about his own hard work someday in the future, of whatever kind that may be, and hoping he will be equal to it. Then he turns away, hoping that the days of toil and care stay far away.

What came first, the chicken or the egg? How do bees and birds and mammals and people procreate? Some parents tell the truth early, some wait and tell tales about storks and angels and seeds and love that manifests itself in ways that you cannot yet comprehend. Every birth is a unique miracle, something so wonderful that no description does it justice. . . . In the end, the child gets somewhat confused for awhile. The process of confusion and unravelling could hardly be better represented than in the *Ballet of the Unhatched Chicks.* Hartmann's sketches for a ballet scene from a work called *Trillby* suggest all this fairly directly, and the very silliness of the costumes evokes the wrong answers with which parents try to delay having to explain sex fully and graphically, for they see almost no way to avoid the child getting the impression that sex is ugly, coarse, and unclean. The uncanny lightness of this scherzo evokes the delicacy of the manner in which this subject is broached.

Of all behaviors taught in childhood, none can be uglier than bigotry. The *Samuel Goldenberg und Schmuyle* movement, as Taruskin has brilliantly pointed out, represents just one Jew, who, no matter how much money and power and respectability he accrues, carries inside him his original self, the humble peddler *Schmuyle* who does whatever he has to do to survive.[20] And no matter how high he may rise, the lowest Orthodox Christian peasant has the right to despise him, to call him "Christ killer," even to kill him without fear of the law. He may feel himself a Prince within the Jewish community, but in the Russian hierarchy he ranks just above an insect. How is prejudice taught to each new generation and what makes it right? During his active, relatively brief career in composition, Musorgskii set music representing Africans, Asians, and exotic people of all kinds, and he set them sympathetically, but he also knew the local taboos about Jews and Gypsies and such. No adult survived in Tsarist Russia without knowing these rules. So the child in *Pictures* learns the following, in the composer's order:

Fear
Courage
Pain
Play
Work
Sex
Hate

No child gets to be an adult without absorbing all of these things, for better or worse. They all helped one survive in that time and place, and in most other times and places, to the everlasting damnation of our species.

The longest *Promenade* of the entire work comes just after *Samuel Goldenberg,* and begins the adult half of the work, the second progression with new and difficult tonal relations; the *Promenade*'s extended final cadence promises almost immediate revelations, and we are not to be disappointed. (The omission of this *Promenade* in some early editions, as well as in Ravel's orchestration, may have played a vital role in the program's not being deduced before now.)

*Limoges* puts us back in France once more, and sounds more like *Tuileries* than we expect. Now the people in conflict have become adults, and the marketplace the real world, the one of work and commerce, the one that chews up its losers as totally as it rewards its winners. Play prepares one for work after all, because success demands frantic, ceaseless activity, and everyone tries to get the best of you, and there seems to be no place to hide, not even in the bosom of one's own family. The mad world of *Limoges* outdoes that of *Tuileries,* and, unfortunately, we do not get to grow out of it — in our society we can retire out of it with some security, while in Musorgskii's Russia, and Europe, and the rest of the then "civilized" world, one participated in this madness all the way to the grave.

We read the Bible, history, and philosophy to search for answers to our deepest problems. *Pictures'* viewer searches the Roman catacombs for such answers and hears voices, but he cannot fathom the applicability of their answers, no matter how hard he tries — he can't even tell what tonality they employ. *Catacombae Romanae* and *Cum mortuis in lingua mortis* both sound profound and important, but sadly enigmatic. Any search for answers in this world meets with frustration, the sense that an answer exists, but that it will remain shrouded and beyond our abilities to fathom. As children, we finally learned not to keep asking *why,* for it tortured our parents past shrieking. Once we become adults, we know that asking that question merely tortures us. We may gain untold amounts of data, much of it useful, but information rarely provides real answers. That explains the message of "speaking with the dead in a dead language"; we do not comprehend what they cannot recall.

The sound and message of *Baba Yaga* seems to mirror that of *Gnomus* in many ways. The witch has great powers, and more specific ones than the old bogeyman. But this particular portrait of her resides within a huge CLOCK, the ultimate symbol of *Pictures at an Exhibition* as a whole. Time may not be the villain, but its lack robs us of our opportunities and hopes. Like the witch, it hurries onwards, paying no attention to us, our cares or needs. We want to accomplish so much, but the witch works hard to prevent us, setting up every sort of obstacle in our path. We persist, and build and draw and design and work, producing wondrous structures like the *Bogatyrs' Gate at Kiev.* Musorgskii portrays its grandeur unforgettably, but we must recall that the gate would never be built. It remained a sketch on the wall of an exhibition, a promise unrealized. The sudden ending portrays the way death cut Hartmann off in a sound as cruel as any since the end of Jean-Philippe Rameau's *La poule,* in which the chicken's head is suddenly cut off in mid-cluck. Finally, the return, within the *Kiev* movement itself, of the *Promenade* portrays the way Musorgskii felt himself drawn into Hartmann's personal tragedy, and of course, Musorgskii too would soon die far too young. The same theme inside *Cum mortuis* signifies that Musorgskii also seeks the meaning of life, and our recognition of all this symbolizes our own fear that we too will be defeated by time, without coming to a glimpse of a hint of any sort of answer, or the full measure of our desired accomplishments.

Thus I view *Pictures at an Exhibition.* Its program, when we think closely about it, differs little from Liszt's *Les Preludes* and many other Romantic compositions that attempt to deal with questions of a philosophy of life, and how we deal with that greatest adventure of all that begins only with death. That one element, falling in love, does not appear anywhere in *Pictures,* typifies Musorgskii, who has avoided matters of love since some of his earliest songs. The so-called love interests in *Boris* and *Khovanshchina* turn sour in every case, except when the lovers immolate themselves. But in all other respects, I think the meaning of the pictures, in their particular order, and set as two adjoining, overlapping progressions, speaks for itself. The titles of the pictures should have been all the clues we needed to work out the rest of the story; if Chopin had given similar titles to his four Ballades, we might have been able to divine a program for them as well. But because Musorgskii has always been regarded as a primitive, a savage who discovers music as he makes it, the idea that he could have housed *Pictures* within a rational and meaningful program, escaped those very diviners.

For those who doubt the division of *Pictures* into three essential subjects: childhood, adulthood, and premature death, the three great song cycles Musorgskii composed in this same era: *Nursery, Sunless,* and the *Songs and Dances of Death,* concern themselves with one or another of the very same issues. Schumann, the likely model for Musorgskii, also dealt with the same subjects at various times in piano and song groups too well known to every musician to need to be cited here. These subjects rank high among those that most interested Romantics in every art, every country, and of every socio-political persuasion. Once one has been shown this program for *Pictures,* one tends to react: "Of course! Why did I not see that myself?" Then one notices how brief and clear all the childhood movements seem, as distinct from the long, convoluted structures of the adult ones. Then one notices how Eb minor and major occur at the vital junctures, dividing the whole into two principal sections. Then one senses how important to the program the motivic connections from aspects of the main *Promenade* idea are to the pictures themselves (a subject Russ handles extremely well). Finally, the level of respect this masterpiece has always been worth, emerges.

# VIII

Michael Russ lives in a galaxy of musical analysis systems in which he grants equal validity to traditional chord grammar, the mechanics of Heinrich Schenker, the modal theories of Balkan folklorists, and the pitch-class castles in the air erected by the Forteans. He moves from one to another with stunning ease and seeming authority. Finding pentatony, octatony, a Lydian or Phrygian usage may strike him as useful, but the sense of the unity of the musical language behind the diversity of sonorities for the many pictures seems to elude him. I find his choice of analytical system arbitrary and most often misguided, and must report that I find not one analytical sketch unequivocally accurate. I find Ex. 6 on page 66 particularly troubling. Why use set identification for a perfectly normal nineteenth-century chromatic procedure, all of which remains locked in an E♭-minor prolongation?

Reading this portion of Russ's seventh chapter reminds me of a lecture I heard many years ago in which a strict constructionist of standard harmony found nineteen modulations within the twenty-five measures of Chopin's Prelude in E Minor, Op. 28, No. 4. The example seems perfectly apt since the descending chromatic scale that produces the wondrous suspension of musical disbelief there does sound like a first cousin of the chromatic manipulations within *Gnomus*. Chopin's harmony comes from linear processes, and makes most "chords" nonfunctional in the narrow harmonic sense; this does not disturb the easy tonal sense of the whole, however, or its antecedent-consequent form. Musorgskii adds to Romantic standard usage of unfolding chromatic material a leaping back and forth among voices that can confound the literal-minded analyst. He transfers register at dizzying speeds and crosses voices in the most unlikely places.

Russ's Ex. 6 illustrates his thesis that Musorgskii's sound-world looks forward to a piece like Schoenberg's *Klavierstück,* Op. 11, No. 1, or Webern's Bagatelle, Op. 9, No. 1, and thus requires pitch-class set nomenclature to make this point. He then concentrates on the overlapping mixture of a Phrygian scale on E♭ with a chromatic tetrad on the scale's high end, and an incomplete (and highly unlikely) whole-tone scale at the low end, within the usual flow of Fortean free numerical interval calculations intended to impede musicianship. In a piece that Russ admits clearly prolongs and remains aurally obvious as

within Eb minor, he remains incapable of seeing that all of this
tangential data misses the main musical point of *Gnomus,* not its pitch-
class content, but its specific spacing, voice-leading, and the harmonic
implications within its textures of many unharmonized but still
functional tones.

The one place a pitch-class might have taught Russ something,
had he chosen to note it, comes in the opening *Promenade* in Bb. A
cursory examination of the chromatic pitch occurrences, in descending
order, even when reckoned by the admittedly rough standard of the
number of measures in which each appears, reveals that the tonic Bb
appears everywhere save in measures 5 and 7 — all in all, in twenty-
two of the twenty-four measures of the movement; the leading-tone A,
avoided at the pentatonic outset, and sidestepped in the inner shift to
Db, shows up in measures 3–4, 6, 12–19, and 22–24 — just fourteen
measures; Ab can be found only in measures 8–11, functioning only as
V of Db. G occupies each and every measure except measure 8 —
twenty-three measures — consistent with its important role in the
pentatonic, for if Bb functions as tonic of the "major" manifestation of
the scale, G serves as tonic of its "minor" manifestation; Gb appears
in measures 9–11, three of the four measures of the Db digression; F
as dominant tone, and putative seventh of G, lasts throughout the
*Promenade* — not one measure lacks it; E♮, as the leading tone to F,
occupies measures 4, 13–14, 16–17, 21, and 23, seven measures in
all; Eb, as the confirming fourth tone of Bb major, gets avoided for the
first six measures, but then interweaves with E♮, in measures 7–11,
16–22, and 24, with the battle between the two Es joined fully in
measure 16; the pentatonic third D fills measures 1–6, 8–19, and 21–
24, twenty of the movement's twenty-four measures, the temporary
tonic Db only appears in measures 8 and 10; the passing second of the
pentatonic, C, can be found in twenty measures, including 1–6, 8–19,
and 21–24. The half-step above the tonic, whether B♮ or Cb, never
appears in this movement, only to be the opening tone of *Gnomus.*
Musorgskii saves this tone to be fresh for *Gnomus,* an action I take to
be purposeful and meaningful, while most commentators, if they had
noticed it in the first place, would regard it as serendipitous. Its
appearance at the outset sets *Gnomus* apart, and helps to shift us from
the pentatonic-diatonic realm of Bb to an Eb minor contrastingly
chromatic and angular.

Russ calls the first seventeen-measure passage "entirely mono-
dic." That both hands move in parallel octaves throughout cannot be
denied, but this is the apparent voice-leading, not the true motion of
structural lines. Three voices in close spacing assert themselves in a
typically Musorgskiian irrational pattern: the opening Cb reasserts

itself on the fourth eighth and then resolves to Bb, while the Eb on the second eighth quickly resolves to a D♮, which reasserts its integrity on the final eighth of the first measure — the third voice does not become manifest until the long Gb that begins in the second measure [m. 26 of *Pictures* as a whole], a Gb that wants to resolve so desperately, that every second the pianist holds it, past the fermata and into the third [27th] measure, its frustration grows greatly. What we have experienced in this opening gesture may best be summarized as a progression from an Eb–Gb–Cb sonority to a presumptive D–F–Bb resolution, in which the opening Cb functions as an incomplete upper neighbor of the Bb that would have completed the tonic triad. And the resolution, by not getting to the F, but sitting on the Gb that creates an augmented sonority with its nearby Bb and D♮, balances the uncertainty of the first chord, with one of its own.

The semidissonant Cb employed here falls into a vi$^6$ tradition that goes back to the opening of Mozart's "Dissonant" String Quartet, K. 465, the very similar opening of *Chaos* in Haydn's *Creation,* and hundreds of nineteenth-century harmonic experiments, perhaps most notably the string of such progressions dominating Chopin's A-Minor Mazurka, Op. 17, No. 4.[21] The two factors that distinguish *Gnomus* from its forbears are the rhythmic grouping of its arpeggiation, and the unwillingness to complete the resolution from Gb to F. In fact, when the Gb finally does move in measure 8 [32], it skips F, going instead to Fb, Eb, and the D♮ that harmonizes the structural Bbs in measure 9 [33] and 10 [34]. The lack of F♮ here continues Musorgskii's idea of saving important tones for dramatic entries noted in the opening *Promenade:* the F finally appears as the first melodic tone of the main theme in measure 19 [43], where it functions as yet another incomplete upper neighbor, this time an accented one fully harmonized rather than arpeggiated. That this upper-neighbor idea dominates this movement can not be noticed in the fundamentalist set mechanics of Russ. His characterization of any portion of this movement as "nonfunctional,"[22] even when it may be just a brief harmonic progression, seems to me a fatal flaw of his analytical procedures, systems, and views.

A reasonable analysis of the basic structural procedures in some of *Pictures'* most experimental moments appeared just as the 1990s began.[23] In a graphic representation of the *Catacombae* section, Derrick Puffett makes one solid musical point after another, particularly affirming the B centrality of the whole, while acknowledging the power of the F♯ dominant as a near-tonic of its own, which almost renders the B as a subdominant at the end of the *Cum mortuis* portion of the compound movement. The most recent exploration of this movement, on the other hand, spends so much time on the foreground level, fighting over almost every Musorgskii choice of chromatic notation, that it loses perspective about the relative weight of the elements cited.[24] Allow me to list and comment upon some dubious assertions by its author, Simon Perry, who generally writes with admirable scholarly caution and care: (1) In *Goldenberg,* measures 26–27 [418–19], he judges the right hand's Fb, which he admits arises from Musorgskii's assignment of functional priority to the directional necessity of the voice-leading of the top line, as weakening the sense of dominant of the tonic Bb.[25] He fails to mention, however, that the F♮ in the left hand anchors the structural tonality in such a way that it reduces the Fb to the status of mere accented passing tone.[26] (2) In *Limoges's* final measure (m. 40 [486]), Perry makes a great fuss about the enharmonic notation of several notes, though he understands that they all function as part of a direct, unimpeded chromatic ascent. He wonders about bimodal and bitonal implications of this very rapid passage — one that goes by so fast that the ear has a hard time picking out any of these details — without realizing that every note in the chromatic spectrum does sound in this measure *except* B♮.[27] Musorgskii saves this tone to be the opening sonority of *Catacombae,* just as he saved it throughout the opening *Promenade* to be fresh for *Gnomus*; that priority colors the peculiarities of this measure far more than any of the factors about which Perry speculates. (3) In the actual *Catacombae* movement, Perry's concern about the relative notations of A♯ and Bb seem misplaced to me, as both seem to have no function besides the basic directional one.[28] (4) The most interesting point he brings up has also long interested me: the C×s in measures 11 and 13 [528 and 530] of the *Cum mortuis* section. His discussion makes a lot of sense, but the D♮s in the bass of each measure tend to make me think that Musorgskii meant D♮ in the right hand as well, and simply erred here.[29] All octatonic, whole-tone, and/or modal explanations seem at best tangential, and most often irrelevant. We clearly hear the notated C×, together with the subsequent B♯, as a double auxiliary, resolving both times to the C♯ in the subsequent measure. Speculation that the C× means to go to a D♯ somewhere in the piece, seems strained. I cannot hear it, no matter how much I try. That the answer may lay in an error by the composer is always the final option for anyone who respects the creator, particularly one so maligned as Musorgskii, and this seems to me the only choice!

# IX

A great deal of work remains to be done about the virtues, character-istics, and limitations of the pianofortes available in nineteenth-century Russia to the heroic generation of Chaikovskii, Musorgskii, Rubin-shtein, Borodin, et al. The very different qualities of the piano works of the St. Petersburg school from those of the Moscow school may in part result from the inspiration of particular pianos, perhaps of varied manufacture. This factor has never been taken into account, though some evidence exists for it. The contrasting ideologies of the two schools has been credited and blamed for everything, though the evidence for that is, and always has been, membrane thin. The great scale in Kiev's measures 111–13 [859–61] that traverses almost all eighty-eight keys, implies a relatively light, quick action, while most of the other sonorous combinations in this *finale* imply the sort of rich, full sonority that nowadays comes about largely by banging on the hard actions of our super Steinways and steely Yamahas. I have always felt strongly that the pianists of my time have had inordinate difficulty with *Pictures* because its many shifting demands, on our "obstacle-course" instruments, simply wears them out. It has been demonstrated that such assertions apply fully to Brahms, Debussy, and Grieg — and now that Russia has opened up to Western musical scholars, I feel confident that we shall learn the same to be true for Musorgskii. In fact, his day seems to be dawning; recent recordings of the long neglected early piano music,[30] of the choral works, the early songs, and the other "lesser" works may be signaling the end of the notion of Musorgskii as "inquisitive savage." This chapter may end up being the useless nail in a coffin already being lowered into the earth. In light of the unwarranted persecution that this man and his music endured for so long, it seems to me that a bit of hyperbolic redun-dancy in the opposite direction is more than warranted. I think of it as a sort of affirmative action, the kind that the dead require less than the living, but require nonetheless, for they can no longer defend them-selves. And how many of the honored dead have needed so much defense, as much from their friends and admirers as from their detractors? A resuscitation of Musorgskii as competent and in control and positive in his artistic results almost parallels the similar revalua-tions of Macchiavelli, Dryden, Nietzsche, and Haydn. Let us all hope that it produces as great a gain in aesthetic insight.

# Notes

The transliterations of Russian names employed here may strike readers as affected and strange, but they follow the usage of the Library of Congress between 1922 and 1973, until negotiated away in an unfortunate Anglo-American set of rules that now apply. The advantage of the previous Library of Congress system, in which every letter of the transliteration consistently and accurately represents one in the Kyrillic alphabet, cannot be gainsaid. In stubbornly sticking to it, I register a protest against the irrational lack of system now in use, and testify to my hope for a return to logic and common sense. I cannot imagine that any reader of this chapter experiences any discomfort with this usage. Why do we have to write "Tchaikovsky" when we no longer need to write "Tchekhoff" or "Chowantshina"?

1. There seems to be little reason to cite the individual items in this bibliography. Suffice it to say that Claude Debussy's *Monsieur Croche* essay on Musorgskii, in which he characterized him as intuitive, one who possesses the "art of an inquisitive savage who discovers music at every step made by his emotions," was meant to praise his genius and its inventiveness, but has been taken up by many as further evidence of Musorgskii's lack of solid musical grounding. This unfortunate result seems sanctioned by the way this quotation appears in Leon Vallas, *The Theories of Claude Debussy,* trans. M. O'Brien (New York: Dover Publications, 1967), 23, but would be best understood if the article were read in its entirety, as in *Three Classics in the Aesthetic of Music* (New York: Dover Publications, 1950), 14–15, or in any of the other English editions of the article. The notion that Musorgskii did not know the best music of the West, and that his "wild" technical innovations represent clumsiness rather than well-calculated, reasonable process, seems not to be in Debussy's mind.

2. The new OCLC bibliographic service lists these and the locations of exemplars of them more thoroughly than I could here. It almost takes one's breath away to discover so very many of them.

3. The orgy of orchestrations reached a new frenzy in this decade when Leonard Slatkin compiled a version in which every movement comes from a different source: Mikhail Tushmalov, Leo Funtek, Maurice Ravel, Henry Wood, Walter Goehr, Leopold Stokowski, Vladimir Ashkenazii, Sergei Gorchakov, et al., in a spirit of good but chaotic fun. I know of brass arrangements, chamber orchestra arrangements, one for solo piano and orchestra by one Lawrence Leonard, an electronic realization by Henry Gondorf, and several organ versions. For many years, Ulysses Kay traveled from college to college talking about the work's gross inadequacies in its piano manifestation, but its perfect reawakening in Ravel's still standard realization. When students suggested that the piano version was growing in popularity since 1965, they were told that "musicians lacking elementary

judgment have always been and will always be with us." Rhetoric on this subject operates at a high decibel level.

4. Richard Taruskin, in several of his recent works, culminating in the collection of articles called *Musorgsky: Eight Essays and an Epilogue* (Princeton: Princeton University Press, 1993), evaluates the composer's work positively but fairly, a refreshing change from four generations of damning with faint praise, and comments throughout on the bibliography in the sort of detail that needs no retelling here.

5. Recording evidence supports tbe growing popularity of the piano version. Alexander Brailowsky's Victor 78s of 1942 seemed to have been regarded as a curiosity, and the Ultraphone set by J. Palenicek did not sell well, but Benno Moisewitsch's *His Master's Voice* release sold very, very well, and seemed to inspire a generation of pianists to undertake a piece everyone had come to believe to have been for orchestra; Vladimir Horowitz came out with his supercharged performance, arranged, like so many of his works, with almost no respect for the text or the composer's intentions, but it drew in the audience that lives for fireworks. This record, first released on RCA Victor 12-0489-92, has been often remastered, as part of the Horowitz Cult. Sixteen recordings came out in the 1950s, with those by William Kapell, Alexander Uninsky, Gina Bachauer, and Philippe Entremont being notable, though the Soviet reading by M. V. Iudina may be the most interesting, especially in its sonorous success with *Catacombae.* The 1960s saw the revival of orchestral recordings and a retreat in the number of piano discs, though Sviatoslav Rikhter, Rudolf Firkusny, and Vladimir Ashkenazii presented credible renditions, all of which contributed at least one sparkling movement and one failed portion. Since 1970, performances have been on the rise, and from all over the world. Many of these sell extremely well, more than holding their own against orchestral versions — the main problem with them seems to be their lack of rethinking the work thoroughly; too many of them sound exactly like each other, though I must admit that I have not heard many of the latest CDs.

6. Musorgskii's partisans either do not talk about this piece very much, like Robert Godet and Taruskin, or seem to see it through smoked glasses as Abraham, Calvocoressi, Swan, and van Riesemann seem to do. The vocal music has been treated with great insight and understanding, but *Pictures,* as well as the other piano music, has been treated as the black sheep of the family.

7. (Moscow: Muzika, 1975). No editor named. 18 pp. music, 16 pp. art reproductions, 12 pp. notes; MS 502–109.

8. The exact wording of this quotation derives from the late Leonard Shure, but I have heard similar pontifications from several other pianists of three generations down to some of the youngest practitioners I know.

9. Michael Russ, *Musorgsky:* Pictures at an Exhibition (Cambridge: Cambridge University Press, 1992). Its ninety-nine pages are available in

hardcover and paperback; it is the eleventh volume of this distinguished series, though not so numbered by its publisher. Unlike Lini Hubsch, *Modest Musorgskij: Bilder einer Ausstellung;* 2nd ed., W. Fink, 1990 (*Meisterwerke der Musik* XV, 77 pp.) which may be characterized as a respectful, technical description of the musical events in the piece with extremely little critical evaluation, Russ *attacks* the many problems of the work and its subsequent history directly and with the sort of forthrightness that one finds far too rarely on this subject; this does leave him open, however, to the sort of criticism offered here.

10. I find the relatively inexpensive edition by Alfred V. Frankenstein (New York: International Music, ©1952), if compared with the facsimile to correct its five or six significant errors, adequate.

11. Russ, *Musorgsky,* mentions this in passing on p. 25, but I have not been able to corroborate it in other sources.

12. This edition does more violence to the original text than any other, especially as it approaches the climax in *Baba-Yaga* and the *Bogatyr's gate at Kiev.* It needs no comment, though one could discuss its excesses endlessly, but to what purpose?

13. The *Meistersinger* example, Act I, measures 1652–3, visible in the standard full score, now available in the reprint (New York: Dover Publications, 1976), 190, upper system, third and fourth measures.

14. In Act III, Scene 2 of *Tristan und Isolde,* the 5/4 appears in measures 1239–45, and again in measures 1270–73, visible in the standard full score (reprint: New York: Dover Publications, 1973), respectively, on pp. 584–85, and pp. 589–90, the original love music began on p. 374 with Act II's measure 1258 and goes on for several pages.

15. Russ and Hubsch do this task best, but leave many details either undiscussed or errantly evaluated, as I hope to demonstrate in the discussion to follow.

16. Russ, *Musorgsky,* 4.

17. Russ, *Musorgsky,* 46.

18. Russ, *Musorgsky,* 46.

19. Teldec Video, 9031-70774-3, with the Swedish Radio Symphony Orchestra; made in conjunction with Allegro Films of London, ©1991 (A Christopher Nupan production).

20. Richard Taruskin, *Musorgsky: Eight Essays and an Epilogue* (Princeton: Princeton University Press, 1993), 382, and especially n. 102. Taruskin reacts to his own observation intemperately, considering the portrayal of the Jew a "brazen insult" so distasteful that it seems to turn him away from the worth of the piece as a whole. But, if the portrayal's very brutality is meant by the composer to redound against the Russians who feel the way they do, as part of this package, of good and evil inculcated into most every Russian child of this era, the ultimate effect is one of guilt and atonement, and thus is positive. Musorgskii's other contacts with Jewish

culture, in both its Hebrew and Yiddish manifestations, reveals none of this venom, and may indicate that my theory is worthy of note, if not of support.

21. See Witten's discussion of this in chapter five, 140–42.

22. Russ, *Musorgsky,* 65, several times, and further on pp. 66–67; for a truly logical and practical analysis of this place, see Gordon D. McQuere, "Analyzing Musorgsky's 'Gnome,'" *Indiana Theory Review* 13, no. 1 (spring 1992): 21–40, which asks all the right questions, answering most of them.

23. Derrick Puffett, "A Graphic Analysis of Musorgsky's 'Catacombs,'" *Music Analysis* 9 (1990): 67–77. That the traditions and methods of graphic analysis Puffett employs follow Felix Salzer more than Heinrich Schenker seems advantageous to me, since Schenker would never have admitted the tonal language of Musorgskii into his narrow canon of musical acceptability.

24. Simon Perry, "Rummaging Through the 'Catacombs:' Clues in Musorgsky's Pitch Notation," *Musical Analysis* 14 (1995): 221–55.

25. Chopin gives a similar priority to the notated E♭s in measures 2 and 3 of his Prelude in E Minor, Op. 28, No. 4, which a few editors, notably Paderewski, saw fit to change to D♯ due to the harmonic function of the sonority in the second half of measure 2. Such details do not seem to me pregnant with information or deep contrapuntal meaning, but several analysts of the present generation have begun exploring them.

26. Perry, "Rummaging Through the 'Catacombs,'" 226–27.

27. Perry, "Rummaging," 230–32.

28. Perry, "Rummaging," 235.

29. Perry, "Rummaging," 239–42.

30. Perhaps the best of these, including all seventeen of the surviving piano pieces, has been recently executed by Boris Bloch, on Accord CD 202152, 1992; unhappily, this also includes a rather pedestrian reading of *Pictures.*

# INDEX